★ A HIT WITH ★
A BULLET

Chris

To Good to Meet You

Best Wishes

★ A HIT WITH ★
A BULLET

**A TRUE STORY OF CORRUPTION, GREED
& THE REAL MURDER ON MUSIC ROW**

SAMMY SADLER

AS SEEN ON UNSOLVED MYSTERIES, A&E'S COLD CASE FILES & ENTERTAINMENT TONIGHT

INDIGO RIVER PUBLISHING

Indigo River Publishing
3 West Garden Street Ste. 352 M
Pensacola, FL 32502
www.indigoriverpublishing.com

Book Design: mycustombookcover.com
Editor: Tanner Chau and Joshua Owens

Ordering Information: Quantity sales: Special discounts are available on quantity purchases by corporations, associations, and others. For details, contact the publisher at the address above.

Orders by U.S. trade bookstores and wholesalers: Please contact the publisher at the address above.

Printed in the United States of America

Library of Congress Control Number: 2019941394

ISBN: 978-1-948080-92-7 (paperback) 978-1-950906-06-2 (ebook)

First Edition

With Indigo River Publishing, you can always expect great books, strong voices, and meaningful messages. Most importantly, you'll always find ... words worth reading

Dedication

This book is dedicated to my friend Kevin Hughes,
who was murdered on 16th Avenue South
on March 9, 1989, Nashville, Tennessee.

It's also for my dad, Jerry, who inspires me every day,
and my mom, Juanita, who passed on August 28th, 2010,
and who was the best friend a son could ever have.

Contents

Acknowledgements

I want to first thank God for saving my life and for saving me. I want to thank my Mom and Dad for all your love and support you've given me all my life. Mom, I miss you and I love you.

I want to thank Jesse Sublett for all your hard work with me on the book. I want to thank my publicist, Shelly Mullins for all your help and belief in me. Thank you, Robert K. Oermann for opening your trove of country music archives to us, and John Wesley Ryles, for your friendship and your sharp, vivid memory. Finally, I want to thank all those who helped with the making of the book and for your interviews.

Thank you,
Sammy

Notes on Sources

This book is a personal memoir of a very public crime. My personal memories and experience have informed many of the places, people, and events described in the book. Whenever appropriate and possible, I sought verification and documentation in reliable sources, in hopes that this book will be of value to other writers, researchers, and historians who may be interested in exploring the events in further detail.

Descriptions of places like Music Row in Nashville are based on my own knowledge and impressions of them and may slightly differ from other sources, and the reader should bear in mind that Nashville has changed significantly in the past couple of decades.

Where chart positions and release dates of songs are used in the text, the information was sourced from *Billboard* magazine, *AllMusic.com*, and individual artist websites. Information from *Billboard* and *Cash Box* was pulled from or verified in the issues of those magazines, all of which are archived and accessible at www.americanradiohistory.com.

Interviews were conducted by Jesse Sublett on various dates in 2017.

"Case no. 89-59058" refers to the murder of Kevin Hughes and is the designation used by the Nashville Metro Police Department for the entire course of the investigation. There are many references to "the case file" in the book. The case file consists of several hundred pages of reports, official documents, memos, notes of interviews with witnesses, and other materials acquired by the murder squad detectives during the investigation. The file was organized loosely (and that's an understatement) when we got it, and there is no sequential pagination. Therefore, it's impossible to give page numbers when the file is referenced in the book.

The vast majority of pages are from the detectives' Supplemental Reports, where they summarize the content of interviews with various individuals connected to the investigation. The coroner's report, lab reports, internal memos, charts of the crime scenes, polygraph exam memos, and various other documents from the case file were an immense help in making this book as accurate as possible.

In source notes, the transcript of the trial of Richard D'Antonio is referred to as "*Tennessee v. Richard D'Antonio,* case no. 2002-c-1280." The transcript is over 1,000 pages long. It begins with pretrial hearings in July, August, and September 2003, continuing with the jury trial September 22-25, 2003, and concluding with the sentencing hearing November 7, 2003.

D'Antonio appealed his case several times. The Court of Criminal Appeals at Nashville denied each one. The rulings contain the basic synopsis of the case, along with excerpts of important testimony, and can be found online using the search term "Richard Frank D'Antonio v. State of Tennessee."

The Nashville daily newspaper, *The Tennessean,* reported extensively on the investigation of the murder on Music Row and the murder trial of Richard D'Antonio; articles from the *Tennessean* are cited extensively in the book.

The Country Music Hall of Fame® and Museum in Nashville (http://countrymusichalloffame.org) was also consulted for various topics. The research staff there was very helpful. Be sure to visit if you're ever in Nashville.

Back issues of *Nashville Scene* magazine were also consulted.

Robert K. Oermann provided us a large batch of materials from his vast archive of country music history.

Print and online books consulted include:

Bill Malone, *Country Music, U.S.A.* (Austin: University of Texas Press, 2002).

Michael Kosser, *How Nashville Became Music City, U.S.A.: 50 Years of Music Row* (Hal Leonard, 2006).

Frances Preston, *BMI 50th Anniversary Book*, https://web.archive.org/web/20030412122819/http://www.bmi.com:80/library/brochures/historybook/index.asp.

Foreword

You've seen the movies that declare they're "based on a true story." And the television shows that are "ripped from the headlines." This is one of those stories. It is a true story of bribery, betrayal, murder, survival and of justice taking a ride on a slow train—a story written in the blood of a rising country music star and in the blood of his friend.

This is an unvarnished account of the premeditated killing now known around the world as the Murder on Music Row. It details how, on March 9, 1989, a man wearing a black mask stepped out of the shadows of a Nashville street to pump .38 caliber bullets into country music newcomer Sammy Sadler and his buddy, *Cash Box* magazine music chart director Kevin Hughes.

Kevin, the actual target of the attack, died on that dark Music Row street, his gushing blood running into a storm drain. Sammy, near death from the attack, survived, fighting, at first, to regain use of his shattered right arm and, then, fighting to regain his stopped-in-its-tracks music career. For years, as the investigation ground on and on, he was plagued by debilitating insomnia and horrific nightmares. "No matter what new corner of the world I woke up in, the man in the black mask was always waiting," recalls Sammy. "You can't outrun a ghost."

The torrent of potential motives for the deadly ambush seemed to match the endless flood of chasing-a-dream singers who step off the bus in Nashville every day. There was the robbery gone wrong motive. The jealous husband mistaking Kevin for his wife's lover motive. The crazed cocaine druggie from the nearby projects motive. The *Cash Box* pay-to-play payola motive. The some kind of grudge vendetta motive.

"Justice delayed is justice denied." Even though British Prime Minister William Gladstone uttered those words a hundred years ago, his observation fits the investigation into the Music Row attack like the proverbial O.J. Simpson glove. As the pursuit of the perpetrator unfolded, justice was delayed and justice was denied for fourteen agonizing years.

After that way-too-long detour, Lady Justice peeked through her blindfold and finally came calling on September 23, 2003, when the trial to discover who gunned down Sammy and Kevin got underway in Nashville's Metro Courthouse. I was then senior editor of Country Weekly, the No. 1 country music magazine in the world. We covered Sammy's tragedy-to-triumph story and the drama-packed trial in our pages.

Country Weekly's Nashville offices were at 118 16th Avenue S., on the northern edge of famed Music Row—the area of the city that is home to record labels, publishing houses, music licensing firms, recording studios, video production companies and other businesses that serve the music industry. Sammy's record label at the time of the murder, Evergreen Records, was also on 16th Avenue S.—at 1021—in the heart of Music Row. That put the *Country Weekly* offices a mere half mile from the murder site and less than two miles from the trial site.

Later, when I became editor-in-chief of *Country Weekly,* I had this famous quote from journalist Hunter S. Thompson on my desk: "The music business is a cruel and shallow money trench, a long plastic hallway where thieves and pimps run free, and good men die like dogs. There's also a negative side."

It is debated by some whether Thompson was actually talking about the television business instead of the music business. Having spent a lot of time in Hollywood during my more than four decades interviewing movie and TV stars as a celebrity journalist and having spent twelve years in Nashville interviewing country stars and covering the music industry, I can attest that the Thompson quote applies to both the TV world and the music world.

In this downright riveting book, Sammy delivers—in his own words—a candid portrayal of the seedy, dark underbelly of the country music business, that "cruel and shallow money trench" where "good men die like dogs."

In the pages you are about to read, Sammy also celebrates the remarkable history of country music and the exhilarating moments he's experienced during his own country music journey. Along the way, he unravels an unforgettable, truly inspirational, story of his struggles to emerge from the brink of death a better man.

The road to justice for Sammy Sadler and Kevin Hughes had so many sharp twists and hairpin turns—along with abrupt, heart-breaking, dead ends—that it was more like a maze than a road. Thank God, as Sammy affirmed after the trial, "There is no statute of limitations on the truth."

Now, fasten your seatbelt. You're gonna need it!

—Larry Holden

Chapter 1

Deep in the Heart of Texas

I GREW UP IN LEONARD, A SMALL RURAL TOWN IN FANNIN COUNTY UP IN NORTH TEXAS BETWEEN DALLAS AND THE OKLAHOMA STATE LINE. If you ask me where I'm from, I'll probably say that I'm from Bonham, the county seat, 16 miles away. In this part of the country, that's about the same as a big-city person going a few blocks over. Bonham is the larger of the two with a population 10,000 versus the humble population of Leonard at 1,975, so there's a better chance that the person asking where I'm from will have heard of it.

They call this land the Blackland Prairie. It's good for farming and grazing livestock, and the gently rolling plain goes on as far as you can see. Someone raised in a big city might think it looks deserted and empty around here, but a lot of history happened in this part of Texas. Named after Lt. James B. Bonham, who was killed in the battle of the Alamo, Bonham was settled in 1836, the year Texas fought for its independence from Mexico.

Although I grew up a Texas boy, a piece of me belonged somewhere else. I was born in Memphis, Tennessee, home of Elvis Presley.

I cried like a baby when Elvis died August 16, 1977, a week before my eleventh birthday. He was my hero and my first huge musical influence. His voice was out of this world. He was a walking encyclopedia of influences and technical abilities—blues, hillbilly, jazz, falsetto, vibrato—he put it all together like nobody before and no one since. He also talked like a Southerner, not much different from the people I grew up with.

Even if it isn't someone you knew personally, it can be hard to process death at a tender age. I know it was for me. Elvis was larger than life. How could the world go on without him? It was hard to wrap my mind around it.

The Sadlers were from Texas, but my mother's family was from Tennessee. My mom and dad, Juanita and Jerry, met when Dad was working in Memphis, where I ended up being born. Mom had family there, so the Memphis connection was always important to us. For me, it reinforced the idea that I would be a famous singer someday.

My parents' generation grew up with Elvis, which sometimes made me feel a little envious. Dad remembers being a teenager when Elvis released "That's All Right (Mama)," "Hound Dog," and "Don't Be Cruel." People were going crazy wherever he played. Sometimes there were riots, and when he was on television, they censored him below the waist because of his scandalous gyrations.

Years went by and Elvis' career had its ups and downs. He did some great movies like *Jailhouse Rock* and *Love Me Tender*, and a bunch of silly ones like *Girls! Girls! Girls!* And *Kissin' Cousins*. Later in the sixties, Beatlemania and the Rolling Stones came along and eventually stole his thunder, but Elvis came roaring back at the end of 1968 with a Christmas TV special recorded live in front of a small studio audience. Originally, the show was just titled "Elvis," but his performance was so electrifying that it became universally known as "The '68 Comeback Special."

The next nine years of Elvis's life was a rollercoaster ride—hit records, legendary acts of generosity, and tragedy. By the time he died, some people had forgotten all about him. Others still regarded him as the once and forever "King of Rock 'n' Roll," including an eleven-year-old kid named Sammy Sadler, who had been singing since he was two years old.

My dad remembers this childhood memory like it was yesterday. "You would sing along with the radio, the television, anything," he said. "You were always singing."

To my good fortune, my parents offered all the encouragement and support I needed. They bought me records, praised my singing, took me to see shows, and helped expand my musical horizons. I became familiar with the music of Johnny Cash, George Jones, Merle Haggard, Marty Robbins, and Hank Williams, to name a few of my early favorites. They took me to country shows in Dallas, Fort Worth, and Houston.

We would pile in the car for the ten-hour drive from Leonard to Nashville just to see country music shows and sightsee. Sometimes we would make it to East Tennessee to visit mom's folks, but many times Dad or Mom would say, "How about going to Nashville next week?" and off we would go.

Nashville was a wonderland for a kid like me. Imagine a star-struck young kid who wants to be a famous actor one day going to Hollywood and visiting Universal Studio with his parents, where they see movie stars everywhere they go. That's how Nashville was for me in those days. You could drive down the streets of Music Row and see famous country musicians coming out of all the different music industry offices. You'd see them all over the place. I remember seeing this guy with long, curly hair walking out to his car, and I'm quite sure, in my excitement, I probably scared my parents when I yelled, "Hey, that's Gary Morris!" Nashville has always been a big part of my life.

I can look back on my childhood and appreciate how lucky I was that we lived so close to Dallas because all the big country people seemed to play there on tour. One place we went to a lot was Granny's

Dinner Playhouse, where I remember seeing Roy Orbison, Marty Robbins, and Jerry Lee Lewis, to name a few.

When I was still a little boy, we saw Johnny Cash in Dallas—Fair Park Coliseum sometime in the 1970s, if I remember correctly. Johnny Cash was a huge international star at the time. His prison albums, *Live at Folsom Prison* and *Live at San Quentin*, hit the top of the *Billboard* Country and Top-10 charts. He outsold the Beatles. My parents told me that I was standing up in my seat during the whole concert, singing along with every song, even the Carter Family songs. I remember the absolutely astonished people around us staring at this little kid singing Johnny Cash. It felt good and that feeling stuck with me.

Then there was my first guitar. Dad got it from mail order, and it was mostly just a prop, something a kid could bang away on. When I got a little older, I got a Yamaha acoustic and took some lessons. I learned the basic chords, picked up the rest on my own, and that's all the musical instruction I ever got. I was in the school band for a little while, but I have to say I didn't learn anything. They didn't need a guitar player or singer, so I played the cymbals. I still can't read music, but I can work out a four-part harmony.

As a teen, I started a little band with some friends, and we played at school and a few other places. I got more serious about music after I started singing at all the local opries. These were regional country music revues, sometimes called a Jamboree, or Barn Dance, Hayride, or whatever. Dallas had their "Big D Jamboree," and there were others in Houston, Mesquite, Wylie, and other Texas towns, as well as in Oklahoma, and Louisiana.

The biggest thing in our area was the "Johnnie High's Country Music Revue" in Arlington, every Friday and Saturday night. Johnnie would always have the current Miss Texas on the show. LeAnn Rimes played it when she was nine years old. We got to see many upcoming artists as well as established country stars—Gary Morris, John Anderson, Tommy Cash, Kitty Wells, Wanda Jackson, and Lee Ann Womack.

Just like the "Grand Ole Opry" in Nashville, the local radio or

TV station often sponsored regional country revues. There would be a house band, and I would go on and sing two or three songs. If you got a good reception, you'd get invited to perform at other opries.

I was singing George Jones, Merle Haggard, and Marty Robbins (the classic traditional country singers). One of my biggest thrills was performing twice on the "Louisiana Hayride." After all, the show, which debuted in 1948, helped make the careers of country music stars such as Hank Williams, Jim Reeves, George Jones, and Faron Young. Elvis made the hay fly there in 1954 and 1955. It was the most prestigious of all country music revues, outside of the granddaddy of them all, the "Grand Ole Opry" in Nashville. Did I fantasize about someday making my way up to that stage? You bet I did.

During my senior year of high school, I realized that I faced a huge decision: Did I really want to do this for real, as a profession? Did I want to commit my life to it? The decision wasn't easy, because I loved sports almost as much as I loved music. I went out for just about everything—football, baseball, basketball, tennis. I trained hard, listened to my coaches, and did my best to excel at everything.

Baseball was my favorite sport of all. One year we made it to the playoffs. We went to bed at night dreaming about bringing home that state championship. We got close but didn't quite make it. My coach, a man named John Kent, not only taught me about baseball but other important things about succeeding in life, and that includes learning how to deal with setbacks and disappointments. Kent almost had a career in professional baseball. He tried out for a big team—I think it was the Cincinnati Reds—and they turned him down because he was two seconds too slow...two seconds. Can you imagine?

I was a pitcher, and I hit well too. When I was a sophomore, I was throwing in the high eighties, and recruiters were coming to check me out. They told me I had a curveball that was hard to touch.

Around that time, I was also playing the opries, and the excitement from performing on those stages in front of all those people was hard to beat. The feeling is hard to describe, but you're up there on stage, singing songs that touch people. You can make them smile, put tears in their eyes, recall happy or sad memories—the emotion and excitement they're experiencing comes back to you. So, as much as I loved sports and valued the lessons that sports taught me, music felt a lot more important to who I was and what I wanted to do with my life.

Graduation Day was approaching, and I was still torn. I asked my dad what to do. "It's your choice, son," he told me. "Your mom and I will support your decision either way. We'll do whatever we can to help you get on your way."

Looking back now, I think one of the most fateful things in my early years was meeting a genuine country music legend who lived in Bonham and worked at the Bonham State Bank. I don't remember exactly how old I was when I met Ruby Allmond, only that I wasn't old enough to appreciate who she was—a champion fiddle player who had played alongside some of the greatest fiddle players in the country, a great entertainer, as well as a successful songwriter. On her first trip to Nashville, she had played a song called "Reno" for Bob Jennings at RCA Records. Chet Atkins liked it, and that was good enough for Dottie West. Atkins, who worked in A&R at RCA, brought hit-makers The Everly Brothers ("All I Have to Do is Dream," "Bird Dog," "Wake Up, Little Susie") to Acuff-Rose, and built the legendary RCA studio also known as "Home of 1,000 Hits" where Elvis Presley, Roy Orbison, Jim Reeves, the Everly Brothers, Dottie West, and many others struck gold and spread the gospel of "The Nashville Sound." With the greenlight from RCA, Ruby Allmond's recording of "Reno" broke the top 10 on *Billboard*'s country music chart.

All I knew was that my mom, who was working at the bank at the time, came home one day and told me that a lady she worked with wanted to meet me. She didn't call her Ruby, because everybody knew her by her nickname, "Chub." Mom had been talking about my obsession with music that day with Chub and another bank employee,

Aubrey Brock, and they wanted me to come over to their studio and do some songs for them.

Ruby Allmond came from a musical family, learning to play the fiddle sitting on her father's knee during family jam sessions on the front porch. During her teen years, she was playing out with a string band that included her brothers, wowing audiences all over the region. She had developed her own unique style with the bow, and in addition her amazing technical skill, she knew how to grab an audience's attention and never let it go. She won National Champion Lady Fiddler award in 1947 and was so popular that another Bonham native, the Honorable Sam Rayburn (long-serving and powerful Speaker of the U.S. House of Representatives), would take Ruby and her band on the road during every campaign.

So that Friday night, we went to meet Chub and Aubrey. Aubrey, I learned later, was an old family friend and neighbor of the Allmonds. She and Chub had built this tiny studio where all of Chub's songs were written and recorded. It was a little freestanding, ready-made building, eight feet by twelve feet, so it was cramped inside. On one side sat Ruby with her guitar, fiddle, microphone, and a reel-to-reel tape recorder. The other side of the room was Aubrey's. She had a little drum set she had bought and learned to play just so she could help Chub write and make demos of her songs.

Chub already had my guitar in her lap as we got settled—she had taken it from me when she came to the door to greet us. After thumping a few strings, she started twisting the tuning pegs and got it sounding sweeter than I had ever heard it before.

"Well, Sammy," she said, "Why don't you sing us something?"

One of my best songs at the time was "Blue Eyes Crying in the Rain," and that's the only one I remember for certain. What Chub said to me that evening was one of the most important moments to shape my future.

"Sammy, I think you have a natural talent," she said. "If it were up to me, I'd tell you that you ought to pursue it."

She also cautioned that while entertaining may look like it's all fun and easy-going, it takes hard work and dedication. "To become a really good musician," she said, "takes more than talent. You've got to give it as much time and effort as you possibly can." How did Ruby Allmond become a great fiddle player? By practicing up to eight hours a day.

The jam session in that tiny studio with Ruby Allmond and Aubrey Brock influenced my life a lot. That's when the "music bug" truly bit me. I took all of Ruby's advice to heart, and by the time they played "The Processional" for the Leonard High School class of '84, I had told everyone I cared about (my family, my girlfriend, my buddies, and probably a few people I barely knew) I was heading out in the world to make it as a country music singer.

Chapter 2

Music City, U.S.A.

My first night in Nashville, Dad rented the limo for us. My parents and I rode around town in a limousine talking about my future. The leaves had turned, and all the Thanksgiving decorations in the store windows and other businesses made the town feel cheerful and welcoming.

It was the fall of 1984, and I was 18 years old. I had graduated from high school a few months earlier. That summer I had decided to leave Perfect Stranger, a professional band I played with for some time during and after high school and move to Nashville as a solo artist.

My parents wanted to help me move in and get settled, and I was grateful. I had lived my whole life in a town of 1,500, and Nashville, with almost a half-million people, was like a different world to me. We had been to Nashville many times before, but just as tourists. I didn't know my way around, didn't know anybody.

Driving up from Texas that day, we were still a few miles outside the Nashville city limits when we spotted the WSM radio antenna. I could feel my heart start to beat faster. The tower is diamond-shaped and 808 feet tall. When it was first built in 1932, it was the tallest antenna in North America. No radio tower anywhere has had a greater effect on popular music or a city.

On November 28, 1927, after being on the air only two years, WSM-AM launched a new, live-in-the-studio music broadcast called the "WSM Barn Dance." The show was an advertising vehicle for the station's owners, National Life and Accident Insurance Co. The call sign WSM stood for the company's advertising slogan, "We Serve Millions."

One night, after just two weeks since the show's debut, "Judge" George D. Hay, the host, took a swipe at the snobby attitude expressed during the opera broadcast that preceded the "Barn Dance" time slot. During the Judge's introduction of DeFord Bailey, "The Harmonica Wizard," he said, "For the past hour, we have been listening to music taken largely from Grand Opera. From now on, we will present the 'Grand Ole Opry.'"

The name stuck, and the show caught on, becoming the longest-running radio program in the world. In the 1930s, the new, monster-sized antenna erected by WSM boosted its broadcasting power to 50,000 watts. The Opry became a Saturday night tradition, reaching nearly 30 states, and in 1939, the show went nationwide on NBC Radio.

In 1943, the "Grand Ole Opry" moved to the historic Ryman Auditorium on Fifth Avenue. Originally built in 1892 as the home of the Union Gospel Tabernacle, the building already had a lively history before it became known as "The Mother Church of Country Music." In its first 50 years, the Ryman had been utilized for boxing matches, Vaudeville shows, plays, presidential speeches, opera, and even religious worship.

Musicians from all over the eastern United States trickled into town, lured there by the possibility of playing on the "Grand Ole Opry." Some of these performers passed the audition, many of them didn't. A good number of them stuck around Nashville and became part of a community of songwriters, performers, record labels, studios, music publishers, and other music-related trades that made Nashville the center of the country music industry—a place where music is so important, they called it "Music City, U.S.A."

Ronnie Cummings, our limo driver on my first night in Nashville, was a very friendly guy, and over the course of our ride, he claimed to know a lot of people in the music business. One of the most interesting names Ronnie dropped was Jimmy Bowen, the producer.

Jimmy Bowen had started out in his teens playing with Buddy Knox in the Rhythm Orchids and had several hit records in the late 1950s. He decided to leave stage performing and work the other angles of the music business such as producing records, starting independent labels, and running major labels. In the sixties, Bowen produced Frank Sinatra, Dean Martin, and Sammy Davis, Jr. He put Nancy Sinatra together with Lee Hazelwood. It seemed like a crazy idea, like combining sandpaper and silk, but "Summer Wine," "Jackson," and "Some Velvet Morning" sold millions and millions of records.

After Jimmy Bowen moved to Nashville, Bowen was President of one record label after another, bringing each one a string of giant country music hits before he moved on. He produced Glen Campbell, Kenny Rogers, George Strait, Johnny Cash, Waylon Jennings, and Conway Twitty.

The point of all this is that Jimmy Bowen was one of the biggest names in the business, and our limo driver turned out to be friends with him. Everything Ronnie told us that night—about having connections with record labels, producers, and other people—was true. He wasn't exaggerating, he knew almost everybody. He followed through on his promise to show me around and make introductions.

Ronnie ended up being my roommate and one of my best friends. He helped me do all the basic things to get a toehold in Nashville: record a demo, write a bio, and start pitching the package around to the record labels. With some money from my dad, we started recording—using a session band, doing some parts in one studio, and then mixing, overdubbing, and mastering in other places. One of the first studios I recorded at was Soundstage on Music Row, a residential area that, many years before I got there, had been taken over by people in the Nashville music industry. One little house after another was home to a recording studio, music publisher, record label, and so on.

Music publishers like Acuff-Rose, Tree, and Almo/Irving had people they called "song pluggers," a term that describes exactly what they did: "plugging" the catalogs of songwriters they represented to all the artist managers, singers, producers, and record labels. Therefore, it wasn't hard to find great songs to record. All over Music Row, every day of the week, great songwriters were creating smartly arranged, radio-friendly songs. I've never been much of a songwriter, and I have great respect for the people who do it well.

I was going to the "Grand Ole Opry" almost every weekend, and as I got to know more people, I got to be a regular backstage visitor. A group called The Four Guys was on the bill almost every weekend. They had started out in 1955 as a group called "The Jets," so they represented decades of music history. We got to be good friends.

I remember being in Roy Acuff's dressing room, talking and joking with Minnie Pearl and Grandpa Jones. I was there the first night Keith Whitley performed on the Opry stage. I stood right beside him before he went on. I'll never forget what Keith wore that night: tennis shoes, solid white pants, and a pink sweater—not your usual country singer look.

I was an eighteen or nineteen-year-old kid, a country boy. Sometimes I had to pinch myself, but most of the time, I was so focused on getting a record deal and becoming successful that I probably took it for granted. I was in the midst of so much history and talent of such magnitude that it was hard to wrap my mind around. If I had really stopped to think about it, I might have been too intimidated to talk to any of them.

You meet one person, and that person introduces you to another. One day, Ronnie and I we went to an office on Music Row where I met a lady named Mae Axton. You may have heard of her since she's the person who helped get Elvis Presley signed to RCA and co-wrote "Heartbreak Hotel," one of the biggest-selling and greatest songs in rock 'n' roll history. When I met Mae, she was in her seventies, and to me, she looked more like a schoolteacher than the "Queen of Nashville," as she was known. She actually had been a schoolteacher for many years before she came to Nashville.

Mae came from Bardwell, Texas, a town about fifty miles south of Dallas that was less than half the size of Leonard. She and I hit it off, and I guess she took a liking to me, because she wrote my first bio for my publicity package. Robert Oermann, the great country music historian, recently found the first draft of it in his own files. They were good friends and used to give each other suggestions on their work.

One day, I had Tony Brown, the president of MCA Records, riding in my truck. I had met Tony through Buzz Stone at MCA Records and found him to be a really nice, intelligent guy. Buzz helped me get in the door to meet a lot of other people. Tony and I were going to watch Steve Earle and his band rehearse. This was right when Steve's *Copperhead Road* album came out, and you could feel the excitement in the air, like just before a powerful storm.

Then there were things like the listening party for a duo called The Vega Brothers, who were being hyped as the next Everly Brothers. If you've never heard of them, it's because they weren't.

I shopped my demo around, and right away, I started getting offers from independent labels. I was hoping to sign with one of the majors like MCA, but you have to start somewhere, and neither country music nor rock 'n' roll would have ever happened if not for independent labels—companies that are small and hungry and not afraid to take a chance.

Ray Pennington at Step One was interested in me. Ray was a singer/songwriter/producer who started out with a western swing band in Ohio in the 1950s and moved to Nashville in 1964. Ray's sense of humor came out in songs like "Three Hearts in a Tangle," "Who's Been Mowing the Lawn (While I Was Gone)," and "This Song Don't Care Who Sings It."

After working with Monument, RCA, and MRC, Ray started Step One Records in 1984 with Melt Holt. Ray Price and fiddler Clinton Gregory were two of the first acts they signed, and before long, *Billboard* was referring to them as "the biggest independent country label in the world."

I really wanted to sign with Step One, but Ray said he wasn't ready to take on any new artists for six to nine months.

"Ray, I don't want to bug you about it." I was antsy. I wanted things to start popping.

"No, I want you to bug me," he said, "I like you, I think you've got something."

I was raring to go. Johnny Morris at Evergreen Records had also made an offer. I liked Johnny, so I signed with them.

When I look back, I can see that things were moving fast. We believe that time is a hard-straight line, marching on like a metronome until we notice the moments that can drag on forever or slip away in a gasp. Being so young, I thought every little step in the process was taking too long. Like staring at the hands on a clock, I was willing it to move forward with every pause. I wanted to get out there and prove myself. I wanted a hit record that would launch my career like a rocket into space.

You always hear about the big stars that struggled for a while and then suddenly they become rich and famous, their lives changed overnight, and you think that everything in their world must feel shiny and special. But it's not really like that. What usually happens is that you move forward little by little. If you do reach the big time, your life may seem a lot more hectic, you might have a big house, a sports car, and a giant closet full of fancy clothes, but you're still the same person. Fame, money, and possessions aren't who you are. You still have to get up every day and put your jeans on one leg at a time.

Six months after moving to Nashville, I had met a lot of important, interesting people and signed a record deal. Soon we would start recording my first album. It was a great feeling just to know that people in the business knew my name and that I was in the game. I didn't know when my next big break was going to happen. Deep down, I realized that it might take years of hard work, with a lot of disappointments and setbacks along the way, but I didn't think about that very much. I had the attitude of an athlete in training: Give it 110 percent, make that goal, overcome the odds, and commit yourself to do the impossible.

When fame came knocking, it was nothing like I had expected it to look or feel. Suddenly, everybody knew my name, and my picture went out all over the world, but instead of fortune and adulation, fame brought years of pain, confusion, guilt, and suspicion. And I was the lucky one—I was the one who survived.

Chapter 3

Evergreen

Standing on the curb at 1021 16th Avenue South (the address of Evergreen Records), you could glance up and down the street and see the offices of Bug Music, Atlantic Records, Emerald Sound Studio, and a dozen or more businesses in the neighborhood known as Music Row. There were two main north-south streets—16th Avenue South and 17th Avenue South—the former, a one-way going north, the latter going south. Looking at a map, you can follow the two of them from the northern edge of Belmont University to the roundabout on the north end of Music Row, where you can turn onto Division or Demonbreun, and Music Circle forms a loop connecting Division Street to 17th Avenue South. The upper part of 16th and 17th avenue is also designated Music Square West and Music Square East, respectively. Long story short, this entire area is almost wholly devoted to some aspect of the music industry.

Almost everyone you ran into in town was involved in some aspect of the music industry. Nashville had long been dominated by country, gospel, and contemporary Christian, but really, you could find people working across the spectrums, pop, jazz, folk, heavy metal, hip hop, rap, and everything in between. Well-known artists, hit songwriters, major stars—some of whom I knew, some I didn't—were always coming and going. Seeing a famous face walking down the sidewalk was no different than seeing a bird in a tree.

Evergreen operated out of a wood frame house with a little front porch under a striped awning. The outside was painted the same light green color as the label on the records. Inside, it was bigger than it looked from the street. In every room, people were busy doing record promotions, songwriting, publishing, and anything else Johnny Morris had a hand in.

Johnny reminded me of William Shatner playing Captain Kirk on "Star Trek," the way he carried himself and the way he talked, like Evergreen was a battleship, roaming the seas, spoiling for a fight. Johnny even had the same haircut as William Shatner.

Johnny seemed to be a jack-of-all-trades, seasoned in every aspect of the Nashville music industry. Before he started Evergreen, he was president of Cinnamon Records, producing John Wesley Ryles and the legendary hit-maker Jerry Foster, among others. Jerry Foster had his first hit as a solo artist when Johnny produced "Copperhead," released in 1973 on Cinnamon.

Johnny had also co-written songs with someone named J.B. Detterline, Jr., a name I later learned belonged to the man everyone knew as Chuck Dixon. Chuck was one half of Morris-Dixon, an independent promotion company that did business with Evergreen. The other half was Johnny's son, Craig. I was acquainted with Chuck, but I was closer to Craig. I thought Craig was a good family man, and as far as I could see, he was honest. Chuck, on the other hand, struck me as a loud-mouthed egomaniac. I had heard that he was crooked and that he fancied himself as some kind of Music Row "Godfather." I didn't know if there was anything to it, or if it was just the way he liked to present himself. For the most part, people on Music Row seemed to accept Chuck as part of their world. Or maybe they just didn't want to talk about anything that would reflect poorly on the community. Better to just ignore it.

After I signed with Evergreen, Johnny put me to work promoting Evergreen's records to radio stations. This might sound like an unusual arrangement, but the practice was fairly common. The job was pretty straightforward. I would come in every morning, sit at a desk, and call radio people—deejays and programmers, mostly—and talk up our records.

You had to have a feeling for people, a knack for reaching out on the phone and striking up a relationship with someone you'd never seen in person. You'd make sure they had the new release, ask how they liked it, and tell them how good it's doing on other radio stations and how well it's selling. You want that person to look forward to talking to you every time you call.

A honky-tonk singer named William Browder was doing the same thing at RCA Records before his single "Devil in the Bottle" hit the No. 1 spot in 1974. Browder was his real name, as well as the name he used as a record company employee, but most people know him by his stage name, T.G. Sheppard.

T.G. Sheppard was a great inspiration, but I chose to use my own name, even when I was calling about my own record. I wanted them to know they were talking to Sammy Sadler.

Since I was coming into the office every day, I got to know the Music Row neighborhood pretty well, and I got to know quite a few of the people who worked there. The Faron Young Executive Building, a few blocks away at 1300 Division Street, was home to a lot of industry offices, including *Cash Box*, one of several weekly trade magazines. *Radio & Records*, *Record World*, and *Gavin Report* also published music rating charts, but *Cash Box* was a magazine we concentrated our energies on, particularly because of the Country Independent Singles chart.

My friend Kevin Hughes had started working at *Cash Box* in 1985 (the year after I moved to Nashville) as an unpaid intern, a member of their chart research team, while he was still enrolled at Belmont University. Kevin had been what they call a "music geek" since he was a teenager. This was a guy who bought all the new trade magazines as soon as they came out and made index cards for every record and CD in his collection. In 1987, when he was still a year away from graduating from college, the people at *Cash Box* convinced him to take over the full-time job of chart director. The decision wasn't easy for him, but he accepted the position with the intention of continuing his schooling later.

Kevin was a guy who made friends easily. We were about the same age, born less than a year apart, and like me, he was from a small rural town. His mother taught Sunday school back in Carmi, Illinois, and he stayed in constant contact with his parents and his younger brother, Kyle. Like me, Kevin was athletic and into baseball, basketball, football, and all the rest. We played racquetball now and then on the courts at my apartment complex, went out to eat, saw movies, things like that. He was easygoing but competitive on the racquetball court and serious about his job.

After I'd been in Nashville a while, especially when I was working on the Row, I got to know so many people that it started feeling more like a small town. You were around people who were working just as hard as you were to succeed, the people Lacy J. Dalton sings about in the song "16th Avenue"—the people who had "walked away from everything/just to see a dream come true."

Naturally, from time to time, you'd feel jealous of someone else's success. Sometimes, when you're struggling to get ahead, you can't escape the idea that success is like a big pie. Everybody else seems to be getting a piece except for you. What if they run out of pie before you get some? But most of the time it wasn't like that. When somebody you knew started selling lots of records, suddenly you'd see their name and face everywhere you look, and you'd think, "I know him (or her), that's my friend," and you're happy for them.

Robin Lee had been knocking on doors at Music Row for a

couple of years before Johnny Morris signed her and put her in the studio in 1983. Over the next five years, Evergreen released her first album, *Robin Lee* (EV1001), and one single after another, "Angel in Your Arms," "Turn Back the Covers," and a lot of other really good recordings. A few of them made the *Billboard* Country Top-100, falling just short of the magical Top-40. If you only make it to No. 51 or so, people at the major labels might grudgingly concede that you had a "minor hit" or that your record "charted," or they might just pretend you didn't exist. The music business can be as icy as any business there ever was.

Everybody knew she would have a big hit eventually, and I was proud to help promote Robin's records. Then in 1988, I believe it was, she went down the street to Atlantic Records and signed with them. Her first three singles on Atlantic didn't do much better than any of the Evergreen releases, but in 1990, she covered the Allanah Myles song "Black Velvet" and scored a top-12 hit. We were all happy for her.

Another great singer who was putting out records with our trademark light green record label was Joe Stampley, from Springhill, Louisiana. Owing to his roots, Joe could knock out a swamp ballad in his sleep, but his music couldn't be pigeonholed by just one label. He was in the tenth grade when he signed a deal with Imperial Records. His band, the Uniques, put out four albums, and between 1971 and 1989, Joe released 53 singles. When I knew him at Evergreen, he was putting out solo records and also performing and recording in a duet with Moe Bandy, billed as "Moe and Joe." Most of their material was satirical. Joe was a person who enjoyed shaking things up.

Like Joe Stampley, Narvel Felts also knew his way around a swamp pop ballad and started out in the music business as a teenager. Whether I'm listening to music with the volume cranked up in my pickup truck or it's background music at a loud restaurant, Narvel's tenor voice cuts right through the mix, and he's got a falsetto that raises goosebumps. The last time I talked to Narvel, he was going strong, playing shows and festivals overseas, 60 years after his first single.

Evergreen may have been a tiny label compared to the majors, but people like Narvel Felts, Joe Stampley, and Robin Lee gave the company real credibility, and being around such talented people was an inspiration to me. Robin was talented, young, and she lived and breathed music, while Narvel and Joe had figured out how to roll with the changing times several generations ago. It was inspiring and educational to be around all of them.

Popular music always goes through cycles, picking up new influences, predicting some trends, and imitating the ones they didn't. In the early eighties, after the hit movie "Urban Cowboy," you saw a lot more country artists scoring crossover hits—records that made the Top10 of the pop charts as well as country. But a lot of that music was country disco, or what the radio stations started calling "neo-country pop." Not to put down anybody's favorite style of music, but it just wasn't for me.

Fortunately, in 1986, as we put the finishing touches on tracks that would end up being my first singles, the old traditional country music band sound was making a strong comeback. I had picked up some new favorite artists, such as Vince Gill, George Strait, John Wesley Ryles, and Steve Wariner. Ricky Skaggs was bringing back the bluegrass sound at the same time those country disco songs were starting to drop off the charts. There was no mistaking the honky-tonk roots in the sound of Reba McEntire, Alan Jackson, Keith Whitley, and Dwight Yoakum. You got the smell of sawdust on the dance floor and the shuffleboard in the back of the room. The chords and the guitar licks spoke the language of the common folks. The slip-note of the piano, the thump and snap of the drums and bass guitar pulled people out on the floor, and the singer poured out his soul. That is what I call country music—the music I love the most, the kind I felt I was born to sing.

In the fall of 1986, Evergreen released my first single, "You Don't Have to Be Lonely," a really fine song written by Dave Gibson and Jimbeau Hinson. Here it was, my first seven-inch slab of vinyl with my name on it, catalog no. EV1045. We had a party to celebrate. I worked the phone, feeling excited, proud, and a little nervous. Once a week, I called Morris-Dixon to follow up on the latest news about how we were doing in *Billboard*, *Cash Box*, and the other trade publications, and asking what kind of feedback they were getting from deejays and station programmers.

When the October 10 issue of *Billboard* came out, I flipped it open and looked for my name. Turning to page 85, under the heading "Recommended," the first thing that caught my eye was the Beastie Boys, who made the list with their new single, "It's the New Style." They also got a line of comment: "Typical taste and attitude from NYC's notorious white rap group." But then I saw "You Don't Have to Be Lonely" under another group of recommended singles. There was no comment, but I figure that was just as good as the lukewarm slug given to the Beastie Boys.

The *Billboard* mention gave us a little clipping to include in my press kit, but after that, the record dropped out of sight. It's been said that failure is the architect of success. You learn from it and try harder the next time. The following summer, we released my second single. "What a Memory You'd Make" (EV1056) was another fine song with a tight, smart arrangement, written by Tommy Rocco, Charley Black, and Rory Bourke.

Once again, we worked the record, looked for parts of the country where radio stations were playing music similar to my own. Every day I'd work the phones and go through the trade magazines to see how our records were doing with music critics, sales, and the various music charts.

A high chart position in *Billboard* meant a record was selling big numbers. *Cash Box* carried less weight in the eyes of the industry, but it was hugely important to independent labels like Evergreen.

Billboard was only interested if your product was the equivalent of Budweiser and Miller, selling by the truckload in every city and truck stop in the country. *Cash Box* put value on the craft-brew style of artists—those that had appeal and quality but weren't pulling in big numbers just yet.

Billboard magazine was founded in 1894, over 50 years before *Cash Box*, which debuted in 1942. *Billboard* didn't publish its first "Music Hit Parade" until the 1930s. There was no demand, really, for a list of the most popular songs of the week until the 1940s when, coincidentally, *Cash Box* began publication.

During its early years, *Billboard* was primarily a supplier of billboards and flyers for traveling circuses and other outdoor entertainment advertising. New opportunities were seized as they came into existence, including vaudeville theaters, the early film industry, and every new field of entertainment and the technologies that delivered it to the public. The earliest charts ranking the most popular music of the time were about sheet music. Before the 1940s, *Billboard* had a list called "Sheet Music Best Sellers," "Records Most Popular on Music Machines," and "Songs with the Most Radio Plugs" (according to a survey of radio stations in the New York City area).[1]

The first national music chart based on record sales appeared in the July 27, 1940 issue of *Billboard*. "National List of Best Selling Retail Records" was a ranking of the top-10, best-selling vinyl records, according to a poll of nationwide music retailers. Tommy Dorsey's "I'll Never Smile Again," with a lead vocal by Frank Sinatra was the first No. 1 record on the charts, where it stayed for 12 weeks that summer. Then came the "Top-200 Albums" and the "Hot 100"; the latter premiered August 4, 1958, with Ricky Nelson's "Poor Little Fool" at the top.

In more recent years, *Billboard* began using Nielson SoundScan technology for retail sales information, and even more recently, expanded its chart menu to include surveys covering social and streaming activity. Streaming also now factors into the tabulation of the "Hot 100." In 2014, *Billboard* added real-time Twitter charts and the "*Billboard* Artist 100."

Cash Box was founded in 1942 primarily as a trade magazine of the coin-operated machines industry. Jukeboxes were in every bus station, bar, and drug store. For a little pocket change, music lovers could hear their favorite tunes or explore the newest releases. Even a ditch digger or a mop lady could choose the music they wanted to hear—at only a nickel a play. Partly because of that image, *Cash Box* always seemed more attuned to the little guy and the street.

Besides being essential to the way that popular music was being distributed and marketed to the public, *Billboard* and *Cash Box* both influenced the way that people thought about the different styles of music they were hearing, along with the artists who were known for particular genres.

In the late 1940s, for example, *Billboard* finally recognized a style of music that was gaining popularity after World War II. At first, they called it "country-western" and labeled the charts "C&W." But even in the late fifties, *Billboard* still seemed reluctant to give country artists more than a sliver of the space devoted to pop music. In the March 3, 1958 issue, for example, news blurbs about Floyd Tillman, Lawton Williams, and Faron Young were all lumped together in a column called "Folk Talent & Tunes."

Another significant change came in 1957 when *Cash Box* dropped the offensive term "Race Music" and replaced it with "Rhythm & Blues." *Cash Box* distinguished itself from *Billboard* in many ways. The most important distinction was that *Billboard* used a combination of sales figures and radio play to compile its Top-100 chart, and *Cash Box* used only radio play. It was a mark of distinction for a radio station to be a reporter to either the *Billboard* or *Cash Box* surveys.

The chart research teams at *Cash Box* relied on airplay reports from independent radio stations in regions across the country. Programmers and deejays at independent stations often had more flexibility in their choice of new records. Some were in smaller, rural markets, where the tastes of the listening audience didn't necessarily follow the mainstream. Independent stations often had much deeper playlists than the stations owned by large, corporate conglomerates. Independents were more likely to play artists on independent record labels.

By the late fifties and early sixties, *Cash Box* was steadily growing in circulation and influence, with offices in New York, Chicago, and Los Angeles, plus bureaus in seven foreign countries. The Nashville office didn't open until 1970 or so, and for the first few years, there wasn't a lot of activity there. For several years, the entire operation consisted of a one-person staff, a woman named Juanita Jones. Her primary job was writing reviews of new country releases, which she shipped off to the main office every week.

The rivalry between *Billboard* and *Cash Box* also extended to the use of symbols: *Billboard* used a star; *Cash Box* used a bullet. Rob Simbeck wrote about the significance of the trades' use of symbols in Nashville Scene in 2002.[2]

Cash Box was once a titan. In 1958, a few months after *Billboard* began placing a star next to titles showing "outstanding upward changes of position," *Cash Box* introduced its own version, called the "bullet." The phrase "with a bullet" would become industry shorthand for a hot record's climb.

It wasn't until the late 1960s that *Cash Box* bothered to use its bullet on the country chart. The bright New York editor responsible for that move was Tom McEntee. McEntee was good at compiling charts; he had a gift for numbers previously working as a code expert with a Special Forces unit in Vietnam. In 1969, McEntee moved to Nashville and quickly found outlets for his skills there.[3]

In 1977, George Albert, President and Publisher of Hollywood-based *Cash Box* magazine, hired Jim Sharp as the new director of the Nashville office for *Cash Box*, with an expanded staff that included two writers. Sharp, formerly with Monument and Columbia Records in California, had visited the *Cash Box* offices back in 1975 when he was working at *American Songwriter* with Tex Davis, a promoter for Monument.

"It was right after I moved back to Nashville," said Sharp. "Everybody in the world loved Tex. He had the new Larry Gatlin record and he said he was going to drop it off at *Cash Box* and he invited me to go along. I'd never been to the trade papers before. *Cash Box* was in a little two-story white building at the time, 21 Music Circle East, downstairs in two little rooms. Juanita Jones was running the office. Tex and I went over to talk to her and Tex says, 'Here's a new record we'd like you to review.' She says, 'OK. What's so good about it?' Tex gave her a little sheet on the record he had written. I never thought anything about it until the next issue of *Cash Box* comes out and they ran the whole thing in the magazine, every word of it, just like Tex had done his own review of the record." Just two years later, Sharp, who had deep contacts within the record industry from the executive side to retail, would replace Juanita Jones as the new director at *Cash Box*, who didn't handle the news well.

"She tried to run over me with her car right there on Music Row," said Sharp. "She was mad. She just barely missed me."[4]

One condition that Sharp insisted on was that George Albert hire a new country music chart director. Incredibly, the country chart was still being done in New York until late 1977.

"They moved Tim Williams, from the New York office down to Nashville to be the first country chart director," said Sharp. "I knew we had to do that after working with the labels in California. If you met with the guys from California, New York, Chicago, all they wanted to talk about was R&B and pop music."

Sharp also insisted on integrity from his staff. He fired one female writer who inappropriately "liked getting flowers from the record company guys" and another writer who went to cover a Willie Nelson and Waylon Jennings Muscle Shoals recording session and accepted an invitation to travel with the entourage rather than filing his story.

From 1977 through 1984, Jim Sharp had done a solid job positioning and relocating the magazine's country division within the country music industry. But by '84, *Billboard* had surged ahead in prestige and influence over *Cash Box* and the other trade publications that compiled charts of the most popular records. *Cash Box* was hurting for revenue Sharpe was ready to move on but promised George Albert, President and Publisher of Hollywood-based *Cash Box* magazine, that he would help find a replacement. The magazine was without a Nashville director until April 1985, when Albert hired Tom McEntee for the job. McEntee scrambled to fill positions and bring in new revenue. The decisions he made would affect the lives of a lot of people over the next several years, my own included.

When I moved to Nashville and signed with Evergreen Records, I didn't know all these details. I knew the name Tom McEntee but didn't know the man himself. If you were in country music, *Billboard* and *Cash Box* were the two most important trades that published charts. —*Billboard* was the most respected and focused on major label releases; *Cash Box* primarily focused on independents.

Most people I knew would pick up a trade magazine and immediately take a look at the charts, then maybe read a couple of the reviews. You had to be really bored to read them from cover to cover. On page nine of *Billboard*, you'd see the name Edward Morris, editor in Nashville. *Cash Box* printed their masthead on page three. If you scanned down the column, you would see "Tom McEntee-Manager, Nashville Operations" in the nineteenth position. A year later, Richard Frank D'Antonio, would replace McEntee. I didn't know D'Antonio, either, except by reputation.

I was watching the charts closely during the summer of 1987, when Evergreen Records released my second single, "What a Memory You'd Make" (EV1056). It picked up some adds on *Cash Box* stations in mid-July and debuted at No. 77 in the country chart for the week of July 25. During August it made No. 10 on the *Cash Box* Independent Top-20. Over the next four weeks, it kept making the

Top-20. We also made No. 67 on the *Cash Box* country chart. The song never made a blip in the *Billboard* charts.

Johnny Morris produced my next single, "You Made It Easy" (EV1093), and was also one of the co-writers, along with Don Goodman and Pal Rakes. Another little black circle of vinyl with a light green label sent out into the world with high hopes and crossed fingers fell between the cracks.

Discouraged? I didn't really know the meaning of the word, or least that was the face I showed everyone. Whenever I went back home to Leonard to visit my family and check up on friends, I ran into people who looked at me like I had dropped from the sky. They seemed to think that playing music was something you did on weekends or with your old running buddies in somebody's garage. The notion of it being a career or a calling just didn't register with them. Was it that they couldn't comprehend it or were they jealous? It was hard to tell and best just to overlook it and say, "Hasta luego, amigo."

Music wasn't the only source of my ups and downs during this time. Sometime after I moved to Nashville, I got married for the first time. Unfortunately, the time wasn't right for us, and by the end of 1988, our relationship was falling apart – out of respect to her, that's all I'll say about it here.

Right after the release of "You Don't Have to Be Lonely," several local newspapers ran a story about me. The headline in Paris, Texas read "Sadler Hopes for Success: Doors Open if You Don't Stop Knocking, Says Leonard Singer." In the picture, I'm strumming an E major chord on my Martin guitar and singing. My hair is a little floppy, and I look nothing but sincere and hopeful. That photo of my younger self reminds me how confident and optimistic I was back then. But it also reminds me of all the hard lessons I had yet to learn.

Chapter 4

Music Row

It's hard to believe now, but I'd never heard of the term "payola" when I first moved to Nashville. During the height of the first teenage rock 'n' roll era in the 1950s, it was revealed that record labels were bribing deejays and other professionals up and down the food chain to play and promote their records, whether the public really loved them or not. Payola is what they called it, but it's just a catchy word for bribery.

If anyone was paying deejays to play my records or report them to the trades, I was unaware of it. As it turned out, my friend Kevin was being pressured by seedy promoters to adjust the *Cash Box* charts for the artists that they represented. Various types of incentives were tried—free tickets to basketball games, cash, and even verbal threats.

When we got together, Kevin and I talked about sports, the music we really liked, and, of course, girls. I had no idea that he was dealing with those issues and that things were so bad he was actually considering leaving his job and finding another profession.

I had been serious about music for a long time, but I had no idea about the lengths to which some people in the music business would go just to get ahead, to control others, or get what they wanted. Some would even commit murder. If that made me naïve, well then you could just call me that.

...

Today they call the Ryman Auditorium the "Mother Church of Country Music" because it was the home of the "Grand Ole Opry" from 1943 to 1974. It's on the National Register of Historic Places, and it's been renovated until everything about it is shiny and welcoming again. There are daily tours and regular live music events. You can still see the "Grand Ole Opry" there, too, during the slow season in November, December, and January.

The "Grand Ole Opry" quickly outgrew its original home in the National Life & Accident Insurance building. Between 1934 and1943, the show moved to several different locations before settling in at the Ryman. But the owners wanted a more modern facility that would be part of a multi-purpose entertainment destination. So, a new theater was built on Briley Parkway, nine miles from downtown Nashville. Besides the Opry House, there was Opryland U.S.A., the Opryland Theme Park, and the Opryland Hotel. This was the "Grand Ole Opry" I grew up with.

By the time I moved to Nashville in the mid-eighties and started working on Music Row, the Ryman had fallen on hard times. It was neglected, decayed, and a magnet for the usual urban critters like rats, bugs, and pigeons. The neighborhood wasn't the kind that cozies up to tourists, either. It was a shameful thing to see. Besides being the historic "Mother Church of Country Music," this was the home of the "Johnny Cash Show" and the place where some of the best films about country music had been filmed: "Coal Miner's Daughter," the Loretta Lynn story; "Sweet Dreams," the story of Patsy Cline; and Clint Eastwood's "Honkytonk Man." Even after the Ryman's owners were persuaded not to demolish the structure, it was another decade before restoration and renovation work began.

The checkered past of the Ryman and other historic buildings and neighborhoods around Music City is a reminder that fame and fortune are slippery things. Even in Nashville, it took more than a love of music to build an industry.

The tempo picked up during the forties and early fifties. Roy Acuff and Floyd Rose founded a music publishing company, Acuff-Rose, in 1942, and it made history as the first successful music enterprise in Nashville that wasn't owned by the people who ran the "Grand Ole Opry." Next, some sound engineers from WSM built a recording studio, and in 1954, Harold and Owen Bradley, a guitarist and his brother, a pianist, built their first studio on 16th Avenue South. More studios followed, spilling over onto 17th Avenue—the two north-south thoroughfares became the twin-axes of what is now known as Music Row. Chet Atkins, the country music guitar hero, was in the middle of it all, too.

Today you can walk north on 16th Avenue South to get a feeling for the neighborhood of Music Row. Continue past the intersection at South Street and the name changes from 16th Avenue South to Music Square East. You might be surprised at how quiet it is, given it's the epicenter of an audio-driven industry. You also might be surprised to find that you're the only tourist walking around. It was the same on 17th Avenue and the connecting streets. You might see the tour groups lined up at RCA Studio B or a double-decker tour bus going by. But for the most part, you'll see some office buildings and little cottages lining the street, and inside almost every one of them, people are conducting the business of music—songwriters, music publishers, music licensing firms, publicity, record labels, studios, etc.

It's not as exciting as going to the Opry or the Ryman, the Country Music Hall of Fame, or strolling down Lower Broadway and its stretch of wall-to-wall live music joints and other Music City-themed attractions. But it's over on Music Row where the gears of the country music industry are rolling, and those streets are the ones that really transformed Nashville from being merely the home of the "Grand Ole Opry" to the heart of country music, "The Nashville Sound," and all that.

Talk about boom times—it happened fast. RCA signed Elvis in 1955. By 1958 there were 500 recording sessions a year in Nashville. Ten years later, there were about 5,000 sessions a year. Just like the recording studio owners, Acuff-Rose and the publishing companies who followed them recognized there was money in all those country tunes that songwriters brought here to play for the folks.

If the prospects for making money by writing songs seems obvious now, it wasn't necessarily so in the forties and fifties. The music royalty affiliate, Broadcast Music Incorporated (BMI) moved to Nashville in 1958 and opened a one-person office. Frances Williams Preston ran BMI Nashville out of her home. By the time she became president of BMI she had her own office. On the occasion of its 50th anniversary, BMI published an online book called *BMI 50th Anniversary History Book,* in which she described that hectic time:

During that first year, I used to meet with writers in coffee shops, because I didn't have an office and a lot of the writers were working downtown at the WSM studios. So, I signed many of the first people at the Clarkston Coffee Shop next door to WSM, because I would meet them after they came off the radio shows…

We signed everybody. I mean, they came in from far and near to join BMI. When the first statements started coming in, some writers came in almost crying, saying, "You know, this is the first time I've ever received any money like this, the very first time."

In those early days, country songwriters didn't know music as an industry. It was strictly an art form. They wrote their songs and kept them in shoeboxes. They wrote about their everyday lives. They didn't think about writing a song as a way to make money. If you had told Hank Williams when he was just starting out that somebody wanted to record his song, he would have paid them to do it.[5]

Even after country music started crossing over to the mainstream, some factions of society pushed back. People who despised country music weren't much different than those who opposed rock 'n' roll. The labels "race music" and "hillbilly music" were meant as shorthand insults for people of color and poor people. As a result, many early performers of blues and country music were greatly underpaid or worse, never paid, for their work. Holdovers from this attitude continued well into the forties and fifties.

The Country Music Association (CMA), founded in 1958, helped rehabilitate the reputation of country music, and at the same time, served as a trade association for the genre, convincing radio programmers, advertisers, and other groups that country music could sell products.

Radio executives, writers, performers, and music publishers led the organization and set about regaining country's place in the public consciousness. From the start, the CMA made sales presentations for broadcasters and advertising executives in major radio markets like New York, Chicago, and Detroit. It aimed to convince advertisers that country music could sell products and brought in everything from market surveys to top country entertainers to prove it. Furthermore, in 1961, the CMA established the Country Music Hall of Fame to instill pride in country music's history.

It's hard to believe now that advertisers had to be convinced that country music could help grease the wheels of commerce, but apparently, it had slipped their minds. Nashville wasn't the only town producing big country hits, either. On the West Coast, Bakersfield, California gave us Buck Owens, who scored with "Act Naturally" in 1963 and had a total of 19 No. 1 hits on *Billboard* in the sixties. A great songwriter, Buck founded his own publishing company in 1965 and wasted no time signing Merle Haggard, who burned up the charts with "Mama Tried" and "Okie from Muskogee."

The CMA was also responsible for the founding of the Country Music Hall of Fame and Museum, which opened at the northern end of Music Row in 1967. The original building looked a lot like a church, with its geometric façade and large stained-glass windows. The founders had lofty goals, which included not only serving country fans who just wanted to see the Nudie suits, custom Cadillacs, and guitars of their idols but also to serve as an educational and research facility. The Country Music Hall of Fame and Museum was a huge hit and soon became one of the city's top attractions.

Years went by, and although the Country Music Hall of Fame remained as popular as ever, the building's appearance looked dated after a decade or so. Next door was a motor hotel and a Shoney's restaurant that catered not only to tourists and wannabe country stars that visited their favorite country stars' vanity museums, but cheap hustlers, drug dealers, and other disreputable characters. By the 1990s, it all looked pretty shabby.

In 2001, the Country Music Hall of Fame moved into its new, gigantic, 130,000-square foot facility in the center of downtown, and in 2015, expanded again to 350,000 square feet of galleries, museum stores, event space, and education facilities. It's mighty grand, created to impress and educate everyone from casual country listeners to steel guitar scholars. And the old area next to the roundabout at the northern end of Music Row, where the original Hall of Fame and motel-complex once stood, has since been demolished, scraped clean, and redeveloped.

Appearances can be deceiving, however. Despite the mainstream respect for the music and the clean up around Music Row, beneath the surface, a seamier side of the music business continues pretty much as it has since the beginning, a side that the tourists never really see.

Payola, or pay-to-play, means some form of bribery or extortion to gain an unfair advantage on a competitor's products. It's a phenomenon that goes on in every business. Call me a foolish idealist, but in the music business it kind of drains some of the magic out of something that ought to be pure and natural. When you hear a song that appeals to you, and you buy a copy, you want to feel as though no one pushed you into it. But unless you're in the room where the artist is playing live, there's a good chance that a record company put some of their muscle behind it getting your attention. The best-known form of music fraud is payola. The term was popularized back in the late fifties when Victrola and Rock-Ola were well-known brand names. Victrola made record players, and Rock-Ola was the name of one of the most common jukeboxes, and the founder of the company that made them was named, believe it or not, David C. Rockola.

The first big payola scandal happened years before I was born. If you've seen *Ray*, the movie about the life of singer Ray Charles, you might remember a scene in a radio station in the 1950s, where someone hands a disc jockey a fistful of money to play Ray's records. That's the most basic, stripped-down example. The movie came out in 2004, a year after the trial that finally brought justice for Kevin's murder. So, when I watched that scene, my pulse kicked up a few notches, and the temperature of the room dropped a few degrees as I said to myself, "That's it. That's payola."

The association between payola and rock 'n' roll music originated in 1960, when two well-known figures, Alan Freed and Dick Clark, were accused of accepting large sums of money to promote certain records. The accusations came to the attention of a committee in the U.S. House of Representatives. A disc jockey in Chicago named Phil Lind told the committee he had been paid $22,000 to play a certain song, but Alan Freed and Dick Clark were more well known. Freed, a DJ from Cleveland, was one of the early exponents of rock 'n' roll music. Clark, from Philadelphia, host of the Top-40 show "American Bandstand" (1956—1989), was still being referred to as "America's Oldest Teenager" until his death in 2012 at age 72.

Dick Clark testified before the committee and impressed them with his all-American looks and his presentation. He claimed he had done nothing wrong, but he divested himself of all investments that had obviously been connected to pay-for-play. Freed, who called himself "the Old King of the Moondoggers," didn't go over as well with the congressmen. He pled guilty to 99 counts and paid a $300 fine, but his career was ruined, and his life cut short by excessive drinking. He died in 1965 at age 43.

Contrary to myth, the payola scandal wasn't exclusively a rock 'n' roll story. The people who wanted to rid the world of rock 'n' roll weren't fans of country, ragtime, jazz, or blues, either. In the 1950s, major labels were upset because independent labels had suddenly gained a toehold in the market. The big labels focused on the idea that their little, independent rivals were hiring promoters to bribe disc jockeys to play their records on the radio, forcing their music on the public.

Strange as it may seem, the group that really pushed Congress into investigating payola in the radio and recording industry was the American Society of Composers, Authors and Publishers (ASCAP). Until BMI was founded in 1939, ASCAP had the market pretty much all to itself for collecting and distributing royalties for publishers and songwriters. Not only was ASCAP hostile towards its rivals, but it was also a stuffy, clubby group that made it really difficult to gain membership. Unless you were accepted by an agency like ASCAP or BMI, there was no real way to make money from airplay. There were plenty of successful artists who weren't good enough for ASCAP, either, according to Francis Williams Preston:

> *"Country artists had access to the public through the Grand Ole Opry broadcast over Nashville's WSM since 1925, and a few artists became nationally-known recording stars, but membership in ASCAP eluded them. Country stars such as Gene Autry and jazz greats like Jelly Roll Morton were rejected for years by ASCAP before finally gaining membership."*[6]

No wonder Frances made so many songwriters happy when she opened the BMI office in Nashville there, embracing songwriters who played country, hillbilly, or blues.

In November 1953, a group of 33 composers calling themselves "The Songwriters of America" initiated a $150 million anti-trust action against BMI, NBC, CBS, ABC, RCA Victor Records, Columbia Records, and 27 other individuals. They were claiming a conspiracy of broadcasters and manufacturers keeping "good music" from being recorded and played on the air. The plaintiffs included some of the leading names in popular songwriting, such as Alan Jay Lerner, Ira Gershwin, Oscar Hammerstein, and Arthur Schwartz, who was the leading plaintiff.

BMI was founded in 1939, shortly after ASCAP came up with "an explosive increase" in the rates it charged radio stations for licensing ASCAP members' music. BMI rates were much friendlier, and radio stations flocked to sign with BMI. ASCAP, however, had a good friend in U.S. Representative Emanuel Celler, chairman of the House of Representatives Judiciary Committee and chairman of the payola investigation in Congress. BMI, he said, was trying to make "good music" extinct and contributing to juvenile delinquency. Billy Rose, an ASCAP songwriter, echoed that opinion in his testimony, saying, "Not only are most of the BMI songs junk, but in many cases, they are obscene junk pretty much on the level with dirty comic magazines."

BMI representatives also testified, explaining the actual ways that music was selected for airplay by radio stations. The way they made it sound, the possibilities for corruption in the process were slim to none. Of course, that was an exaggeration, too, but it wasn't on the level of hysteria being expressed by the other side. Tennessee Governor Frank Clement also came to the defense of BMI. Clement truly appreciated the way that BMI supported the Nashville music industry. He also took a poke at the Songwriters of America by asking if their high standards were really and truly represented by the popular song co-written by ASCAP member Billy Rose, "Does Your Chewing Gum Lose Its Flavor on The Bedpost Overnight."[7]

The first big payola scandal blew over without any Congressional action against BMI or, for that matter, the musical styles that ASCAP disliked. The practice, however, has continued in various forms ever since. Every few years, a record label or radio station is slapped with a fine, or some politician stakes his future on a high-profile investigation of payola practices in the music industry.

Meanwhile, on Music Row, life goes on. People keep writing songs, making music, trying to get a break, looking for a little secret that will help them get ahead of the competition.

Chapter 5

With a Bullet

As the Sadler family celebrated the Christmas holidays in 1988, we nervously waited for news on how my sixth single "Tell It Like It Is" (EV1088) was doing. The song is a personal favorite of mine——a beautiful swamp pop ballad that had launched the career of Aaron Neville. Neville was working as a longshoreman the first time he heard a demo of the song. Neville's recording was released on Par-Lo Records in the fall of 1966 when I was three months old, and by early 1967, it was No. 1 on *Billboard*'s Hot R&B chart and No. 2 on the Hot 100.

John Wesley Ryles covered it in 1976. It was a single on Music Mill Records. That's actually the version I remember hearing first, the way I came to know the song. John was good at everything: singing, playing guitar, songwriting. He was only 17 when his first single, "Kay," was a Top-10 hit on the *Billboard* Country chart. In Nashville, I felt privileged to meet him, work with him, and become his friend.

"Tell It Like It Is," asks the age-old question, "How deep do your feelings go? Are you ready for commitment?"

"If you want something to play with," the singer says, "go and find yourself a toy..." I guess that attitude might have reflected my desire to have people out there to love my music, and for recognition by the Nashville music industry, but I don't remember thinking about it that deeply. I just wanted a hit record.

We recorded "Tell It Like It Is" in Waylon Jennings' studio. I had injured my back, so I was sitting on a stool with an ice pack on my back while we were recording. I remember it was late, about two or three in the morning when we started on this one, and I did the vocal in one take. I didn't even know about Aaron Neville's version until later on. Maybe when I was a baby, just a few months old, the song became imprinted in my brain.

Christmas morning, we had presents under the tree, mistletoe in the doorway, and the No. 44 spot on the *Cash Box* Country Independent Chart. And on page 20, they gave me an "Indie Spotlight" blurb, with a photo. "A perfect musical vehicle," they said. "Sterling production highlights Sadler's adept vocal ability. A warm song to slow dance to during these wintery nights." The next week, it climbed to No. 8 on the Independent chart and it debuted on the Country Singles Chart at 76. Radio stations in three different geographical regions reported that it was one of their "most-added" singles of the week.

Happy New Year, 1989. Nashville weather turned cold and rainy and stayed that way the whole month of January. "Tell It Like It Is" inched up to No. 68 on the *Cash Box* Country Singles chart and moved up to No. 7 on the Independent chart. We crossed our fingers as it debuted at No. 90 in *Billboard* and climbed to No. 77.

In February, it snowed a little, the rain stopped, and the temperature rarely got above 70 degrees. There was an extra chill in the air as we learned that Billy Joe Royal had recorded his own version of "Tell It Like It Is." Royal had started out as a pop singer and had his first hit ("Down in the Boondocks") the year before I was born. To our misfortune, Royal's record label, Atlantic, chose this time to release the single and the album of the same name. Atlantic was a powerhouse and compared to Evergreen; it was a blue whale, and ours was a little catfish.

Marie Ratliff, a writer for *Billboard*, wrote several paragraphs about what happened in the February 4, 1989 issue. "It's not often that two different artists get the inspiration to do a remake at the same time," she began. "Unfortunately, it has happened with Aaron Neville's 1967 pop hit, 'Tell It Like It Is.'

"Sammy Sadler's version on Evergreen had a few weeks of lead time in its release date and bulleted up the charts for three weeks before the Billy Joe Royal cut on Atlantic America hit the streets.

"Because of Royal's strong fan base, most programmers are making the switch, which resulted in Sadler's record peaking at No. 70 last week and Royal's taking the Hot Shot Debut honors this week at No. 54."

Billy Joe Royal was a great singer, but was his version of the song that much better than mine? I didn't think so, and I didn't want to give up hope on my single just yet.

At the beginning of March 1989, "Tell It Like It Is" was still clinging to the *Cash Box* Independent chart, but it was fairly certain that it wasn't going to earn either a bullet or a star. I felt a little kicked in the gut by Billy Joe Royal, but I knew better than to take it personally.

I still had an album's worth of songs, but if we kept putting out singles and each one of them fizzled out, I wondered how we could expect much excitement for the release of the first Sammy Sadler LP. Johnny Morris said he had confidence in me. The way he had stuck behind Robin Lee was reassuring, but I couldn't help feeling frustrated.

Thursday, March 9, started off cold and foggy. The sun didn't come out until the afternoon when the temperature peaked at just over 50 degrees and then started falling again. During the day, I made some business calls, ran some errands, and worked out. That afternoon I made some more calls and ran more errands. When I got home, my wife and I got into an argument. It was one of those disagreements that cools down for a little while and then blows up again. After nightfall, I realized it might be best for both of us if I went out and got some air.

Cash Box came out every Friday, and anybody who knew Kevin Hughes knew that on Thursday evening, he'd be slaving away on his charts long after everyone else went home. The annual Country Radio Seminar (CRS) had taken place the previous weekend, which added some additional workload. CRS was one of those must-attend gatherings for anyone who had any connection at all to country music radio. It was the equivalent of Music Row's junior-senior prom.

I knew Kevin would still be in the office, so I called him. I knew he might have plans already but sometime after 8, maybe 8:30, I called him anyway. The phone rang a bunch of times, and I was hanging up when I heard Kevin say hello. I asked him what he was doing, and he chuckled since it was such a dumb question. He said he was pretty close to wrapping things up. "Come on down," he said. "I'll leave the door unlocked so you can get in." So, I put on a warm jacket, grabbed my keys, and left.

People didn't hang out on Music Row after dark. You'd hear the police sirens just about every night heading to the projects just a few blocks away. Derelicts would show up out of nowhere and go through your trash. Muggers, armed drug dealers, and the occasional sociopath came down there because it was full of targets.

Back in 1987, a suspect dubbed the "Music Row Rapist" had terrorized the neighborhood. An ex-convict living just two blocks south of our office was finally arrested, tried, and convicted. At least half a dozen women had been attacked, including several in the nearby Edgefield neighborhood.

"Back then, the Row really wasn't all that safe after dark," said Monte Warden, whose band, the Wagoneers, were working there in February 1989 at Emerald Sound Studio on 16th Avenue South. "I remember at the end of the night when we were finished working for the day, before we went out to our cars, somebody would say to the session engineer, Jeff Copek, 'Jeff, you have your gun? Somebody with a gun needs to walk these boys to their car.' And Jeff would do it, because he always had a gun when he was working."

Truthfully speaking, sometimes when you heard about musicians getting mugged on Music Row and other sketchy parts of town, the victims were in the wrong place at the wrong time for a reason—typically to score some drugs.

I never messed with drugs, not even when I was a teenager, not ever. I didn't hang around with those people. I didn't get into the kind of trouble other young people get into because they're unhappy or poor, they don't fit in, or they just want to be different. This story might be more dramatic if I said I was a miserable kid at war with society, but it wouldn't be me. I was happy growing up. My parents were always proud of me. I never wanted to let them down.

Kevin was cut from the same cloth. He was a straight arrow—religious, sensitive, honest, and down to earth. A country boy who never dropped the habit of saying "please" and "thank you." On paper, we could have been the same man.

It was a real dark night, just a day or two after the new moon. Music Row was quiet except for all the big cars around Emerald. Earlier in the week, Willie Nelson, Johnny Cash, Waylon Jennings, and Kris Kristofferson had begun recording their second *Highwayman* album. Chips Moman was producing again. Famous musicians and in-crowd types were dropping by to visit every day.

Even though Kevin had let his hair grow long and had a semblance of a beard, he still looked like a Boy Scout. This was a guy who wore white socks to work.

Kevin looked up and smiled at me when I got there. He was on the phone with somebody, but he waved me in and wrapped up the call before I had a chance to sit down.

"Hey man, how are you?"

He said, "I'm good, but I'm ready to get the heck out of here. Where you want to go?

"I don't know. What do you feel like?"

He said, "I don't care."

I laughed, "I don't care, either."

Kevin said he'd drive. He had a little Pontiac Sunbird that was practically brand-new, and he was proud of it. I remember he had his racquetball stuff in there, sweatshirt, shoes, and a bunch of cassette tapes. He wore a big, brown leather coat. After we got underway, we decided on Captain D's, which was over on West End. We ordered sandwiches or something like that and talked and laughed for an hour or so. He didn't let on that something dark was brewing.

Later, other people who talked to Kevin that week said he was worried or upset about what was going on at work, but he didn't mention any of that to me. It's a fact that guys will sometimes confide things to their female friends that they won't even bring up with their male friends. Maybe that was the case with us, or perhaps he was just all talked out.

On the way back, we stopped to use the phone at the Evergreen office. It was my idea because I wanted to talk to my parents before they went to bed. This was before everyone had cell phones and free long distance, but I could call for free at the office.

I called and talked to Mom and Dad both. They had heard me talk about Kevin, but they'd never met him, so I said, "Want to talk to Kevin for a minute?" and handed him the phone.

He talked to them for several minutes before handing it back to me. I was still talking to them when we heard a rattling at the front door. Kevin went to the door and looked out.

"What was it?" I asked.

"It looked like a black guy walking down the street," he said. "But it's dark out there. It's hard to tell."

By then, it was about 10:30 p.m., so I told my mom I'd call her tomorrow and said goodbye. Before leaving, we looked out the front windows and on the side of the building. I locked up, and we went out and stood on the front porch for a minute to look around and didn't see anything. As I've explained before, the office was really just a little house that had been converted for business, so I felt kind of like a homeowner worried about a burglar or a window peeper.

Evergreen is on the west side of 16th Avenue South, a one-way street heading north, and Kevin had parked his car on the other side. We crossed the street, talking back and forth (most likely about nothing extraordinary), and laughing.

Both car doors were open, and we were still talking, then everything got real weird real fast. The man in the black mask came out of the shadows, and suddenly he was right on top of me. I had no idea what color his skin was, I don't even know if I saw his eyes, but I did see the gun. Dark metal, a little gun with a short barrel pointed right at me.

Here is when time becomes an odd thing; it tilts and a second crawls by like an hour. Later it races away in the memory of the moment.

"Look out, he's got a gun!" I yelled, my voice sounding like a scared child. I threw up my hands, saw a flash, and fell sideways and flopped on the floorboard. The right side of my body seemed to have caught fire or something.

Doctors told me later that throwing up my hands probably saved my life; otherwise, the gunshot might have hit me in the head. Instead, the bullet had entered my right arm, traveled through my bicep, scrambled a big nerve bundle, ruptured an artery, and finally lodged in my shoulder muscle.

I tried to get up, but the seat was slippery, and blood was going everywhere. The gunshots were loud. Lots of people on the block had heard the shots and my shouts and were looking out their windows or standing outside. One woman pulled up and parked three car-lengths behind us and saw the whole thing. Fearing for her own life, she scooted down in her seat as the masked gunman ran past her car.

Meanwhile, I heard a voice shouting at me, asking if I needed help. It came from a second-floor apartment in the little building at 1020 16th Avenue South, almost directly across the street from Evergreen. Phillip Barnhart was his name, I learned later. He was in his apartment, where he lived with Connie Gaddis when they heard loud voices and then gunshots. Phil went to the window, looked out, and saw my feet sticking out of the car.

I don't remember running up the stairs, but I made it up to his apartment somehow, and after I got there, I fell on the floor. From there on, everything that happened is a scrambled bunch of puzzle pieces. The account of that night you're reading now was drawn from information I learned from eyewitnesses, televised news reports, newspapers, and the criminal case file.

My body was going into shock. I was bleeding to death.

The people in apartment No. 6 at 1020 16th Avenue South, Phillip Barnhart and Connie Gaddis, looked after me until the ambulance came and took me to the emergency room at Vanderbilt Medical Center. I owe them my life.

Apparently, I asked if I could use their phone, then I called my parents back to let them know that I'd been shot, but I was alive and that Kevin might have been shot, too. I didn't know what had happened or why, and I didn't know a whole lot more about it for a long, long time.

Officer David Williams was almost at the end of his shift when he heard the dispatch call.[8] It was 10-52, 10-64, the police codes for *ambulance needed* and *crime in progress*. The address given was 1020 16th Avenue South. The dispatcher immediately came back on and said, "multiple calls"—another indication that it was a bad situation. Williams answered the call and lit up his cruiser. It only took between two and three minutes to get there.

Williams had joined the force in 1986 and would serve another 17 years before retiring in 2004. During his 20-plus years as a policeman, he saw a lot of the worst things that people can do to each other, but the memory of this crime scene would haunt him for the rest of his life.

"I had five or six people in the street flagging me over," said Williams. "When I pulled up, there were civilians standing around everywhere, coming out of the studios. Somebody had been shot. I saw a body in the street. Both doors were open on the car, a blue Pontiac Sunbird."

Among the people gathered around was a registered nurse named Diane Palovich. She was trained in CPR and was attempting to revive Kevin.

"Kevin Hughes was the victim lying in the street," said Williams. "I checked his vitals, but he was dead. He wasn't coming back. I told these people, step back, he's dead, you can't help him. I've got to get this area cordoned off."

As the first officer at the crime scene, Williams knew he had a protocol to follow, but this was a special situation.

"I called for backup, but I knew it would be a while before anyone got there," said Williams. "The blood coming out of Kevin was horrific. There was blood everywhere, blood all over inside of the car, blood flowing down the sidewalk on the passenger side of the car. Kevin's blood was just running out of his body. His blood was running down the concrete next to the curb. I've seen a lot of stuff in my twenty years in law enforcement, but I can still see that. His blood was flowing down the street into this storm drain. It was unnatural."

A woman grabbed Officer Williams' arm and said she'd seen the suspect. She pointed out the direction he had fled—south on 16th Avenue South. Then another civilian told Williams about the other guy, the one who'd been shot and then ran the other direction (north).

Williams was faced with a tough decision: Should he try to pursue the shooter, protect the crime scene, or find the victim (me) and render aid?

"If someone is injured, the first duty of a police officer is to render aid," said Williams. "So, I told these people, 'back up, keep this area clear, and wait for the police.' Then I ran up the sidewalk. Sammy was losing so much blood I just followed the trail. He was just a few doors down in this building on the second floor. I found the stairs and saw the blood spatters going all the way up. I ran up there and saw all these people in this little apartment, and they were taking care of the shooting victim. He had crawled under a desk and was curled up in a fetal position. A girl was on the floor with him, applying direct pressure to the wound to stop the bleeding."

Seeing that the shooting victim was in good hands, Williams cautioned everyone there to wait for the police to come and take their information, because he needed to get down to the street and secure the crime scene. "I hated to leave him, but for all I knew there was still an active shooter running around down there," said Williams. "But when he heard me saying I was going to leave, he just went into a complete panic mode. He was reaching out saying 'No, you can't leave me. He's gonna come back and finish me off.' He doesn't remember any of that now, but he was in such shock he thought the guy would come back to kill him. At least he was still conscious. I told the girl, 'This guy's not coming back, trust me. You all are doing a good job. Keep applying pressure, but I've got to get back to the crime scene."

The crime scene was secured a few minutes later. Additional police cars were arriving, as one witness later described, "from every conceivable direction." Paramedics from the Fire Department secured me on a stretcher and loaded me into the ambulance for the short ride to Vanderbilt Medical Center. They immediately determined that I was in critical condition. I was in and out of consciousness and was unaware of how badly I was injured.

The Metro detective on call that night was Detective Bill Pridemore.[9] He was notified of the shooting at 11 p.m. and arrived on the scene 45 minutes later. A veteran detective named Lt. Pat Postiglione, who would be second in command on the case, joined Pridemore. Officers at the scene were already taking preliminary statements from witnesses. A number of people had seen the shooting and, except for being able to see the suspect's face, the descriptions were fairly detailed.

Witnesses said they had seen a man wearing a black ski mask, black clothing, a dark ball cap, and black gloves. All of them said he was a white man, about 5' 10" and stocky. Apparently, the shooter was right-handed, because he held the gun in his right hand. The gun was described as being dark and small, with a short barrel, probably a .38. Every witness who saw him said that there was something strange about the way he ran. Some of them called it a limp; others just said it was just weird. On the police reports, it was described as "an odd gait." No one recognized him.

As hard as it is now to go through the descriptions of my own shooting, it was much more disturbing to learn the details of Kevin's murder. They say the whole thing happened in about seven seconds. If the killer shot me in the first second, it took another six seconds to chase Kevin down and fire the four shots that ended his life.

Blue Ridge Publishing operated out of the converted residence at 1024 16th Avenue South. An employee, Rita Alcorta, was the woman who had just parked her car when the shooting started. Detective E.J. Bernard questioned Alcorta at 10:44 p.m. that night, less than 15 minutes after it happened.

Alcorta gave Bernard what was probably the most detailed description of the shooting of any of the witnesses. She said the masked man was definitely white because she could see the skin around his eyes. He was between 5'8" and 5'10" and "chubby." The gun was small and dark.

According to Bernard's notes, Alcorta witnessed the following:

> *Victim [Kevin Hughes] was standing beside the driver's open door. Suspect was standing beside the open passenger's side door… the victim appeared to sit in the seat, then jump or roll out onto the street. At the same time the suspect appeared to lean into the passenger side. After the victim rolled out of the vehicle, he began running away from the car, toward Edgehill. The suspect chased him and fired two times, causing the victim to fall. The suspect fired these two shots with his right hand. He then fired three times, using both hands, into the victim's head… he then ran in the direction of the projects.*

Several witnesses saw the masked man chase Kevin and shoot him to death. They said he fell after being hit by one of the shots, and after that, the suspect calmly walked over and fired three more shots, aiming at his head. The killer then paused for a moment looking down at the body and fled the scene on foot. Several people told police they saw a dark colored Nissan on Tremont Street drive away with its lights off.

Four days later, when detectives Pridemore and Postiglione re-interviewed Rita Alcorta at her office, she gave them the following detail:

> *[It] appeared that the suspect had tunnel vision on the victim and it did not seem like he cared who was watching him, he was so determined to get the victim and kill him. Ms. Alcorta also states that she never heard the suspect say or yell anything to the victim.*

The death of a friend or family member can be a hard thing

to understand and accept, even when it was caused by a terminal illness or old age. But for a guy like Kevin Hughes to be stalked, run down, and executed in such a cold, inhumane manner, it was just gut-wrenching and awful. I felt so bad for his family. Their lives had been turned upside down by a killing that made no sense. They were coming to Nashville to identify Kevin's body, talk to the police, and gather up his belongings.

The criminal case files gave the cold details of Kevin's death. On a chart with silhouette drawings of a generic male body, medical examiner Dr. Harlan drew two arrows pointing to the back of the head, another one to the left shoulder, and two others to fingers on his right hand.[10] Each arrow was labeled "G.S.W. entry" (G.S.W. stands for gunshot wound). And there were deep abrasions on both knees.

> *This 23-year-old white male was shot multiple times, with the gunshot wound to the head causing injury to brain, vital structures of midbrain, internal carotid arteries, and death. The blood alcohol is negative.*

Each of the body's organs had been removed, examined, and weighed. Kevin's heart, for example, weighed 345 grams.

Meanwhile, I was in a hospital bed at Vanderbilt, registered under a fake name. There was a policeman outside of my room at all times. They were concerned that someone might come in and try to finish me off—it was like something out of a movie. The only visitors allowed were my mom and dad, a couple of friends, and detectives from the Metro murder squad.

I was heavily sedated. My right arm was wrapped up, swollen as big as two basketballs. One thing I remember is when they took me into the X-ray room, they put a catheter in my arm and shot me up with contrast dye for the X-ray. Then a doctor took my arm and yanked it straight out, and it sounded like tree branches breaking. I screamed. The pain was off the scale. If there's a worse level of pain, I don't want to know anything about it.

The next few days were surreal. The pain drugs made one day

melt into another and time felt as if it kept falling out of tempo. The detectives came to interview me several times, and during their visits, I know I was alert because I have strong memories connected with them.

A few days after the surgery, the phone on the bedside table rang. Someone handed me the phone and I said hello. It was Chuck Dixon of Morris-Dixon. They partnered with Evergreen for promoting, and Dixon was the man who thought of himself as the "Don" of Music Row.

"Sammy, I just want you to know I'm so, so, sorry," he said. "You call me if you need anything. Money, whatever it is, you let me know."

I was shocked. I don't remember what I said. After I hung up, I was petrified. Chuck Dixon wasn't on my list of visitors; he wasn't supposed to know how to find me. Why did he sound so worked up about the shooting? Maybe I was just feeling paranoid, but it didn't feel like he was calling because he was worried about my health.

Later on, I remembered that Craig Morris was the first person I saw at the hospital that didn't work there. He rushed down there and saw me before they took me into surgery. Craig was Chuck's partner, so it was only natural for him to call Chuck and tell him what happened. But the phone call still bothered me. The tone of Chuck's voice, the things he said—there was something off about it.

At the time, I didn't know that Kevin had died. They weren't telling me anything. One day the following week, the two main detectives on the case, Pridemore and Postiglione, came in to ask some more questions. One of them said something about a funeral.

I always addressed them as "sir," answering "yes, sir" and "no, sir" whenever it was the appropriate response, just as my parents had taught me when I was little. But in my surprise, I forgot all that.

"What funeral? Who died?"

"Kevin," said Pridemore. "He died that night you got shot."

Everything was surreal, and I knew it wasn't because of the pain and the medications they were giving me.

Chapter 6

Under Suspicion

I REMEMBER BEING ON THE OPERATING TABLE WITH ALL THESE DOCTORS AND NURSES WORKING ON ME. I saw my mom and step-sister Detra walk through the door of the operating room, and I said, "I'm gonna be OK." Then I floated up and out of my body, hovering there, watching them operate on me, and then I went into a white light—he brightest I'd ever seen—and I was in total peace.

After the surgery, I awoke and saw my arm, it was wrapped tight and as big as a tree trunk. The doctor came in and told me that I had suffered a serious gunshot wound to my right arm. The bullet had severed the main artery and they had to operate on me right away to stop the bleeding and save my life. They took an artery out of my leg to graft into my shoulder and worked on me, using a microscope, for over 18 hours.

"A serious gunshot wound," he said, "does a lot more than just drill a hole through tissue and bone." The word "trauma" came up several times. "The tissue around the bullet wound was so swollen that the X-ray was hard to read," he said. They didn't know the full extent of the damage until they operated.

After rupturing the artery, the bullet slammed into a bundle of nerves in my arm. He ticked off the names of nerves that might have been destroyed or severely affected, explaining that they were all involved in moving my hand. The nerve bundle was now wrapped in synthetic fiber, like a tiny burrito in my arm. The bullet was left in place, since trying to remove it would do additional damage to the muscle.

The bad news was the bullet had blown apart the ulnar nerve, the one that directs any kind of pinching movement with your hand. That included holding and maneuvering a guitar pick. From now on, I'd have to let somebody else do all the guitar work when I performed. Physical therapy would also be a big part of my recovery, along with another surgery to finish the job. For that one, we would have to wait six months or so.

I felt bad for Mom and Dad. Getting to Nashville on a moment's notice had proven difficult. Thursday night, after driving pedal to the metal from Leonard to Dallas-Fort Worth airport, they found out that there were no flights to Nashville until Friday. They tried to rent a private plane, but there were none available. So, Mom stayed there at the terminal all night, waiting for the next flight out.

Meanwhile, Dad decided to drive. They figured they would be in Nashville for a while anyway, and they would need a car. They were worried as hell about me and bewildered about the whole thing; so was I. But I was alive, and for that I was thankful.

The few friends allowed to visit me brought me messages from all the people who cared about me. Flowers started arriving. A big bunch of flowers and a nice card came from Jimmy Bowen, the president of MCA Records.

The "Murder on Music Row" story went out on the wire and appeared in headlines from coast to coast, and it made its way to Europe, as well. Reporters seemed to love dropping catchy phrases like "Murder on Music Row," "Murder in Music City," and clever puns using the word "hit."

Television crews came down to Music Row that night to broadcast live footage, showing all the music people crowded on the sidewalk on 16th Avenue South. The police and ambulance lights were still flashing, there were cops everywhere, and every other face on the sidewalk belonged to a famous musician. It was crazy. There was Kris Kristofferson, tall and skinny, and Willie Nelson, both of them with serious looks on their faces, watching as my stretcher was loaded into the back of the ambulance.

One of the crucial eyewitnesses was Donnie R. Lowery, who lived at 1030 16th Avenue South.[11] You'll see Donny's credits as a songwriter on hit songs by artists like Alabama, Kathy Mattea, and New Grass Revival, but when the police asked him about his occupation, he said he was employed by the Tennessee Valley Authority as a fisheries biologist. You don't run into a lot of ichthyologists on Music Row. Donnie and his girlfriend, Kathy Hunter, were listening to a tape when they heard the first gunshot. They went to the window and saw everything that happened next. Sometimes I wonder what song they had been listening to, and if it later became one of Donny's big hits.

The press worked the story like a dog chasing a car. Saturday's headline in Nashville's *Tennessean*, "Music Row Becoming Murder Row," was just the beginning.[12] The photo of Kevin was an old one, taken before he let his hair grow long. The picture of me was from my press kit. I had a big smile on my face as if nothing could go wrong. A map of the crime scene named all the businesses on the block, from Evergreen Records to Emerald Studio on one side, and Celebrity International down to Bug Music and Kim's Market on the other. Arrows and numbers traced our last steps:

1. Kevin Hughes and Sammy Sadler leave Evergreen Records.

2. Gunman opens fire. Sadler seeks safety in 3rd floor apartment.

3. Gunman fires on Hughes as he runs south down 16th Avenue.

4. Hughes collapses behind car where Rita Alcorta cowers.

A word balloon next to Emerald Studio read: "Country music stars Willie Nelson and Kris Kristofferson record tracks for their upcoming album, *Highwayman II*." Readers of the *Tennessean* would probably want to know that information, even if it had nothing to do with the murder.[13]

The shooting was the "latest in a series of murders and rapes that have hit the Music Row area over the past three years," the article said. The people who lived and worked there were practically on the verge of panic. One of them was Gayle McMinn, who ran an agency called Events Unlimited from her office at 1022 16th Avenue South. McMinn said to reporters that she had always told her employees to be extra careful and to always park their cars in front of the office. But after seeing what happened in the street that night, she was terrified and didn't know what to tell them anymore.

The paper also interviewed Candy Parton, a singer and songwriter. Yes, Candy and Dolly Parton were related, but not closely related. "We saw this guy in the street," said Candy. "His feet were jutting out into the lane...There was blood everywhere." Candy and her drummer were driving to an audition when they drove up on the murder scene.

Murder squad detective Terry McElroy told the reporters that the police didn't have much to go on. "We really don't have a motive," he said. "It could've been robbery related. We just don't know."

The final paragraphs in the article were given to Kevin's father, Larry Hughes. "Kevin had always been obsessed with music," he explained. He had even dropped out of Belmont College to work at *Cash Box*, because "charting music was kind of his love."

On the morning after the murder, eleven witnesses were driven down to Metro Criminal Investigation Division (CID) for formal statements that would be tape-recorded. In their interviews, Phillip Barnhart and Connie Gaddis told the police what I had said to them after I collapsed on the floor of their apartment: "He just walked up and started shooting."

But that particular statement was never fully accepted by Pridemore and Postiglione. The public line they gave out was that they suspected it was "an attempted robbery gone wrong" or some kind of grudge or "vendetta" related to the music industry.

The first theory was ridiculous. They wanted to find a motive, and I understood that, but to call it a robbery attempt contradicted what I had told them, along with the accounts given by all the other eyewitnesses.

Over and over they asked if Evergreen employees or *Cash Box* employees like Kevin ever carried large sums of cash when they left the office at night. Were we having business troubles? Was Evergreen heavily in debt to someone? Drugs? "No, no, and no," I told them.

I didn't have any enemies that I knew of. How could anyone in his or her right mind hate Kevin Hughes? Vendettas? Neurotic, oddball music people were out there, sure, but I'd never met one crazy enough to shoot someone over a bad review or a record that didn't make the Top-40.

In the first two weeks or so after the shooting, Pridemore and Postiglione questioned me at least four or five times. They always came back wanting more details about this or that, but it always seemed to be the same question over and over. They seemed to think I wasn't telling the truth, but if they asked me in a different way on a different day, they might get a different answer.

Nashville Metro Police Department definitely devoted a lot of manpower to the case. Besides lead detectives Pridemore and Postiglione, there were two other teams from the murder squad, helping with the workload as well as pursuing some of the more far-out theories they were investigating.

Postiglione was the politer and more sensitive of the two detectives. He was slender, with black hair and a push-broom mustache. He talked fast, with a heavy accent from his upbringing in Queens, New York. Pridemore was taller, bald-headed, and spoke with a mild Southern drawl.

After looking at newspaper files on the criminal history of Nashville, I've learned that Postiglione is a legend. He retired after 33 years on the force in 2013, having cleared many of the most major cases in the city's history, including 55 cold case files.

Pridemore and I never hit it off. He was aggressive, blunt, and didn't seem to worry about asking something that might embarrass me or make me mad. When I gave him an answer, he'd get a blank look in his eyes, as if whatever I said had to be weighed with a grain of salt. Maybe they were just playing good cop/bad cop, and perhaps they were just doing their jobs the best way they knew how.

Friday morning after the surgery, when my head was still cloudy from anesthesia, they came in to question me. Monday morning, they were back again, asking the same questions, wanting more details. The second interview was tape-recorded. The summary of the interview, written by Postiglione said: "Sammy knows of no one who would do something like this and stated that neither he or Kevin had any known enemies…" he wrote. "Sammy gave the impression of being honest and concerned about the outcome of this case."

On the Monday following the shooting, Detective Pridemore had a meeting with Bill Wence, a music promoter from Nolensville, Tennessee. Wence had phoned him, suggesting the meeting. He said he had important information about the murder of Kevin Hughes.

At the meeting, Wence admitted that he didn't have any direct knowledge about the murder. He actually wanted to enlighten Pridemore on "the inner workings of the music business." The meeting lasted approximately one hour, according to Pridemore's supplemental report. Exactly what Wence told them, I don't know, but Pridemore and Postiglione started digging into more corners of the Nashville music business, especially *Cash Box*, independent record labels, and independent promoters. They seemed more suspicious toward me than ever.

The police department's official statements in the media hadn't changed. Suspects were being looked at. They didn't have a motive. The robbery-gone-wrong theory kept being mentioned.

The police hotline collected a mix of helpful tips and the usual wacky calls from people who wanted to get revenge on someone by reporting them for murder. A lot of these were from women reporting their husbands or exes.

One individual called a number of times to offer new information that supported his theory that Kevin's murder had something to do with fraud at *Cash Box*. This person wasn't in the music business, but he did know Kevin. According to the criminal case files, the murder squad followed up on several of his tips—some of which were more like idle gossip from conversations he'd overheard.

The same person also set up a midnight meeting between Pridemore and a college student who claimed to have spoken with Kevin on the phone the night he was murdered. The student told Pridemore that he was working the night shift and had called to ask Kevin if he could give him a ride.

"He was told by Kevin that he was not able to give him a ride home," wrote Pridemore, "because Sammy was coming to his office, was upset, and they had to get it worked out. Kevin did not tell him why Sammy was upset."

The student went on to say, "he had been told by Kevin that he (Kevin) had been taking payoffs from promoters in the music business." Kevin didn't mention any names, the student said, but another friend of his told him that Chuck Dixon was the one paying him off.

More than one caller to the police hotline said that Kevin was killed over payoffs or some other kind of fraud, but informants like the college student working on the nightshift and the eavesdropper sometimes did nothing more than muddy the waters in the case.

Many years later, Pridemore and Postiglione admitted that before 1989, they knew very little about the music business in Music City, U.S.A. Sometimes I wonder why the Chief of Police didn't think of assigning some detectives who did know a thing or two about the industry that put Nashville on the map.

The people working on Music Row were still in shock about the murder. Now, even before they could deal with their grief, these stories were going around like a bad virus, creating paranoia and confusion.

The idea that Kevin was dishonest, that he was taking bribes, went against everything I knew about him. Chuck Dixon was a different story. He was a hustler, a wannabe gangster-type, a guy who really knew how to work a room, but he also kept a lot of things close to his chest. I talked to him on the phone weekly, but I realized that I didn't really know him at all.

The bullets fired from the suspect's gun had come from a .38 caliber revolver. Three bullets had been recovered, two from Kevin's body and one found on the pavement nearby. The bullets were sent to the TBI (Tennessee Bureau of Identification) lab for identification. Six handguns from the Metro evidence room, each capable of firing .38-caliber ammunition, were also sent to TBI for examination.

One of the top suspects in the Music Row murder was Milton Santiago Reyes. He was 26 years old and was enrolled at Belmont University in 1985, the same year as Kevin. Reyes told police that he was a "writer," but they were more interested in his career as a small-time cocaine dealer. His friends were cocaine dealers. So was the woman he lived with.

The detectives began looking at Reyes after a caller on the hotline reported that on the night of March 9, Reyes was going around saying he needed to buy a gun because someone had ripped him off. Later that night, he told several friends he had to leave town because he'd shot two people on Music Row.

The caller mentioned one other detail about Milton Santiago

Reyes that everyone remembered about him: He drove a red '79 Pontiac Firebird with a "Free Charles Manson" sticker on the bumper.

During the first two weeks of the investigation, a spin-off branch began focusing on a 52-year-old real estate agent named Ken Matthews. Sherry Matthews, his wife, also a real estate agent, reported that Ken was stalking her and the man she'd been seeing for the past two years. She said that Ken had threatened her, had a bad temper, was violent, and a heavy drinker.

The main instigator of the spin-off investigation was a Metro patrol officer named Chuck Lewis. He was assisted at various times by officers Gene Donegan and Kevin Fowler. It was an unusual situation for someone who wasn't a member of the murder squad to investigate a homicide. Lewis had a checkered history in law enforcement. After working as a patrol officer for Metro for a short time, he resigned to serve as chief of police for Berry Hill. The job didn't last long. According to Bill Pridemore, he was fired. Berry Hill is a small, incorporated neighborhood in Nashville, home to about 537 residents.[14] They have a mayor, a commissioner, their own police force, and trash pickup. According to Bill Pridemore, Chuck Lewis and Assistant Chief of Police, John Ross, got to know each other during the brief time that Lewis was chief of police in Berry Hill. Once he got fired and went back to Metro patrol, he was assigned to patrol in Music Row. When Lewis approached Ross about taking part in the Kevin Hughes homicide case, Ross gave Lewis special consideration and okayed it.

Chuck Lewis learned that Sherry Matthews's not-so-secret-lover was David Shearon, who lived at 1020 16th Avenue South, apartment No. 4, the same building where I had run upstairs to safety after being shot. Was Kevin's murder a case of mistaken identity? Chuck Lewis believed that it was—-so did Gene Donegan and Kevin Fowler.

Sherry Matthews told Lewis and Donegan that her husband had also publicly threatened to kill David Shearon just days before the shooting on Music Row. He had bragged about it to other people.

When Sherry saw Kevin's picture in the paper, she thought he looked almost exactly like David. That's when she called the police.

Lewis and Donegan discovered that Ken Matthews's first wife, Norma Jean Matthews, had died in 1979. Her death certificate listed drug overdose as the cause of death, but there had been no autopsy and there were rumors of foul play. The family's housekeeper, Maggie Harrison, told the detectives that Matthews was at his office the morning she discovered the body. Mrs. Harrison had worked for the Matthews for 18 years. She had her own house key. After letting herself in at 10:30 that morning, she thought it strange that the house was so quiet. She found Mrs. Matthews in bed, unresponsive, and she didn't appear to be breathing. Mrs. Harrison immediately phoned Mr. Matthews at his office.

"Kenneth, I think something's wrong," she told him. "I can't wake Norma Jean."

"Don't worry, Maggie," he said. "She's probably dead."

When she asked if she should call an ambulance, Matthews told her not to, that he'd be there shortly and take care of it.

Sherry Matthews told the detectives she was worried about what her husband might do next. David Shearon was just as worried. He shaved off his beard and slept with a gun nearby, a .38 caliber revolver. The night of the murder, he had been staying at his brother's place, which his brother confirmed. At some point, David decided that the gun was making him even more fearful, so he turned it over to his estranged wife, Patti, for safekeeping.

Meanwhile, on March 17, Postiglione and Pridemore came to see me again. They never brought flowers or balloons.

"The reason we're here," said Pridemore, "is that we want you to tell us about the dropped radio stations."

I'm sure I looked surprised. I'd never heard them use that kind of music biz lingo. Years later, I learned that this was right after their midnight meeting with the college student who told them that I was upset on the night of March 9.

I said, "What do you mean, 'dropped stations'?"

"In the last couple of weeks," said Pridemore, "Kevin dropped some radio stations from the *Cash Box* chart."

"Well, sir, I guess he did," I said.

"We have information about that," he said. "Did you discuss that with Kevin?"

"Yes, sir, I did," I said. "Kevin told me earlier that day that he had dropped some more stations from the Independent chart. I think he said he had dropped four stations." It wasn't anything new. Kevin had his own ideas about which stations should be on the *Cash Box* list for country music airplay data collection, just like *Billboard*'s country charts director (I believe it was Marie Ratliff at that time) did with their stations. But I didn't know much more about the job than that. Kevin and I never really discussed it.

"Did he tell you why he did it?" said Pridemore.

"No, sir, he didn't," I answered. "He just told me."

"Is that why you were upset that day?" he said.

"I don't remember being upset that day," I said. "I don't remember anything in particular, anyway. Why would it upset me?"

Postiglione asked, "Did you discuss that with anyone else?"

"Not that I remember," I said.

"Chuck Dixon was mad about it, wasn't he?" said Pridemore.

"I didn't talk to him about it, not that I remember," I said.

Chuck did have a temper anyway. I could've told them about that. I could've said he was the kind of guy who might fly off the handle at the littlest thing, but they seemed smart enough to figure out things like that on their own.

Why should these corruption and murder plots reflect on me? Because I was with Kevin the night he was murdered, and because I was an artist on an independent label, promoted by independent promoters, and played on a lot of independent radio stations. That's why. But if I was involved in a crazy plot to set up my good friend to be murdered, was my getting shot something I volunteered for to make it look real, or was that bumbling on the part of the hitman? That part I never could figure out.

Reporters and photographers were camped out at the hospital. From the look of the crowd waiting at my apartment, you'd think I was a major superstar. I already knew I'd have to move when they let me out of the hospital.

Even though I still looked like hell and was still in shock to boot, the hospital and the media got together and decided we should have a little press conference. The reporters and TV camera crews crowded into a waiting room and blasted their bright lights in my direction. There I was, my eyes glazed, a bathrobe thrown on, sitting in a wheelchair with Mom, Dad, and my stepsister Detra at my side.[15]

I told them, "We just stopped by to use the phone to call my parents. We were heading home. We're just real good friends and we were together that night and we were fixing to get my truck and go home."

Of course, they wanted to know details about the shooting and the investigation, but I told them I wasn't going to discuss it yet because it was just too early.

"This is the kind of thing you see on TV," I said. "You never expect it to happen to you."

I said how grateful I was for all the people who had sent flowers and other messages of love and support.

According to my doctor, there was an 80 percent chance I'd be able to use my right arm again. "It's a good percentage, it's given me a lot of hope," I said.

I looked forward to performing again, I told them, but it would probably be six to eight months from now, and I hoped to be back in the studio sooner than that. The half-page story in the *Tennessean*, written by reporter Sheila Wissner began with: "A Nashville singer wounded in a Music Row shooting that killed his friend made his first public statement yesterday as police continued to search for the killer."

The photo they used was taken when a reporter was asking

me a question. Mom is standing behind my wheelchair. She looks tiny, and we both look tired and drained, but you can tell what she's thinking: *You people better not mess with my son.*

Chapter 7

The Murder Squad

A FRIEND WHO ATTENDED KEVIN'S MEMORIAL SERVICE TOLD ME ALL ABOUT IT. The funeral had been in his hometown in Illinois, and the memorial service in Nashville was held the following Friday, but I still couldn't go. The people there, I was told, were still completely stunned by the shooting. The ones who saw it happen with their own eyes had as much trouble believing it as those who'd only read about it. Chuck Dixon had attended the memorial, but he sat by himself, in the back row, and he never took off his sunglasses. People probably talked about that even more than they would have if Chuck hadn't shown up at all.

Kevin's mom and dad were torn up, and that was to be expected. Everybody felt bad for his brother Kyle, especially those who had met him when he came up and spent the weekend with Kevin. Although I never met him, I almost felt as though I knew him already, because the two of them talked on the phone nearly every day, and I knew how much Kyle looked up to Kevin. They were about as close as two siblings could ever be.

On my bedside table was the new issue of *Cash Box* magazine, which still had Kevin's name in the masthead as the chart director in Nashville, and an entire page two of the magazine was a remembrance of Kevin, signed at the bottom *"Cash Box* Staff, Nashville."[16] It was hard to read the memorial. Every time I opened the magazine and turned to that page, I saw the photo of Kevin, seated at his desk, smiling, and my tears started all over again.

One of my most frequent visitors was Scott Morris, who was another one of Johnny Morris's sons. Scott, who was married to Robin Lee at the time, promised that he would help me with my physical therapy after I got out of the hospital. It was another month or month and a half before I was up to it, but he was there every day, without fail, helping me so that I could use my arm again. When I got out, my arm was in a metal brace and my hand wasn't much more than a fleshy claw. We had to start our physical therapy routine doing really small stretches and simple exercises, repeating it every day before I could move my arm at all. Of course, there was a lot of pain involved. But Scott kept giving me pep talks, just like a high school coach. He said, "We're gonna work on you until we get that arm moving and we're not gonna quit." That's what we did. He didn't let me get away with any slacking.

The doctor said I could go home a little over three weeks after the shooting, but the police wouldn't allow it. They put me up at the DoubleTree Hotel, guarded by a police officer 24 hours a day. It was for my own protection, they said, but it was also to keep me from going anywhere except to see my doctor. A whole lot of people did want to get in to see me, judging from all the reporters who were waiting to get a peek of me at the hotel, and then later, after I went home to my apartment. For a while, I was a real celebrity, just like the pop stars and movie stars you see on TMZ, with paparazzi following them everywhere. I'd never pictured having that kind of fame, not in my wildest dreams, nor in my worst nightmares.

About two months after I got shot, I felt well enough to get back to work. Mom and Dad drove me down to Evergreen Records and came in the office to visit with Johnny Morris and his wife. Johnny was still recovering from injuries he'd gotten in a car wreck. He was still hurting, but like me, he was hardheaded and determined, so the two of us shared a few jokes about our experiences before we got around to catching up on business.

After only a few minutes of conversation, we had some un-expected company. Detectives Bill Pridemore and Pat Postiglione walked in, and everyone stopped talking. Postiglione said "good morning" and then asked if I could step outside for a minute. "There's something we'd like to talk to you about," he said.

If they had good news about the case, they could've told me inside, on the front steps, or in the yard, but when they put me in the back seat, I knew not to expect a positive outcome. The two detectives sat in the front seat—they turned around so they could look at me.

Pridemore spoke first.

"Now, what we've got to tell you, you can't tell anybody," he said. "You can't tell your mom and daddy, your friends, you can't say nothing to nobody."

"Well," I said, "All right, sir."

Postiglione was the one with the big news. He looked me in the eye and said, "Sammy, people tell us that you were supposed to get Kevin down here that night to be shot and killed."

Even though I was sitting just a couple of feet away and I was looking straight at them and watched their lips form the words, I thought I'd heard him wrong. "What did you just say?" I asked.

"If it wasn't a robbery attempt, and it was somebody who wanted to take him out, they had to know where he was going to be," said Postiglione. "How did they know? It doesn't make sense that they would follow you here."

"Bringing him here was your job, in other words," said Pridemore. "Somebody told you to make sure he was here at a certain time. Maybe they didn't tell you they were planning to kill him."

Before Pridemore finished speaking, I could already feel the blood rushing up to my face, going redder and redder. All this rage was boiling inside me. I felt like I was on fire.

"You're crazy," I said. "If you think that, you guys are crazy. I don't believe this. You guys are just crazy...*crazy* or just plain stupid."

There was no "yes, sir/no, sir" left in me. If they said anything else, I don't remember it, but the interview was over. They left me alone for a few days. Around this same time, there were a couple of other interviews that verged on the ridiculous, but the one on my first day back at Evergreen was the worst.

One time they took me down to the Criminal Investigation Division (CID) for a polygraph exam. The lazy name for a polygraph is *lie detector*, but that makes them sound more exact than they really are. A polygraph measures a person's physical reaction to questions or statements. If there's a strong reaction, it suggests that the person is being deceptive. Maybe the person is lying, or maybe they're telling the truth but withholding information about something that may be of interest to the police.

After the exam, the police officer in charge of the polygraph told Pridemore and Postiglione that, in his opinion, I was telling the truth.

Not long after that, they decided they might learn something new if they tried hypnosis on me. The detectives took me somewhere on the Vanderbilt campus to be hypnotized. I don't remember a thing after that, except that they told me afterward that I had told them that masked man was wearing a heavy coat. Before that, I hadn't said anything about it being light or heavy, just that he wore a coat. Otherwise, they said, all my answers were just the same.

After the session wrapped up, we were on our way out the door when Pridemore stopped and said to the analyst, "He wasn't really hypnotized, was he?" The hypnotist said, "Absolutely, he was."

The murder squad kept the polygraph machine busy on this case. Had I known how many tests they were doing on people, I might have felt less paranoid. They were giving polygraph tests to suspicious people they picked up for months and months afterward.

The questions on the polygraph exams given to suspects consisted of four basic questions:

Did you shoot those men on 16th Avenue? (YES/NO)

Did you shoot those men on March 9? (YES/NO)

Were you present when those men were shot? (YES/NO)

Do you know who shot those men? (YES/NO)[17]

To help separate the reliable witness statements from the not-so-reliable ones, some of the witnesses were also subjected to polygraph exams. On the night of the shooting, they took at least 13 witnesses from 16th Avenue South down to CID for taped statements. Reading through the case files, we learned that Rita Alcorta's statement was given voluntarily and tape recorded at 1:06 a.m. Katherine Hunter gave her statement at 2:04 a.m., Donny Lowery at 2:20 a.m., and so on.

We had gone over the contents of this particular folder several times before a name jumped out at us: Faith Audrey Hill, age 21. Back in 1989, Faith Hill was like many of the rest of us, a musician who was playing around town, doing backup singing gigs, and trying to carve out a career. At the time, Faith was married to music publisher Daniel Hill (this was seven years before she and Tim McGraw met and got married). On the night of March 9, 1989, Faith and Daniel happened to be on 16th Avenue South when the masked man jumped out of the shadows with his gun.

Daniel's statement lists his employer as Act III, the talent agency on 16th Avenue South. Faith may have been visiting him at the office when the shooting started. Faith gave her recorded statement at 2:06 a.m. on March 10; Daniel gave his at 1:27 a.m.

Meanwhile, other detectives on the murder squad were running down other leads. Lewis and Donegan seemed fixated on Milton Santiago Reyes. On March 22, the two of them reported finding a piece of physical evidence that appeared to tie the suspect to the scene of the crime.

That day, during a search of the crime scene, they had found a key lying on the narrow strip of ground between the buildings at 1020 and 1022 16th Avenue South. It was a Sargent brand key with the "1812" stamped on it. Before the key was touched by anyone, officers from Metro Identification were summoned to take photographs and precise measurements of the location.

In their March 22 report, they noted that the key was found "27 inches from outer edge of 1020 16th Avenue South. There are 28 inches between the two buildings," and made the following dramatic conclusion: "This is possibly the place where the 10-52 suspect stood."

The key was rushed to the chief of security at Belmont University. The security chief determined that the key had been manufactured by Florida Steel and sold to the Residence Inn at 2300 Elm Hill Pike. The detectives went to the motel to meet with Manager David Nelson, who showed them room 1812. The key fit.

The motel register was checked against the list of suspects. The only name in the register that sent up a red flag was Marion DeCastro. According to their notes on Milton Santiago Reyes, he sometimes went by the name DeCastro.

The details didn't match up perfectly. The name Marion De-Castro was on the register for February 24, 1989, over two weeks before the murder—but it was enough to keep Milton Reyes on the suspect list for a while longer.

Detective Bill Pridemore wasn't happy with the direction or the progress of the investigation. Postiglione, the more experienced detective, wasn't either. When asked about the case in May 2017, Pridemore said that the machinery of the Metro police department at that time had a few loose gears and squeaky wheels.

"At the time we had some internal political crap going on," Pridemore explained.[18] "Some other officers who had connections wanted to get into our unit. So, basically, they were put on special assignment by our department to investigate the case, so they could, quote/unquote, 'help us,' you know. The way we finally had to deal with them was, we would just give them assignments on certain aspects of the case that we knew wouldn't lead us in the right direction, but we were obligated to eliminate them. So, what happened, these guys would come back all excited, acting like there was some sort of big connection to the case, and that would just muddy up the waters even more."

The room key found on the ground at the crime scene was one piece of evidence that kept Lewis and Donegan busy. Even when it failed to link Reyes to the crime directly, they seemed confident that it would unlock some other door. Reyes and his friends certainly seemed to have things to hide. Besides Reyes trying to buy a gun on March 9, one of his friends had offered to sell a .38 caliber revolver to someone for $60 three days later. Reyes's roommates, relatives, and other dope dealing acquaintances were questioned repeatedly, and their statements were compared.

Marion DeCastro turned out to be a real person. Lewis and Donegan started looking harder at DeCastro and his past, along with the four friends he'd been with at the Residence Inn on February 24. Lewis and Donegan pursued this lead all through the week ending Friday, March 24. That day, Milton Santiago Reyes and the whole parade of characters associated with him were hauled down to CID to give statements about their activities on March 9. Some of them were given polygraph exams.

Detective Postiglione talked with the subjects again after their polygraphs. Later in the day, with the approval of Detective Pridemore, Detective Postiglione drafted a report in which he shared some conclusions regarding the status of the investigation.

"I feel that these subjects are not being totally honest with us about their actions on 3/9/89," Postiglione wrote, "but I also feel that their reasons for not being truthful are not connected with the [the Kevin Hughes case], but rather, other illegal activities that they are involved in and were trying to keep us from learning about. Unless other information becomes available… [they] will no longer be considered suspects."

Pridemore and Postiglione were a long way from solving the case, but they felt they were experienced enough to tell the difference between viable leads and square pegs in round holes. Some of the other team members were inexperienced and lacked judgment, and one of them "really liked conspiracy theories," Pridemore said recently. "If you really know what you're doing, you don't have to make a square peg fit a round hole, and that's what they were doing. The truth is the truth, so when you find it, it's going to fit. But these guys were so anxious to make a big case, they were trying to shave a little off the square peg and say, 'Is it possible it could have been this or that?' You shouldn't be doing that."

Around the same time, Lewis and Donegan were focusing on the room key, a dark blue baseball cap found at the crime scene next to Kevin's body was being investigated as a potentially valuable piece of physical evidence. The cap had gold lettering on the front that read "*World War II Veteran and damn proud of it!*" and a scowling soldier wearing a combat helmet. Who dropped it there? That was the question.

Follow-up interviews were conducted with all witnesses. I knew Kevin wasn't wearing a hat, but I had no idea what the killer had on his head. I saw the mask, the gun, black clothing, and then the flash. *Boom!* That's all I remembered and all I could tell them.

Some witnesses couldn't answer the question. Rita Alcorta, who recalled almost everything else she'd seen in sharp detail, could not say one way or the other. A confidential informant (CI) claimed that Kevin was wearing a cap before he fell in the street. Certain parts of the CI's statement were verified as being correct; some could not, and some, including the assertion that Kevin wore a hat, were proven untrue.

Other witnesses set the story straight: The shooter was wearing a dark-colored baseball cap when they saw him chasing Kevin down the street, shooting. When the suspect stopped and leaned over

Kevin's body to fire the final shots, the cap fell off and landed on the pavement next to Kevin.

Everyone now realized that the cap was an important piece of physical evidence that could potentially prove that the suspect had been at the crime scene—if they ever found a suspect. Photos were published in the *Tennessean* with information about the crime and the question, "Have you seen this cap?"[19]

In the first 24 hours after the photo of the cap was published, more than 50 people called the hotline. At the Metro Identification Lab, an examination of the cap turned up one partial fingerprint, but not enough for fingerprint identification. Under a laser light, one strand of hair was found in the inside fold of the crown. The strand of hair was sent to the TBI lab, and from there, it was forwarded to the FBI lab in Quantico, Virginia. The specimen was analyzed and determined to be of animal origin—specifically, it was from a black cat.

As the hat investigation was heating up, another mystery was solved by a phone call from David Shearon to Chuck Lewis. David admitted to Lewis that he and Sherry had recently enjoyed a secret rendezvous in room 1812 of the Residence Inn. He'd been holding onto the room key as a souvenir of that happy weekend, but recently he'd become so paranoid that he'd thrown it out the window.

Even after the key lost its relevance to the case, Lewis and Donegan remained confident that Ken Matthews was their man. When Matthews was brought in for questioning, he said he had been under the impression that he and Sherry were working things out. She was going to be faithful, and he was going to stop losing his temper so much. Matthews readily admitted that he had told David Shearon he was going to "beat his ass." He had an alibi for March 9, but it had to be checked out. Lewis and Donegan would be following Matthews and examining his life in even greater detail for months to come.

David and Sherry claimed they used all kinds of ruses to keep their affair from Ken, but it couldn't have been very difficult to discover. Sherry told the detectives when she and David went out, they usually drove her car, and afterward, she often dropped him off in one of the alleys off Music Row. The alley behind Evergreen Records was close to his apartment, and it felt secluded, so they used it a lot. From there, David could walk across the street to his apartment.

Ken Matthews followed them more often than they knew. He admitted catching them together before, searching David's apartment, and seeing them in the alley behind Evergreen Records.

When Kevin and I left Evergreen that night, was Ken Matthews waiting in the shadows? On that nearly moonless night, did he mistake Kevin for his wife's boyfriend? From all the media coverage of the case, we knew that the police were looking at possibilities. Was it a grudge shooting or a case of mistaken identity? They were exploring all possible motives and potential suspects. But they never shared any of that information with us. They just left us hanging.

Friends and acquaintances told us about what the detectives had asked them and what they'd heard from other people who had given statements. The mood on Music Row was dark and strange. People were paranoid and anxious, double locking their doors, looking over their shoulders. One of my friends, who didn't want her name used, said people were just traumatized by the killing, and by that, she meant scared, nervous, depressed, and confused.

Sometimes when I'd go places, rooms would suddenly get quiet when I walked in. People would stare at me when I wasn't looking their way, and then avert their eyes when I looked at them. Maybe they were just staring because my arm was in a brace, wondering what kind of accident I'd had.

The man in the black mask was still out there somewhere. Would he come after me again, or was he satisfied now? The cops never offered an opinion on that. The people who whispered behind my back didn't seem worried about my peace of mind, either.

Winston Churchill once said that there's no experience quite as exciting as getting shot at and missed. That might be true on the battlefield in wartime when both sides are shooting at the other.

This was a little different. I didn't know who'd shot me or why. I never expected Music Row to be a combat zone.

Chapter 8

Cash Box

RUMORS WERE BUZZING AROUND MUSIC ROW LIKE ANGRY WASPS. Everybody had a theory about why Kevin was killed. Some agreed that it was a paid hit, then argued about who had hired the hitman and why. Rumors about fraud, chart manipulation, and corrupt record promoters were tossed around like softballs at a picnic, but truthfully, no one in the world could say they actually knew why Kevin and I were shot except the masked man, and he wasn't participating in the discussion.

All this talk was hard on the people who worked at *Cash Box*, the ones who showed up every day, met their deadlines, and as far as I could tell, were dedicated music business professionals. Apparently, the entire staff was aware that their work had to please a particular couple of guys (Chuck Dixon and Tony D'Antonio) who, officially speaking, didn't even work there. A couple of characters that came and went whenever they felt like it because they had the keys to the office. George Albert, President and Publisher of *Cash Box*, knew all about this arrangement and was pleased with it. Keith Albert, his grandson, supposedly Vice President of the company, never made a peep about it, either.

Everybody was assuming that the *Cash Box* charts were being manipulated to a certain extent, including all the staff. Only a very small number of people knew how it was being done, and they kept their mouths shut. Everybody seemed to believe that Kevin Hughes was honest and full of integrity. But if that was true, some other part of the corruption charges had to be false.

The scandal cast a shadow over Kevin's reputation, but to some extent, it also tarnished everybody else on Music Row. The independents looked bad, but you'd have to be extremely naïve to think that the majors always played fair.

The major record companies and the radio station conglomerates had the power and the money, and they loved to flaunt it. Whenever one of them got caught up in a scandal, and it was usually more than one at time, their go-to tactic was to deny, deny, deny. Often, they would try to minimize the damage by picking a fall guy. There's always a bad apple or two in the barrel. Next thing you know, it's back to business as usual.

I think some people believed that Kevin's murder was part of something rotten going on in the music business; therefore, Sammy Sadler was just collateral damage, or he was in on the plot. But I couldn't afford to dwell on that, or I would have gone crazy. For one thing, you'd have to be an idiot to volunteer to get shot like that, and you'd have to be really, really evil to take a friend out to eat and then set him up to be shot to death in front of a bunch of witnesses—or you'd have to be a figure in a gangster movie. I wasn't in the Mafia; I was just a country boy who followed his heroes to Nashville, hoping for a chance to show I had good music to offer people.

An article in the *Tennessean* said you could hire a local hitman for between $500 and $1,000.[20] Not much for taking a human life, but compared to Kevin's salary, that was a lot of money. If Kevin were making enough money to get killed over his job, you'd think it would've shown in his lifestyle. So many things just didn't add up.

A month or so before the shooting, maybe right after Christmas,

I remember Kevin wanted to go home to visit his parents, but he didn't think the tires on his car would make it. He couldn't even afford new tires. When you rode in his car, he always had some new music going in the cassette player. Working for a trade magazine meant you got to take home copies of all the new releases that came in the mail every day. Kevin had pennies in his bank account, but he felt like a rich man because he had all the music he could ever want.

On April 5, a fringe character named Scott Holland was arrested on 16th Avenue South carrying a pair of loaded pistols (357 magnum and 9- millimeter automatic).[21] Although the murder weapon was presumed to be a .38-caliber revolver, they sent both guns to the FBI for testing. The projectiles recovered from the Music Row shooting had been identified as .357 "wadcutter" ammunition.[22] A .357-caliber bullet can be fired from either a .38-or .357-caliber gun. A wadcutter bullet has a flat front and is usually all lead, as opposed to having a tapered shape and copper jacket. Wadcutter rounds are good for target shooting because they're cheap and make a clean, round hole in a paper target. At short range, they can be very effective against a human being.

Pridemore and Postiglione questioned Holland in his jail cell on April 6. Holland told them that he'd stolen the guns in Florida and then hitchhiked to Nashville. According to his story, he hadn't even spent a full day in Music City. The FBI lab cleared the weapons and Holland was released.

Meanwhile, the police were trying to find the person who owned that World War II cap. A waitress at Captain D's named Sherrie Davids had something to say about it. Sherrie only worked until 9 p.m. on March 9. By the time Kevin and I got there, she was gone for the day. The next night, March 10, she worked until closing time, and during that shift, she said, she waited on a particular customer that seemed worth mentioning to the police.

Sherrie told Detective Postiglione that the man was heavy-set, about 5'5" in height, with brown hair and mustache, wearing a dark-colored cap. He was creepy. Sherrie said he passed her two notes, written on napkins, with his phone number. She promptly threw them in the trash. One of them said something like, "I'm a World War II vet, but don't tell anyone." She also remembered that he walked with a limp.

Lewis and Donegan made follow-up visits to Sherrie the waitress working on the idea that the Music Row shooter could have been the flirting guy in Captain D's. Maybe, on the night before, he was stalking someone besides waitresses.

Now that the baseball cap was considered a major piece of evidence, the suspect's hat size was an important factor to consider. Donegan and Lewis strongly suspected that Ken Matthews, the jealous husband, might also be the flirting Captain D's customer, as well as the Music Row shooter. Ball caps and hats recovered from the Matthews home were examined by the Tennessee Bureau of Identification and recorded as being between size 7 3/8 – 7 ¾. That was a problem. The World War II ball cap from the crime scene had been adjusted to fit size 6 ½, big enough to fit over the shooter's ski mask.

A front-page story in the *Tennessean* on April 9, 1989, exactly one month after the shooting, seemed to swing the spotlight right back to Music Row. The headline "Chart Fraud Hinted in Music Row Slaying" gave the impression that the chart-fixing angle was a slam-dunk. At the same time, Metro police officials seemed to be throwing cold water on that theory: *Yes, we've found that there definitely might be a connection,* and then, *No, we have no real reason to think there is one.*

Assistant Police Chief John Ross told reporters "police are investigating a theory circulating on Music Row that Hughes was killed either because the *Cash Box* charts were being manipulated, or because Hughes refused to tamper with them." That sounded wimpy enough, and it was immediately followed by another denial from Metro Captain Pat Griffin: "There is no indication whatsoever that the homicide came out of the music business."

The Pridemore-Postiglione team was investigating the possibility of a music business connection, Ross said, while two other teams looked into theories that the shooting was a "domestic situation" or some variety of "street crime."

The article went on like that for the first ten paragraphs—-the part that appeared on page one, above the fold. But the greater proportion of the story, continued on page four, was all about the music industry. Reporters Robert Oermann, Sheila Wissner, and Thomas Goldsmith put teeth in the headline with one example after another of bad behavior and corruption on Music Row, the majority which centered on a handful of disreputable figures.

The first music business professional quoted was Bill Wence, the promoter who'd consulted with Detective Pridemore back in mid-March 1989. Wence told the reporters he believed *Cash Box* had been playing favorites with certain promoters and locking others out. The individuals behind the pay-for-play schemes, Wence claimed, were also capable of much more serious crimes.

"On Friday [the day after Hughes's death] I had nine or ten calls," the promoter said. "I believe this kid [Kevin] was killed because he knew things about *Cash Box*."[23]

Gene Kennedy, promoter and head of Door Knob Records, said he believed Kevin was "targeted for death because he discovered *Cash Box* chart irregularities."

Kennedy became suspicious, he said, because his clients were getting airplay, but it wasn't being reflected on the *Cash Box* chart. It was as if his artists didn't exist, so Kennedy did some investigating on his own. When he examined the airplay reports that radio stations were making to *Cash Box*, he was able to confirm that his artists' records were getting airplay. Those records should have appeared on the charts somewhere.

"A lot of the reports were somehow missing for a six to eight-week period," said Kennedy. "Maybe Kevin found out why."

Most people in the business that I knew looked at trade charts each week with a skeptical eye. Sometimes it was total disbelief. It's a little like when a study comes out claiming that broccoli is the No. 1

food. But no one you know eats broccoli, so how can it be so popular?

Nobody I knew thought that *Cash Box, Billboard, Gavin Report, Radio & Record*s, or any other trade chart was the absolute truth. Just like nobody completely believed the guy on the corner with the billboard reading "Honest Abe's Used Cars, No Credit? No Problem!"

"Chart Fraud Hinted in Music Row Slaying" looked quite sensational at first glance, but you had to read carefully to tell the difference between allegations of wrongdoing and simple comments about the quirks of the music industry. Just like with Honest Abe's Used Cars and a smelly landfill, most people just drove through Music Row and didn't look too hard at the seedy parts of the neighborhood.

For example, the story didn't claim that the country chart in *Cash Box* was 100 percent fraudulent. The main chart in question was their Country Independent Singles chart, the one that originated from the magazine's Nashville bureau, and was compiled from radio stations all over the country. The *Tennessean* had conducted its own analysis, comparing that chart with *Billboard's* Top-Country chart. Their study found that the top 50 records in both charts were practically the same. Major label stars like Conway Twitty, Reba McEntire, and Randy Travis dominated both lists.

The major differences were in the bottom 50. During the first part of 1989, the reporters said, "*Billboard's* lower chart positions were more often occupied by major label acts on their way up or down the charts," said the *Tennessean*. In *Cash Box*, "more than 20 percent of the country records listed weekly were small label releases which did not appear on *Billboard's* Country chart."

The article never came out and said that a 20 percent difference for "small label releases" meant something suspicious was going on, but why would anyone expect the two charts to be the same? *Billboard* and *Cash Box* got their data "from two completely different panels of radio stations," as Marie Ratliff pointed out. Ratliff knew a thing or two about the subject—she handled the Country chart for *Billboard*. Additionally, *Billboard* also used sales figures in their calculations.

Not surprisingly, the sales of independent releases were rarely ever as high as major label records—another reason *Cash Box* had started the Country Independent Singles chart.

Cash Box had been more "indie" than *Billboard* for a long time, maybe even since it was founded in 1942, primarily to serve the jukebox industry and owners of other coin-operated machines. It wasn't exactly a secret that the 100-something radio stations accredited by *Cash Box* included a significantly higher ratio of independent stations than the list of stations surveyed each week by *Billboard*. Independent stations tended to play more independent label releases. Independent record labels didn't have big promotion departments like the major labels, so they hired independent promoters to promote their records to radio stations.

Probably the single best thing about the article in the *Tennessean* was the way it explained how important charts were to the music business.

In the world of commercial country music, the charts of popular records play an almost incalculably important role. A position on these weekly lists, compiled for trade publications by Kevin Hughes and others like him, is supposed to reflect airplay at radio stations all over the country.

An appearance on the charts is the first real step toward record sales, tour dates, and eventual stardom. As the country music industry is structured now, there is virtually no way around it....

The *Billboard* chart is the industry's most closely-watched barometer of airplay, but an extended appearance on it is almost out of reach for new, independent label artists such as Sammy Sadler. Thus, the lower reaches of the *Cash Box* chart are the chief national outlets for the independents.

Robert Oermann, one of the main contributors to the story, had been following my career ever since 1986 and my first single ("You Don't Have to Be Lonely"). Oermann has a phenomenal memory, so I am sure he remembered that *Billboard* had given it a "Recommended."

And I know he was watching as my sixth single, a cover of "Tell It Like It Is," made it to No. 70 on *Billboard*'s Top 100, only to be knocked off by Billy Joe Royal's version of the song, which Atlantic had released a few weeks later.

One of the other main points the reporters made was that there was money to be made in record promotion, even if you were signed to the smallest record label in town.

Record promoters charge these artists as much as $2,000 to push their single releases to *Cash Box* for as little as four weeks. The promoters will earn bonuses from the artists or labels if one of their records ends up above a specific position on the chart.

Thus, an active promoter with a dozen or more clients would have a deep financial stake in any manipulation of the *Cash Box* charts.

The article said that a position on the *Cash Box* chart could be bought for as little as the promoter's weekly fee plus a $75 ad in the magazine. Some busy promoters supposedly handled 40 records at a time. Forty multiplied by two-grand sounded like a reasonable motive to commit an even more serious crime. But was it enough to kill someone? A desperate drug addict might shoot a 7-Eleven clerk for $10 to buy another dose, but this was about music. It was still hard to accept.

Several people contacted for comment clearly rejected the music fraud connection. Chuck Dixon was asked about his theories on motive, but Chuck, who was normally very talkative and opinionated, barely gave them enough for a paragraph.

"'Maniac' is the best word I can think of for it," said Sadler's record promoter, Chuck Dixon.

Chuck Dixon was probably the first name that came to mind when people in the Nashville music business saw the headline. I can imagine them rereading the article several times, wondering if they missed something else about Chuck. My opinion: The writers cleverly made him notable by his absence.

George Albert, President of *Cash Box*, apparently wasn't very generous with his time or insight, either. Albert said he did not know why the police or reporters were looking into allegations about the country chart.

"I can't understand this whole thing," he said. "I don't know why the police, or you, or anybody else are going into a story that is something that nobody, or that we, know nothing about."

He said the talk related to possible chart manipulation was being concocted and spread by the media.

Keith Albert, George's grandson, was currently overseeing the Nashville office. The reporter seemed to have caught him at a bad time:

"I'm tired of all these calls coming in," he said. "It's nothing but a pain in the neck. Let the police do their jobs."

Jim Sharp, director of operations for *Cash Box* in Nashville from 1977—1985, was much more cooperative and insightful. Being offered cash bribes wasn't unusual, he said, but some were more creative than others. "I had one that came right out and said that since we wouldn't take money, he would pay $2,000 a week to my wife as a secretarial fee," said Sharp. "But I refused that."[24]

On other occasions, certain unnamed record promoters had threatened Sharp when he refused to "falsify" the country chart. "Those promoters… are still in town," he said, believing some to be capable of violence. "There were a couple of times I had to call other people in the industry to try to find out if the individuals were serious [about the threats] or if they were just mad."

Sharp told the *Tennessean* that, as of April 1989, he believed that no one currently employed at *Cash Box* was responsible for any chart fixing. Other sources in the article agreed.

While everybody was busy talking, the murder squad detectives were knocking on doors, taking music people to CID for statements. Idle gossip and hearsay are one thing, but certain witnesses had heard Kevin say things that trumped all the gossip and idle speculation. Sharon Pennington was one of those witnesses.

Sharon was a friend of mine. When I found Bill Pridemore's

report of her March 16 interview in the case files, I paid close attention. She told them that Kevin was upset the day of March 9, but it took a while before he came out and admitted it. Possibly it was the reason he agreed to go see the 5:30 showing of a movie with Sharon that day, even though he had work to do later that night.

While driving to the movie, she had told Kevin that Chuck had called her during the day. He asked her about Kevin dropping several radio stations from the radio survey. He laughed and told her that Chuck had called him three times that day. She asked him why he had dropped the stations. ... [He said the] stations were padding their playing of records [so] he had decided to drop them. She told Kevin that Chuck was very upset. After the movie, they drove back to the office and sat in the parking lot for several minutes, and Kevin then went inside his office building to return to work.

The blow-up from Chuck over dropping stations wasn't the only drama in Kevin's life Sharon told them about. During the Country Radio Seminar, held the previous week, there had been a strange scene over Kevin's scheduled speech. At one point, she said, Kevin had tried to back out of the speech, and then he decided to go ahead with it, and then changed his mind again. She said that Kevin had some qualms about giving a speech in the year 1989, representing a magazine bureau that didn't own a single computer.

He had a good point. Even with the minimal computing power available in the late 1980s, even the smallest business offices were using computers to make crunching numbers faster and more accurate. Kevin had even taken a break from the seminar that day to call George Albert at the Los Angeles *Cash Box* office and asked him point-blank if he ever planned to buy a computer. Albert told him "no," and that's when Kevin decided he wanted to walk out of CRS.

A loyal employee, Kevin was planning to go through with the speech when Chuck intervened again. He took Kevin aside and told him that some of the other professionals were planning to ridicule him during the Q&A after his speech. Whether it was supposed to be a simple prank or a plot by belligerent rivals isn't clear, but for Kevin, it was the last straw.

After learning this, Kevin decided not to speak. He called the owner of *Cash Box* in L.A. asking not to speak. He was told to speak. Kevin then asked Chuck Dixon and Dan Mitchell to call the owner of *Cash Box* and convince him not to have Kevin speak at the seminar. He did not have to speak.

Cecilia Walker Bragg started out in 1987 as the receptionist at *Cash Box*. Later she was promoted to Editor. She'd already told the detectives about Chuck Dixon burning up the phone lines all day March 9 because he was mad at Kevin for dropping stations.

Chuck acted as if he and Kevin had a special relationship because he was one of the biggest local advertisers in *Cash Box*. He brought advertising revenue to the magazine every week and had been one of their best accounts for years. He acted like he owned the place, and according to observers, like Kevin was his young apprentice.

Kent Crawford, one of Kevin's best friends in Nashville, wasn't the only person who described the relationship between Chuck and Kevin as awkward. Crawford told Pridemore and Postiglione that in the last few weeks before the shooting, Kevin had referred two different artists to Chuck Dixon for his promotion services. Chuck slipped Kevin a couple of C-notes to show his appreciation. Kevin took the money, Crawford said, but he felt crushed with guilt later.

"He was very upset about this," Crawford told them, "but after talking to his parents in Illinois, Kevin felt OK about it."

He told the police that he and Kevin were so close that Kevin would tell him things of this nature. I still have trouble believing it.

Crawford also told the detectives that Kevin once said that since he had no family in Nashville, "Chuck was like a big brother." That part makes me cringe, too. The way I read Pridemore and Postiglione's notes in the case files, though, they seem to have had the impression they were onto something.

What didn't surprise me was that Chuck had tried to buy Kevin's loyalty in other ways. Several sources in the *Tennessean* article assumed that Chuck had used a combination of intimidation and bribery to get Kevin to manipulate the charts in whatever way he desired. Pridemore and Postiglione were hearing the same reports from people they were interviewing.

The real story was probably much more complicated than that. When I look at all the evidence now, I believe that Chuck was using Kevin in an even more devious way than the insiders on Music Row suspected. Out of the roughly 125 radio stations that reported to *Cash Box*, many of them were "pocket stations," meaning Chuck controlled them either through bribery or some other means. With so many stations in his "pocket," Chuck was, in actuality, manipulating airplay figures before the stations made their reports to *Cash Box*. When those numbers didn't match promises he'd made to his clients, he would direct last-minute changes to them after Kevin had turned in his charts, but before they were sent off to George Albert for publication.

Kevin was being used like a tool. Chuck and his henchmen probably figured that using Kevin as their cover would throw people off the scent or confuse the issue just enough that they could keep the scam going.

When the detectives interviewed Music Row professionals, they found that there was always another Chuck Dixon story that topped the last one. There were stories about intimidation tactics, accusations of chart fixing, freezing other promoters out of *Cash Box*, and various other allegations, including stories of people getting beat up when they didn't cooperate. A lot of it was garden-variety thug behavior, only with a Nashville twang.

The most basic form of racketeering in Chuck Dixon's catalog went like this: If an independent artist wanted a place on the *Cash Box* country chart, they had to hire Chuck Dixon to promote the record, and they had to buy an ad in the magazine. No wonder you heard people around town calling the magazine "Chuck Box."

Since Postiglione and Pridemore were such fish-out-of-water in the country music business, Chuck Dixon must have had them scratching their heads. I know they had heard all about Chuck's shady dealings and tactics, but when you were in his presence, he could pour on the good-ole-boy Southern charm. He'd ask about your family, and tell you he was a family man, too.

Chuck Dixon was actually born John Blayne Detterline, Jr., in 1941, and he grew up in the area around Philadelphia, Pennsylvania. In the 1950s he was singing in a popular rock 'n' roll band called the Rocketones. By the mid-sixties, he was in Nashville working in the music business. Another promoter, Gary Bradshaw, said that Chuck lived in the projects for a while and that he never got over the feeling of being poor and powerless.[25]

J.B. Detterline, Jr. has credits on quite a few songs, including some big hits in country music. One of the most successful was "The Ride," co-written with Gary Gentry. David Allen Coe scored a No.1 hit with it in 1983.

Even back in Philadelphia, "Chuck" or "Chucky" was his nickname, but J.B. Detterline, Jr. was the name that always appeared in songwriting credits. In 1967, a singer from Westchester, Pennsylvania named John Poole paid J.B. Detterline, Jr. $1,400 for "Shakin' an' a-Twistin'" and three other songs to be released on K-Ark Records. Two years later, Poole sued Detterline and K-Ark, complaining that they hadn't delivered much of anything. It was the first in a long line of fraud complaints against the man eventually known exclusively in Nashville as Chuck Dixon.

In their supplemental reports on the case, Postiglione and Pridemore said that Chuck Dixon denied having called *Cash Box* more than once on March 9. He also provided an hour-by-hour accounting of his whereabouts that day. They made repeat visits to Chuck's office, asking him the same questions they had asked previously, kind of like they did with me.

Of all the people who were suspected of having killed Kevin,

Chuck Dixon was tied for first place with one other guy, Richard F. D'Antonio, Dixon's right-hand man.

Most people referred to D'Antonio as "Tony," even though there were times he wanted you to call him "Tony D," or "The Tone," or "D," and so forth. It was some kind of gangster thing, like the way he and Chuck carried themselves, the gold jewelry, expensive watches, and all that. When you saw the two of them together, Chuck was obviously the dominant one, bigger, older, and bossy. Later, I was surprised to learn Chuck was only five or six years older than Tony. He was born in 1940, Tony in 1946.

Chuck and Tony were always watching "The Godfather" movies. They would watch "Godfather I, II, and III" over and over on a continuous loop like it was their religion. The two of them would strut around with their gold chains on their necks, puffing out their chests, talking out the side of their mouths, acting like they owned the whole town. It was a little bit comical, but you never knew what they were truly capable of doing.

Like Chuck, Tony was originally from Philadelphia, so they had that in common. Before moving to Nashville, Tony was a blackjack dealer in Las Vegas. He got married, had a kid, and moved to Nashville around 1983, joining the sprawling local population of hopefuls who had a notebook bulging with songs that were crying to be heard by the right person. Fast forward a year or so and Tony is pushing 40, his wife wants a divorce, and he's passing out business cards that identify him as a music promoter.

Valentine's Day 1985 found Tony with a bad case of the blues. His mother in Colorado was sick, his last employer had gone bankrupt, his car needed new brakes, and his seven-year-old boy needed food and clothing. He did have custody of his seven-year-old boy, thanks to the divorce decree, which also awarded him the four-bedroom house in the Inglewood neighborhood of Nashville, not far from the "Grand Ole Opry," which he needed to sell pronto. Kirk Loggins, a writer for the *Tennessean*, thought Tony's plight would be interesting to readers because, in his desperation, he was selling raffle tickets for his house at $100 a pop.[26] The newspaper wasn't the only party who took notice of Tony's newspaper ad, titled "4 Bedroom House $100." The Davidson County district attorney's office informed Loggins that the raffle constituted "an illegal lottery" and that the penalty for it could include a hefty fine and jail time. Tony said he wasn't worried.

"It's a one-time thing with me, I'm not running a scam on it or anything," he said. He hoped the police and the D.A. had "better things to do than hassle me. Hopefully, they'll be out chasing robbers or something."

Here he was, one year short of 40, and his main gig was driving an ice cream truck, his son riding along on his route, learning the trade. At times when he had a babysitter, Tony hung out in the bar in the United Artists Tower, playing the Pac-Man machine and trying to meet somebody with a connection to the industry. One day, he met a fellow Pac-Man ace named Tom McEntee. It was a very lucky day for Tony and an unlucky one for the rest of us.[27]

Tom McEntee was the guy at the New York office of *Cash Box* who had coined the term "with a bullet." McEntee could tell you about working for *Cash Box* in the 1960s, when, in contrast to the late 1980s, the publication carried a lot of weight in the industry, almost on the same level as *Billboard*. In contrast to Chuck Dixon, McEntee was a respected promoter with platinum selling records to his credit. The Southern super group Alabama had him to thank for their unequaled string of No. 1 hits, and if you were sick of hearing Jimmy Buffet's "Margaritaville" on the radio and in bars around the world, you had Tom McEntee to blame.

In 1969, McEntee traded New York for Nashville. During his first year he started a radio tip sheet called the *Country Radio Sheet*, then he organized an event with the same initials, the Country Radio Seminar (CRS). Hosted by the Opryland Hotel, the first one lost money. Only 70 radio professionals showed up, but word of mouth was overwhelmingly enthusiastic, so another gathering was organized for the following year. Now approaching its 60th anniversary, CRS is known as the country radio event of the year.[28]

Tom McEntee and Tony D'Antonio first met each other some-time in 1984. Late that year, McEntee was recruited by George Albert to take the helm at *Cash Box*. Office staff had to be hired, so Tom called Tony and talked him into giving up his ice cream route for a job as a chart researcher.

McEntee later explained that he had heard Tony's stories about being a Blackjack dealer in Vegas, a job that requires great skill with numbers. With each hand dealt, the dealer must remember the hand shown by each player around the table, plus the house hand, the bets, the odds, the payoff, etc. Those skills, McEntee surmised, could also be applied to crunching radio play data for music charts.

McEntee was right. Tony learned quickly. He quickly rose from being a member of the research team to chart director. McEntee left *Cash Box* a couple of years later due to health reasons. Tony D'Antonio took his place. On the surface, things looked great. The Nashville division was swimming in red ink before Tom and Tony came onboard, and nowadays George Albert was smiling whenever he looked at a balance sheet from Music City—these were good times. The increased business meant that more hands were needed in the office. Tony scouted for college interns. Kevin Hughes applied. The Illinois farm boy and the Blackjack dealer hit it off. Under Tony's training, Kevin was an eager student and was soon able to teach his own assistants.

Kevin quit school and moved into a salaried position, but then Tony was forced out because of scandals and threatened civil or criminal legal action. There were accusations of sexual intimidation of female employees, blatant drug use, and extortion. As further details came to light, the question wasn't why he was terminated, but why it took so damned long.

I never liked Tony D'Antonio. I kept him at a distance. Maybe it was just instinct. I never understood what Tom McEntee liked about him, either.

Postiglione didn't have kind things to say about Tony, either. "People didn't like Tony," the detective told us in 2017. "He was always inappropriate. He was sexually inappropriate with women. I remember him in his little fleabag office when we questioned him. He was rude and bossy, always trying to push people around."[29]

Cecilia Walker Bragg said Tony was obnoxious about drugs around the office. He always let it be known that he could get you drugs, she said, that he sold drugs to this or that person, and so on. And when Tony was around, there were always guns in the office.

So, Tony was fired, more or less, but he never really left. Chuck was at the office a lot, and Tony hung around with Chuck. They took calls at *Cash Box* and took meetings there.

Apparently, it was during Tom McEntee's time as director of the Nashville office that *Cash Box* started having a much more flexible attitude about honesty and ethics. McEntee seems to have stepped back and let Chuck Dixon and Tony D'Antonio do whatever they wanted. Tom seemed to have enjoyed a lot of respect in the business, despite what was going on under his nose. Although some of the employees under McEntee probably suspected that Chuck and Tony were behind the shooting of Kevin and me on March 9, 1989, apparently, they were afraid to talk about it until years later.

Chuck could come off as a good guy—a person who really cared about his family and friends. Tony got a kick out of bringing his baby daughter to the office. They also got a charge out of bullying people, especially business rivals.

The Chuck and Tony show didn't impress Pridemore and Postiglione. Postiglione took notes the first time they questioned Tony. The location of the meeting was Tony's office in the Young Executive Building. Tony was full of denials. "He states that he liked Kevin and never had any problems with Kevin as far as he knew," wrote Postiglione. D'Antonio repeated that he "did not have a problem with him" and also that he "was unable to explain why several people have told us that [he and Kevin] did not get along and that Kevin was not able to work with D'Antonio."[30]

Even in these brief notes, certain lines suggest bad chemistry between the detectives and their interview subject: "D'Antonio stated that the nature of his business caused people to think he was pushy, and they tended to dislike him for it."

Other reports in the case file indicated that D'Antonio's physical profile was a good match for eyewitness descriptions of the suspect: 5'11" and 180 pounds. Tony was thick around the middle. Although he was "cooperative," Postiglione writes, he also appeared to be "nervous."

Near the end of the interview, D'Antonio said he was experiencing back pain. The detectives had already noticed his physical discomfort when he stood to greet them.

Ironically, years later, in 2017, when Pridemore was interviewed about this case, he was being plagued by lower back pain. A herniated disc between the vertebrae in the cervical spine and back can cause muscle spasms that make walking painful. It can become difficult to walk in a straight line, resulting in the kind of "strange gait" that had been described by witnesses of the shooter on Music Row. Pridemore and Postiglione were decades younger in 1989, and possibly blissfully unfamiliar with these painful conditions and their physical effects. In any event, neither of them commented on the physical symptoms shown by D'Antonio in their interview reports.

So, the investigation continued. More people on Music Row were questioned about what they knew and what they suspected. Lewis and Donegan kept on the trail of jealous husband Ken Matthews and looking into reports of disturbed war vets.

I had a lot to learn, too. Looking back on that time, I can't believe I didn't go completely crazy. I was hurting all the time. There were bad feelings in the air, and bad news all around. Some people said they were in a state of shock about the shooting and the sorry state of things, and some of them weren't even in town when it happened. Lucky for them they didn't have to take a bullet over it.

My career, my reputation, and everything I'd worked to accomplish seemed in danger of slipping away. I tried to keep my chin up, go to work every day at the record label, and finish my album. I couldn't sleep at night—I'd lay my head on the pillow and see the man in the black mask coming out of the darkness, and I'd just come flying out of the bed. My parents said I would jump two or three feet in the air. Maybe that was an exaggeration, but I know living with that kind of terror wrecks your nervous system and everything else.

Sometimes, just as I began feeling a little more at ease, the police would come to ask more questions. Most of the time, they were the same old questions, just worded a little differently.

Chapter 9

Dark Days

WHENEVER I CAME BACK TO 16TH AVENUE SOUTH, IT WAS ALMOST
IMPOSSIBLE NOT TO LOOK ACROSS THE STREET TO THE EXACT SPOT
WHERE KEVIN AND I WERE SHOT THAT NIGHT. Even if I hid my
eyes, I could see it clear as day. There was no escaping the memory.
A lot of other people had the same problem—the eyewitnesses who
saw it, the ones who came out on the sidewalk later, the paramedics,
the television crews, and dozens of police officers, detectives, and
investigators from the district attorney's office.

When you have been a victim of a violent experience like that, it
can be difficult to return to the place where it happened without re-
living the experience. All of these tiny details about it come charging
back at you like a wild horse, including things that possibly didn't
register at the time. You only need to see a little fragment of the place
it happened, hear a similar noise, or smell a familiar smell, and your
heart starts racing, and the tape loop starts to roll in your mind.

So, whenever I went back to Evergreen Records, I would try not
to look across the street to the spot where Kevin had parked his car,
but then, maybe a twig would snap, or a car would backfire. That's

when my pulse would quicken, my mouth would go dry, and the whole thing would flash before my eyes. I could see the man in the black mask and his gun in front of my face. Sometimes, I could see the whole street, like from the eyes of a bird overhead—me running up the stairs and Kevin running down the street, and this sense that everything was flying apart like a bomb had detonated. I could see the ambulance taking me away, Kevin's body covered by a yellow sheet, cops, and bystanders everywhere.

I never wanted to see it all, but sometimes I couldn't help but take that memory and examine it and be impressed by how terrifying the scene looked to everyone. There was so much blood. Mine was splattered all around the inside of Kevin's car. On that block of 16th Avenue South, the trail of blood spatters and pools of blood stretched for 100 feet, from the parking spot across the street from Emerald Records down to 1026, where Kevin fell in front of the Bug Music office. Arterial blood, the reddest kind, squirted from my arm as I crawled from Kevin's car, marking my path up the sidewalk, up three flights of stairs, across the floor of that apartment, and under the desk where I lost consciousness. Blood from Kevin's head wounds flooded out onto the pavement and ran into the storm drain. There was more than enough blood to shock even the hardened policemen who came down to 16th Avenue South to try and make some sense of the situation.

You try to forget what you can, concentrate on positive things, and find ways to cope with the rest. Whenever I walked out of the record company office, for example, I could turn right on the sidewalk and keep my eyes fixed in that direction. It was just a short walk down the block to a little convenience store called Kim's Market, at 1028 16th Avenue South. It took concentration, but after walking past the office of Bug Music, I could cross the street and avoid seeing where Kevin had fallen.

Inside Kim's Market, Min Duc would see me and say hello. He always seemed glad to see me. Our difference in size made me feel a little like a giant. Min Duc always asked how I was doing, if my arm was getting better, things like that. He always said things like, "Sammy, if I would have been there that night, I would have helped you. I'm sorry you got shot. You be careful, Sammy." A lot of people used to call it the Murder Mart, and some still call it that, but you'll never catch me saying it.

The International Market was another place I liked. It was over by Belmont. For years and years, even after I moved away from Nashville and came back for business, I'd stop in there to eat. They always recognized me and would come out and make a big fuss over me.

Belmont is a small college, and the first year or so that Kevin was enrolled there, modern gospel music was the thing he was most enthusiastic about. Modern gospel was a big element in the Nashville music industry.

What if Kevin had stuck with gospel music, or if he'd been somehow steered in the direction of Metallica instead of Alabama? Maybe none of this would've happened. And what if I'd been content living in Bonham, playing with a country band on weekends? I could've spent my spare time practicing my fastball or learning how to fingerpick like Chet Atkins, and Kevin might still be here today.

Driving down the "if only" road is a miserable trip to Nowheresville. It's a pity party. "When you're in a hole," they say, "first thing to do is stop digging." I was in the ditch, physically and mentally, and the only thing to do was claw my way out, recuperate, and rebuild—think positive thoughts, acknowledge my misfortunes, but be grateful for my blessings, not the least of which was the support of my family and friends, who refused to entertain any notions of me giving up.

Scott Morris kept coming over every day to be my personal coach and attitude adjuster. He kept telling me we were going to get there someday; we just had to keep training. Even after I was able to start moving my arm, my hand was still mostly useless. Because of the nerve damage, I could not make a fist, and because my ulna nerve was severed, I couldn't do any kind of pinching motion with my fingers. Scott kept working with me, trying different exercises on me.

Scott wasn't a doctor or trained physical therapist, either. He just liked sports, working out, and muscle training. He just figured out how to help me and did it out of the goodness of his heart.

One morning, after a couple of months of therapy, I took my brace off and when I tried to flex my hand, all of a sudden, I was able to move it a little bit. It was a great feeling, like the sun coming out on a gray day. Scott kept working with me, and eventually, I was able to make a fist again.

I got better and better, not back to where I was, but much improved. Today, I still have some deficits of motion. I can't hold a guitar pick well enough to do much more than beat on a guitar, but it's not a huge loss to the world of music. There's always a guitar player who's ten times better than me anyway, so I just let somebody else be the guitar hero, and I'll do the singing.

Living in Nashville, I always had some good neighbors. One of my neighbors at Polo Park Apartments was Skip Ewing. We were practically the same age. Skip had a contract with MCA, and when he wasn't working on his own records, he was busy writing with other people or plugging his material around town. His first album on MCA, *The Coast of Colorado*, had five singles that made the Top-20. He's a very, very well-respected songwriter. Every year, he runs a songwriting retreat called Horse & Writer. You go to this ranch in Dubois, Wyoming, and for six days, you get to work with a songwriting giant like Skip. And if that doesn't do anything for you, you should probably stick to writing emails and grocery lists.

Another one of my neighbors had sung with Dave & Sugar. They were a hugely successful pop-country group in the late seventies and into the eighties. Their first giant hit was the 1975 cover of a Shel Silverstein song, "Queen of the Silver Dollar." Between 1976 and 1979, Dave & Sugar topped the charts again with "The Door Is Always Open," "Tear Time," and "Golden Tears."[31]

Dave was Dave Rowland, who had toured with Elvis and as part of the Four Guys when they were part of Charley Pride's roadshow. Dave was the only permanent member of the trio, and "Sugar" was more or less a revolving door for pretty female singers who worked hard to make Dave look and sound good. One of them was always blonde, the other a brunette. If all that sounds sexist, you don't know the half of it. Dave took all the credit and did all the interviews, and onstage Dave was way out front, and Sugar was far behind him, even though they sang the lead part on a lot of the songs.

One of my neighbors was a very attractive blonde woman named Sue Powell. She was one of the three or four different blonde singers who sang with Dave & Sugar. I hope she found success because all the women who helped Dave earn his millions deserved better. I recently heard that Dave was driving a tour bus for somebody. It would be interesting if he ended up driving for a female superstar like Taylor Swift or Lana De Rey.

You learn that life is full of surprises. I learned, for example, that doctors don't like to reveal the entire protocol of your treatment, that is, the next steps you'll have to face later down the road. I suppose they just don't want to hit you with every single scary detail at once.

Anyway, they waited a while before telling me that I'd need a second surgery on my arm. So, the whole time we were doing therapy with my arm and trying to get back into fighting shape, I had another operation to worry about, and I wasn't looking forward to it.

Fortunately, I met another special neighbor when I moved to Donelson, a suburb of Nashville. Mitzi was her name, and she worked for Nashville Metro. One day, Mitzi told me I should call the surgeon who had operated on Al and Tipper Gore's son, Albert. The story of the Gores' six-year-old son was an emotional one. They had gone to a baseball game, and as they were leaving after the game, Albert saw a friend across the street. He ran over to talk to him and was hit by a car. The impact threw him 50 feet. His injuries were severe.

At the time, Al Gore was still a U.S. Senator, and like his father, he was an influential and popular figure in Tennessee. Coincidentally, Albert's accident happened less than one month after the shooting on Music Row.

When Mitzi heard about the highly respected surgeon in New Orleans who had operated on Albert, she knew he was the surgeon for me, so she set about convincing me to hire this big-time surgeon for my own surgery.

She brought it up every time I saw her. I should call that surgeon, she said, because he was the best there was. But this doctor was in New Orleans, and I lived in Nashville. Al Gore was a U.S. Senator, and I was just a poor country singer from Bonham, Texas. Even if I called this big-time surgeon, I didn't think he would call me back.

But she wouldn't leave me alone. "You just need to pick up the phone and call Al Gore," she said.

"I don't know how to call Al Gore," I said. "He's a Senator."

"You just call his office," she said. "Whoever answers the phone, leave a message. Tell them you read about their son's surgeon and you need that kind of expertise, too."

"I guess I might try it," I said.

"Sammy, he's a servant of the people," she said. "Just do it."

"All right, Mitzi," I said, "I guess I will." I didn't do it that day, however. I put it off for a day or two and then managed to forget all about it. But I kept running into Mitzi. I couldn't seem to avoid her.

"Have you called Al Gore?" she asked.

"Not yet," I said. I was out of excuses. "I'll do it tomorrow. Thanks for reminding me."

She handed me a piece of paper with a phone number on it that said, "Office of the Honorable Al Gore, Jr."

"It's still early in the day," she said. "Why don't you call him right now?"

Just to get her off my back, I called the number and left a message. No more than 15 minutes later the phone rang.

"Sir, I know you don't know me," I said. "But I'm a singer from Bonham, Texas, originally, and I—"

"That's OK, Sammy," he said. "I know who you are. I've heard all about you."

We talked for maybe a minute or two more, and he said, "All right, I'm going to call you back." Less than a half hour later, he did. The doctor in New Orleans who had operated on Al Gore's son was Dr. David Kline, and he was one of the top neurosurgeons in the nation.

Senator Gore had already made the call to Dr. Kline and told him about me. Normally, he said, they didn't take out of state patients, but after discussing my case with Al Gore, Dr. Kline said he would be happy to take on my case.

"It's all set up," said the Senator. "All you have to do is fly to New Orleans and check in with Dr. Kline's office."

Dr. Kline performed the surgery, grafting some nerves together to improve my arm and hand flexibility and strength. The procedure took 13 hours. Afterward, I found I could move my arm and hand better than before the operation, though it didn't bring me back to 100 percent. At least I knew I was in the hands of an expert in the field.

There was a big article in the LSU paper about the operation. When the medical field makes a big fuss about you, it's not something you want to put in your press kit as a musician. People don't usually make their music choices based on what they read in medical journals.

Years later, however, I did get another reminder that I was semi-famous in the neurology community. I had made an appointment with a neurologist in Dallas for some reason or other. At some point during the appointment, I asked this neurologist if he'd ever heard of Dr. Kline.

"Yes, in fact, I studied under Dr. Kline," he said excitedly. "We heard all about you, Sammy. It was a big deal!"

...

During the first eight to ten weeks after the shooting, I was often distracted by my efforts to recuperate and rehabilitate, but the murder investigation continued, and it was hard to tell if they were making progress or just stumbling around in the dark.

Over in the Young Executive Building, the staff at *Cash Box* kept up with their work, selling ads in the magazine and compiling country charts under a new Chart Director, Steve Hess. The operation continued despite all the negative talk in the media and local watering holes about a link between Kevin's death and chart-fixing allegations.

By this time, Cecilia Bragg had been promoted to Nashville editor. Joe Henderson, the former director of the Nashville office, who had worked there at least as long as Kevin, resigned at the end of February 1989, after only two months in his new position. The vacancy wasn't filled until May.

Joe Henderson was a longtime member of Nashville's army of aspiring songwriters. But after leaving *Cash Box*, he didn't stick around town, working the singer/songwriter field or plugging his songs to Music Row. Instead, he moved his family far away from Nashville, changed his name, and left the music business. Years later, he said that after Kevin was murdered, he felt unsafe in Nashville. Independent promoters, he claimed, had threatened his life.

Steve Hess told the detectives that when he was hired for the chart research team, Tony D'Antonio was brought back to the office to train him. This sounds strange to me since Tony had been forced to resign in late 1988 for sexually harassing female employees. In the weeks after Kevin was murdered, there was a complete staff turn-over. According to some ex-employees, they walked out; George Albert claimed they were fired. I guess by May 1989, no one working at the office remembered or knew anything about the harassment charges, they didn't mind, or Tony claimed to have rehabilitated himself.

Despite Tony's unsavory reputation, Hess claimed that he "was not instructed to manipulate the charts" by Tony. Hess also told detectives that "to his knowledge, [the charts] were compiled legitimately during his tenure."

Cash Box was a mysterious operation before Kevin was murdered, and it kept getting weirder after. Tony didn't work there, yet he trained Kevin's replacement. Chuck Dixon didn't work there, either, but he seemed to be running things. According to Hess, "George Albert, the owner of *Cash Box*... made it clear that Dixon was in charge."[32]

I started feeling very uncomfortable about working for Evergreen because Chuck Dixon was still our promoter. I'd never liked Tony to begin with, and whenever I saw Chuck Dixon and Tony D'Antonio together, I got an awful feeling in my gut.

When Chuck and Tony were doing their Nashville gangster impressions, it was hard to know whether they were just playing around or if they were truly capable of doing the terrible things to people that they joked about doing.

Many years had to pass before people who'd been next to Chuck Dixon started talking and verified that Chuck and Tony's gangster routine wasn't all fiction. Most of these witnesses only testified after being offered plea bargains in their own criminal cases.

One of them was Gary Bradshaw. I didn't know him at the time, and from what I learned during my personal investigation, I feel it's just as well that I didn't know him. Bradshaw was a promoter in Nashville who came to work at *Cash Box* a few months after Kevin's murder. Bradshaw understood at the time that he would be working for Chuck Dixon. In 2003, Bradshaw testified in court about their first face-to-face encounter, when Chuck's "henchmen" had frisked him for weapons. Bradshaw also testified that when Chuck got extremely angry with someone, "he would comment that their fate could be the same as Kevin's."[33]

But back in 1989, people like Gary Bradshaw weren't saying a lot to the murder squad detectives. Pridemore and Postiglione knew enough to feel that the music business in Nashville was dirty, but they had no evidence against the biggest dirt clods they had questioned.

On June 6, less than two months after publishing an article entitled "Chart Fraud Suspected in Music Row Slaying," the *Tennessean* poured cold water on the idea with another article, "Music Link Lacking in Music Row Slaying."[34] Every quote from a Metro official sounded dejected. "We don't have any evidence yet for any of the theories," Captain John Ross told reporters, adding, "It's a tough nut to crack." The possible motives still being investigated were pretty much the same: Kevin was murdered either because he was manipulating the charts or because he refused to cooperate in manipulating the charts; because of a domestic dispute involving either Kevin Hughes or Sammy Sadler; or because we were at the wrong place at the wrong time.

According to the article, police were now leaning in the direction of the street violence theory, having apparently "exhausted the music industry link." Pridemore said, "No links connecting the shootings to the music industry" had been found, and currently, they were "hitting the robbery theory hard."

"We have had very little luck with any of the physical evidence in the case," said Ross, possibly referring to the motel room key from the Residence Inn. David Shearon had already explained how the key ended up on the ground so close to the site of the shooting, but this did not discourage Lewis and Donegan from pursuing the jealous husband/mistaken identity theory. Ken Matthews, they believed, still had a lot of explaining to do. Each time something incriminating against him was eliminated, another strange circumstance or accusation surfaced.

So far, findings on the World War II cap had been disappointing. The investigation had been unable to determine where the cap had been purchased or manufactured.

Lab results of the hair found in the cap (which in many instances, can be as useful as a human fingerprint) determined, unfortunately, it was from a house cat, not a human.[35]

Some of us wondered if the police were just being clever, trying to give the perpetrator a false sense of security. In fact, the murder squad detectives were probably busier than ever. For one thing, they were sifting through the tips that came in daily on the Crime Stoppers hotline number and investigating a handful of them that couldn't be immediately dropped into the "Looney Tunes" file.

In this case, the Crime Stoppers hotline and other, alternative sources of information did a great deal to help the investigation move forward, eventually to a successful prosecution.

In addition to the usual media sources that covered the case from the beginning, "Entertainment Tonight" (ET) broadcast their own investigation on April 22, six weeks after it happened. The murder case was in the "Inside Story" segment of the program, during the first part of the show. Garrett Glaser did the reporting. They hyped my interview as the first one I'd done since getting out of the hospital.

ET reporters also interviewed a record promoter, though I don't remember who it was, and gave screen time to detectives and people who had worked with Kevin and Jim Sharp. Jim took credit for steering the interviewer to the dangerous figures he had encountered during his five years as the Nashville division manager for *Cash Box*.

It was kind of ironic that most of the conventional reporting, including the *Tennessean's* "Chart Fraud Links Hinted in Music Row Slaying" and "Music Link Lacking in Music Row Slaying" insisted that the music angle was only one of several theories, but really, that was the one that got everyone's attention. And that was the one that hooked the editors at the nation's most prominent newspapers, including *Boston Globe* and *Los Angeles Times*, who all ran new coverage of the story.[36]

"Unsolved Mysteries" rolled into Nashville in July. The producer said they first heard about the case from the latest *Los Angeles Times*. The format used by "Unsolved Mysteries" was a combination of taped interviews with witnesses and other real people, including yours truly once again, with a dramatic reenactment of the crime. The host,

Robert Stack, did the voiceover narration and cameo bookends to the episode. Stack had played the FBI agent Eliot Ness on "The Untouchables," a popular TV series that had debuted seven years before I was born and had been on late-night cable TV ever since.[37]

You never want to get your hopes up too much when television producers tackle a true story. Real life often just doesn't fit into the standard format of television and movie ideals of drama. Some of the true crime shows, however, try to be faithful to the facts and respectful of the victims without over-sensationalizing the story.

When you're in the entertainment business, you learn to look out for mentions of your name in the media and try not to get too puffed up over the positive reviews or too angry about the negative ones. But I didn't think I'd ever get used to seeing my name in connection with a murder being investigated by the police, or a murder case being adapted to a true crime television series. It just bugged me. I couldn't help it. Here's an example from an entertainment column in the *Tennessean* called "Namedroppers," published July 23, 1989:

> *Metro detective Mike Smith, handsome in a tux, left Un Ete du Vin's wine auction early to go to Music Row where NBC's "Unsolved Mysteries" was filming a segment on the Music Row murder of Kevin Hughes and the shooting of Sammy Sadler. Metro detectives Bill Pridemore and Pat Postiglione were there as technical advisers. Smith worked until dawn as a prop person. "I'm really glad a national Crime Stoppers program came to town. Hopefully it will help us in the case," Smith told "Namedroppers." This is the second television show Smith's worked on this year. In May, he was technical adviser for TNN's "Nashville Beat," which will star Martin Milner and Kent McCord.*

The synopsis of the "Unsolved Mysteries" segment (I found it on a site called *The Unsolved Mysteries Wiki*) illustrates that the writers had a pretty good grasp of the case:[38] At the end of each episode, viewers were given a toll-free phone number and urged to call if they had any information that might lead to the resolution of the crime. Maybe true crime television producers would have more luck solving Kevin's murder than the ones who wore the badge. To find out, we'd just have to wait. The episode was scheduled for broadcast on January 17, 1990. The title for the segment was "Nashville Hits."

On the inside at least, the official investigation was uncovering more than enough strange leads to keep it interesting. All through the hot and humid weeks of August 1989, Metro officers Chuck Lewis, Gene Donegan, and Kevin Fowler were bird-dogging Ken Matthews, the betrayed husband of Sherry Matthews. Judging by the details of the supplemental reports they filed, they kept up a hectic daily pace.[39]

They followed Ken Matthews, photographed the love notes he left for his straying spouse on the family refrigerator, skimmed the titles of the self-help books he was reading, questioned the neighbors, obtained a subpoena for his cellular phone bills, and around August 23, seized "three white, round pills" that he had in his pocket.

On the other side of the love triangle, Patti Shearon, David Shearon's wife, turned over David Shearon's phone bills covering a four-month period. After leaving Mrs. Shearon's residence, Lewis and Donegan met with Sherry Matthews.

[We] picked up a pair of blue slacks with stains on the pants legs below the knees. She stated that they belonged to her husband and she noted the stains after she picked them up from the cleaners. Subject also turned over hair from the family dog, two cats, and five fur coats belonging to her. She also took officers back to the place where her husband had caught her and David Shearon getting out of her car. The location was in the alley behind 1026 17th Avenue South, which is across from where Mr. Shearon's apartment is. Subject stated she had to drop Mr. Shearon off there several times before. Also, she stated that she had dropped him off

in other areas, but he would always come out and across to his apartment house on 16th Avenue South from behind Evergreen Records.

Investigation continues.

Sherry Matthews also turned over a black ski mask and a handful of caps and hats, which she took from his closet. Everything was turned over to the TBI lab and tested, but there were no breakthroughs in the case from this evidence. The hats and caps were too big. The ski mask did not match the witnesses' description.

Ken Matthews' credit card history turned up the fact that on March 9, he had made a trip to Service Merchandise on Nolensville Road and charged several items to his CitiBank AAdvantage card. Steve Stanley, one of the managers of the store, was able to give the detectives the details they wanted. Officer Lewis then called Mr. Stanley at which time he gave the following info:

Mr. Matthews purchased on 3/9/89 an AM/FM radio & GE brand Spectra telephone & some 9-volt batteries. On 3/18/89, he purchased a portable AM/FM cassette player & three (3) sets of D-size batteries & replacement cutters for electric razor.

By the month of August, David Shearon had given up his apartment on 16th Avenue South and moved in with Sherry. Ken Matthews had moved out, but he kept driving by the house, spying on his ex and her boyfriend. Some days, when Sherry and David were at work, Ken came by the house and let himself in with his own key. Usually, he only stayed a few minutes—probably just enough time to leave a note on the refrigerator, pleading for her to take him back.

Chuck Lewis and Kevin Fowler were carrying most of the load at this point. They staked out the Matthews house, followed Ken Matthews, and carefully examined his credit card purchases.

On August 18, Fowler and Lewis were at the Cellular One office speaking with an employee when Ken Matthews entered the building. In his report of the incident, Fowler excitedly described what happened next:

> When Officer Lewis noticed [Matthews], he stated, "Look at that hair." I noticed Mr. Matthews did not have any visible gray hairs and [his hair] had changed to a walnut brown color.

> The Lewis-Donegan-Fowler team was newly energized by every new detail observed of their favorite suspect. In recent weeks, the officers had conducted several follow-up interviews with Sherrie Davids, the waitress at Captain D's who told them about the flirting, dark-colored-cap-wearing customer who had passed her notes claiming to be a World War II vet during the late shift on the night of March 10. Under subsequent questioning, Sherrie had added a few more details about the customer's appearance. On August 16, 1989, Lewis noted, "Ms. Davids also remembers very distinctly that the person giving her the notes had brown and gray hair."

Two days later, when Lewis and Fowler saw Ken Matthews in the Cellular One office, all traces of gray in his hair and mustache were gone. The love-triangle detectives also spoke to Sherry Matthews's neighbors, who reported seeing David and Sherry meeting in a school parking lot and other public places. Patti Shearon admitted that she had hired her own private detective to follow David and Sherry. Every person in town seemed to have someone shadowing them.

On August 22, Chuck Lewis was able to speak with the private investigator, Dorothy Brown. Brown and Pruitt confirmed that her firm had been hired by Patti Shearon to spy on David and Sherry. The time period stretched over three months, from December 31 through March. Brown said that she initiated the surveillance, but hired another agent, Kay Pruitt, after sensing that her cover had been blown. Pruitt then posed as a prospective homebuyer in order to strike up a friendship with Sherry. By January, Kay Pruitt had gained

Sherry Matthews's confidence. Although their marriage was on the rocks, Ken and Sherry were still in the same business, and so Pruitt also made Ken's acquaintance and became known to him as one of his wife's friends.

Dorothy Brown brought copies of all her notes from the investigation. The highlights recorded by Lewis in his reports included the following: Ken Matthews was the person who convinced Patti Shearon to hire a detective. Ken Matthews had a vile temper and drank a lot. Sherry Matthews was "not happy" about her marriage. Over the course of their investigation, Brown and Pruitt became convinced that they were being subjected to counter surveillance. Among other things, they had spotted a white Ford Mustang following them around. Their cell phones had been hacked. The spies were being spied upon.

Or maybe this whole wing of the investigation was a mass hallucination, a trip to Alice's Wonderland to chase rabbits.

Chuck Lewis did put a lot of hours into the case, but a lot of his time was wasted when different subjects of the investigation jerked his chain in one direction or the other. Several of them seemed to be constantly one step away from needing a Thorazine drip. One day, Patti Shearon had him come over to her house to check it for bugs. The next day, Sherry Matthews would call and leave a message that she believed that Ken was about to kill her. On August 22, the day Lewis spoke with Dorothy Brown for the first time, David Shearon called him and sounded, according to Lewis's notes, genuinely concerned for Sherry's safety.

> On 8/22/89, at approximately 2055 hours, I received a call on my beeper. I called, and David Shearon stated that Sherry Matthews was meeting Kenneth Matthews at the Baskin & Robbins on Franklin Road at that time. Mr. Shearon stated that Mrs. Matthews had asked him to call me because Ken was very upset and [Sherry] was in fear for her life. He also stated that Ken had been drinking and he

did not know what was going to happen. Myself [Lewis]
and Officer Fowler went to that location and observed Mr.
and Mrs. Matthews inside the address, talking. Both left
the area at 2205 hours in different vehicles.

Eventually, Bill Pridemore lost his patience with Chuck Lewis and his colleagues. I don't know exactly what Pridemore said to them, but during our interview in May 2017, he was clear about his frustration with detectives "who want to make a square peg fit in a round hole by shaving off some corners." Most of his frustration seems to have been directed at Chuck Lewis.

Years later, after Chuck Lewis had retired from Metro, the two men had an occasion to speak to each other again. "Eventually, we met up again," said Pridemore. "He didn't apologize, but we made amends."

On Monday, September 11, 1989, six revolvers were delivered to the Metropolitan Police Department, all addressed to the attention of Detective Bill Pridemore. Five of the handguns were .38 calibers and one was a .357. Each weapon had been used in a crime in Nashville. The guns had been sent to TBI for testing to determine if any of them had been used in the shooting on Music Row. The results were all negative.

...

One sunny day a couple of months later, between Thanksgiving and Christmas, I was driving my truck, listening to the radio. Despite all of the young, new faces in country music in '89, a lot of the old-school artists had enjoyed a very good year. Johnny Cash, Willie Nelson, Dolly Pardon, and George Jones were playing back-to-back, or so it seemed, and then Clint Black, Randy Travis, and Garth Brooks, and their songs all fit together just like a conversation between a few life-long friends. I heard that Tony Joe White, the man who introduced the world to "Poke Salad Annie" and had survived in Nashville longer than I'd been alive, had just produced the new Tina Turner album.

The idea of Tony Joe White in the studio with Tina Turner was something that tickled my imagination. At some point during the sessions with her, somebody would have to break down and play a few chords from "Proud Mary" or "Nutbush City Limits." The temptation would be great, but you never know how a superstar is going to react to something like that. It could possibly be a career-ender.

At some point on that drive, the deejay put on "When You Say Nothing at All" by Keith Whitley and it took me back to the beginning of my life in Nashville, just like a time machine. I saw Keith playing the "Grand Ole Opry" right after I moved to town. Even though he started out as a bluegrass singer, his solo style wasn't much different than my own, that is, the mainstream, traditional country sound. Keith was an electric performer, hitting the stage with a fiery gleam in his eyes and colorful stage outfits.

Keith Whitley and Ricky Skaggs were just teenagers when they were hired to play in Ralph Stanley's band. It was 1970, and Stanley walked into a club, late for his gig due to a flat tire, and when he heard Whitley and Skaggs playing. He thought it was the Stanley Brothers on the jukebox, so he hired them.

Whitley hit it big in 1986 with his second album, *Don't Close Your Eyes*, which had four singles hit No. 1. One of them was "When You Say Nothing at All," which came out on Christmas Eve 1988. Two other great singles, "It Ain't Nothin'" and "I Wonder Do You Think of Me," were released after his death.

Whitley's death was hard to take. It was no secret that he was an alcoholic, but he was kind of a loner drunk, so the severity of his problem wasn't as well known. Lorrie Morgan, his wife and mother of their child, said she used to have to tie their legs together at night so that he wouldn't slip off during the night. Keeping booze out of the house didn't always help since he would guzzle her perfume or nail polish remover just to get a buzz.

Hailing from Kentucky, Keith and the other reckless Sandy Hook teenagers used to drink bootleg bourbon and race cars down the mountains. One time, he drove off a 120-foot cliff into a frozen river. He survived that and numerous other close brushes with death, but he couldn't outrun depression and alcoholism. He died of alcohol poisoning on the morning of May 9, 1989. He was only 33 years old.

Music can take you out of one place, fly you to another and back again. On this day in late 1989, the music on the radio was taking my head back to Nashville and an earlier, more innocent time, but I was in my truck driving down State Highway 121, across the flatlands of Texas. I had moved back in the fall.

I had not given up on Nashville or my music career. I just felt like I had to come back to Texas for a while. My body and my spirit still had to heal. This was my home. My family was there. It felt like the right thing to do.

Chapter 10

True Crime TV

HERE IT WAS, 1990, A NEW YEAR WITH A ZERO AT THE END OF IT. Whenever I read the 1989 year-in-review stories that mentioned the murder on Music Row, I couldn't help getting the same old lousy taste in my mouth. Robert Oermann listed the crime near the end of his recap piece about 1989's biggest country music stories, referring to it as "a dark cloud" on Music Row, just before the closing of the Lone Star Café in New York City and Gilley's in Pasadena, Texas.[40]

A three-part series in the *Tennessean* about unsolved killings in Nashville, "Murder in Music City," called it "'89's most speculative case." Sixteen homicide cases out of 72 killings that year were still open.[41]

Writers, I found out, enjoy writing about crime, especially murder, but some of them do it with more class than others. One local reporter confessed to readers that he was "excited by the adrenaline rush and challenge of an unusual accident, an exciting murder, or a particularly excruciating rape." I wondered if he was still close to his mother, or if he had a wife or daughter, and how they felt about that.[42]

On Christmas Eve, the *Tennessean* unveiled its top 10 local Nashville stories of the year. Out of five crime stories that made the list, "Music Row Shootings" came in last. "Landfill Search," the city's long, suspense-ridden search for an alternate municipal dump, took first place.

At some point, the reward offered for a tip leading to the solution of the case went up from $1,000 to $5,000. Immediately after the broadcast of "Unsolved Mysteries" on January 17, 1990, the calls started pouring in on the Crime Stoppers hotlines. Within five weeks, hundreds of people had called. Some used the toll-free number on the show; others called the Metro line directly. Transcripts of every call to the Unsolved Mysteries" line were turned over to the murder squad.

Many of the tips were complete fantasy. Pat Postiglione released a few of the choice ones to the media, including a caller who theorized that the suspect must be in the navy because the re-enactment actor wore bellbottom pants and another who wanted to turn in a 30-year veteran mail carrier in Oshkosh, Wisconsin, who had never been to Nashville.

"Ninety-nine percent of the people who call here are very serious and they believe it was the mailman, or it was someone they saw on the 'Gong Show,'" said David Rajter, a telecenter administrator from "Unsolved Mysteries." "There are some people who apparently cannot tell the difference between reality and what are enactments of a crime."

The day after the show aired, Pridemore collated the transcripts of eleven calls and organized them in order of priority. Two of the messages had accused a black man named Aubrey Moore. One of the callers, identified as a white male, had dialed Nashville Metro PD's central records office.

"Listen, I need to tell you something," said the caller. "I know who killed Kevin Hughes. Kevin was killed by a man named Stan, and Aubrey Moore. They work at a printing company."[43]

The other accuser of Aubrey Moore, described as a black male, left a message on the answering machine of a Music Row talent agency.

> *A male black named Aubrey Moore who drives a blue van, works for the Metro Board of Education as a printer on Bransford Avenue, and a subject named Stan killed Kevin because Kevin refused to accept packages sent from L.A. to Nashville to Cash Box or Evergreen any longer.*
>
> *[When] Kevin informed Stan of this, Stan called Aubrey Moore. Mr. Moore drove to Evergreen [where he] met Stan. Stan then shot Kevin and Sammy as they were exiting the building. Aubrey Moore then took the package...*

One of the messages about Aubrey Moore and Stan contained several warnings. "Be careful," said the caller. "Both those guys are very dangerous."

The third call on the Pridemore's list was from a female in the Nashville area who said Kevin was killed because he had refused to cooperate in a chart-fixing scam with the backers of a new record label called Air Advantage Records.

Another caller said he believed that the killer was a former employee of B.N.T. Car Hauling Company named Donald White, from Alaska.

Four callers claimed to have the answer on where the World War II cap had been made or purchased.

The other two calls from the first 24 hours after the airing of "Unsolved Mysteries" were confident that Tony D'Antonio had murdered Kevin because of conflicts over Tony's interests in chart-manipulation at *Cash Box*.

The calls about Aubrey Moore moved to the top of Pridemore's priority list, but not necessarily because he thought they were solid leads. From the beginning, witnesses had mentioned seeing suspicious black males. It was a fact that many African-Americans lived in the subsidized apartment buildings a block or so away, and any African-Americans in the area could easily have been law-abiding citizens going to or coming from work or home.

When we were still inside Evergreen Records and heard a rattle at the door, Kevin told me that he thought he saw "a black guy" on the street. I repeated what he said to the police, but when we were getting into Kevin's car, I didn't have time to notice the skin color of the man who shot me. Other witnesses, including Rita Alcorta, who had the clearest view of any witness, said the killer was a white man.

Several other witnesses reported seeing "suspicious" black men on that block of 16th Avenue South at the time of the shooting. Valerie Pearson, who happened to be an African-American woman, was one of them. Valerie worked at Homeland Recording Studio at 1011 16th Avenue South. When initially contacted by Detective Jerry Moore, Valerie said she didn't want to get involved, but the next day she changed her mind. Valerie told Detective Postiglione that she had just gotten off work and was waiting for her fiancée to pick her up when she heard noises outside that sounded "like fireworks." Looking outside from the front door of the studio she saw "three male blacks walking from the west side of 16th Avenue South toward the east side and then up Grand Avenue toward the projects…" It wasn't until the next day that she heard about the shooting.

Research has shown that what we regard as "suspicious" is often affected by ingrained racial stereotypes. Even people who try to be totally color-blind often sense danger when they see a person of another ethnicity in an unfamiliar or threatening situation. Pridemore and Postiglione may have been newbies to Music Row, but they were aware of the likelihood of racial profiling in witness accounts. Pridemore and Postiglione were anxious to investigate the calls about Aubrey Moore, not because they felt they were probably valid, not because they were eager to pin the shooting on a black man, but because it was something they had to do.

Pridemore met Aubrey Moore at his place of employment, the Metro Board of Education Printing Shop. Moore had worked there for 26 years and also, as a supervisor for an office cleaning company for the past 21 years. His third job was a printing business, M&T Printing, which he owned with a friend, Robert Tucker. Pridemore asked Moore if he owned a handgun. Moore said no, he did not, although he used to have one, years ago. And no, he had never shot anyone before.

What about the mysterious and dangerous individual named Stan? Moore said he only knew one person named Stan--Burt Stanley, who worked for the Metro School Board. Moore had been separated from his wife, Margaret Moore, since April.

While Pridemore was questioning Aubrey, Postiglione was visiting Margaret Moore. Margaret told him that she was now driving Aubrey's blue van. She was shocked Aubrey was accused of murder.

"There is no one more law-abiding than Aubrey," she told Postiglione. "He does not condone drugs or any type of illegal activity... Aubrey does nothing but work."

The same morning, Postiglione interviewed Francis Eleam, the landlady at Wedgewood Towers Apartments. Eleam wanted to report one of her tenants, a World War II veteran who, she claimed, suffered from mental disorders and was "very violent." Mrs. Eleam also stated that her tenant "has a WWII ball hat, wears a ski mask, and walks with a limp." Detective Postiglione left the apartment building and hurried to rendezvous with Pridemore at their next appointment. If every caller was as flaky as this one, they could probably knock off a dozen false leads per day.

On February 5, Detective Pridemore was handed a Crime Stoppers tip sheet that suggested a new love triangle theory. This caller blamed Michael Harris for the murder and alleged that Kevin had been killed because of his involvement with Harris's lover. Calls were made to Kevin's parents to get information on his past relationships, but there wasn't much to go on. As most of Kevin's friends were aware, he was looking for a long-term relationship, one that meant marriage, a family, and the whole nine yards.

Sharon Pennington and Joe Anderson suggested that the detectives talk to Kim Buckley. Kevin had shown a little keener interest in her than his other female friends, they said. Perhaps he had confided in her about a relationship unknown to his other friends.

Detective Pridemore met with Kim Buckley at 8:50 a.m. on Tuesday, February 6, 1990.[44] Kim had been questioned during the investigation at least once before. She and Kevin got to know each other when she had worked as an intern chart assistant at *Cash Box* in the summer of 1988. The two of them also saw each other outside of work, she said.

"What was the nature of your relationship?" Pridemore asked.

"We did a lot of things together," answered Buckley. "Went to the movie and dinner, but we were just friends."

"So, the two of you weren't dating during that time, or later?" said Pridemore.

"No," she said.

Kim Buckley said she did know Michael Harris, that he had attended Belmont with him.

Pridemore then tried another line of questioning.

"To your knowledge," he said, "Was Kevin ever offered cash or merchandise in exchange for manipulating charts?"

Her answer to that question was no, but she told Pridemore that she did know something that might be related to his question.

> She did not know of any voluntary chart manipulation, however, the last two weeks of her internship [which ended in either October or November of 1988], Kevin became very upset because he was ordered to change the charts by the owner of Cash Box. I asked her to explain the entire situation. She stated when Tony D'Antonio was the director of Cash Box, he had made a deal with a recording artist. This deal consisted of Tony taking cash in exchange [for] having

the artist's record higher on the Cash Box charts. Sometime
after this agreement was made, Tony was fired for taking
funds from Cash Box and purchasing cocaine. Later, when
the artist did not receive his end of the agreement, he called
the owner, George Albert. George Albert called Kevin and
asked that he change the charts. Mr. Albert stated this would
be the last time he would have to do this. Kevin was very
upset but he did change the chart.

Buckley's answers helped the detectives gain a clearer picture of the environment at *Cash Box* in the months leading up to the murder. If what she said was true, Kevin had been under pressure from Tony, Chuck, or both, along with George Albert, who had the last word. But every accusation against Kevin felt like salt in my wounds. I didn't want to believe it.

Two of the first batch of Crime Stoppers calls had named Tony D'Antonio as the killer. Both were from Nashville. One of them said he had worked with Kevin at *Cash Box* in 1987.

He states Kevin and D'Antonio hated each other because Kevin would not alter the charts. Kevin stated D'Antonio was taking money to alter charts. Kevin did not say from who or how much.

The only loose thread from the Kim Buckley interview was Michael Harris, and how he might fit into the puzzle. In the weeks following the "Unsolved Mysteries" broadcast, dozens of callers had named Michael Harris as the killer. There had to be a reason.

It wasn't until late on February 7 that Pridemore obtained a good photo of Michael Harris to show Kim Buckley. Buckley was able to come down to Pridemore's office at 8:15 that night. According to his summary of the meeting, it was short and disappointing. "Kim viewed the photo and stated the Michael Harris she knows is not this person," he wrote. "She has never seen this man before."

The question of Michael Harris's real identity and his role in the case was finally answered on February 22, after four weeks of detective work. The place it all came together was the office of country singer

Tanya Tucker. Even Bill Pridemore, who didn't know much about country music, knew who she was.

Pridemore's appointment, however, was with Susan Baker, who worked there. Susan was the ex-wife of Michael Harris and had since remarried. "As soon as I identified myself," Pridemore noted in his report, "she asked if this was concerning Kathy Russell." By this time, Pridemore had been informed that Kathy Russell was Michael Harris's ex-girlfriend.

Susan Baker explained that she and Michael Harris had been divorced for three years now and they had a nine-year-old son. Michael had once owned a .357 magnum, but she didn't think he would ever kill anyone over a girlfriend. He had no connection to the music industry whatsoever, she said, and if he had known Kevin Hughes, Sammy Sadler, or anyone else in the music business, it would have been a surprise to her. He'd always been a chemical salesman, except when he was unemployed, and that was most of the time. He was also a habitual liar and he cheated on her a lot.

Michael and Kathy began seeing each other in the summer of 1987 and broke up at the beginning of 1989. The reason, Susan stated, was that Kathy had become too possessive, maybe a little crazy. No one knew just how crazy until later.

After the break-up she had made hundreds of phone calls to Michael, Michael's family, to hers (Mrs. Baker) and her husband of three years. She has been evaluated as being mentally ill. She has made threats to Michael, his family, and friends. Mrs. Baker states Kathy had been arrested during the holiday season this year and has been indicted by the Davidson County Grand Jury for harassing communications.

Detective Pridemore called the district attorney's office to inquire about Kathy Russell and learned that she had been indicted for approximately 300 harassing communications—a figure that did not include all the calls she was making to the Crime Stoppers hotline accusing Michael Harris of murder and assault with intent to murder.

The next day, the district attorney's investigator made a personal visit to Pridemore's office at Metro, so they could exchange information. The district attorney, he said, would be glad to know about these other charges. Kathy Russell was in even deeper water than before, but at least one more mysterious knot in the murder on Music Row had been cleared up.

At the time, I was still down in Texas working on my health. I watched the "Unsolved Mysteries" segment, and during the part where Robert Stack told people to call if they had any information about the case, it was hard for me to feel much optimism. From what I'd heard, the phone lines at Nashville Metro lit up every time one of these true crime programs came on the air, and it happened whether the crime had occurred in Nashville, Tennessee or Natchitoches, Louisiana. Pridemore wasn't calling me with updates, either, so I didn't have the slightest insight as to how the hundreds of potential tips they got through the Crime Stoppers numbers were panning out.

Years later, after we obtained the case files, then read them over a couple of times, I kept wondering why they didn't arrest Chuck Dixon and Tony D'Antonio right away. If they didn't have enough incriminating evidence on them after a couple of months, surely, they could've figured out a way to send them up the river before a whole 12 months went by, much less 14 long years.

Remember, at least two of the people who called in during the first 24 hours after they saw "Unsolved Mysteries" had pointed the finger at Tony D'Antonio. Most people who were familiar with Tony knew that he and Chuck were practically joined at the hip, so if one of them was guilty in this case, odds were that the other one was at least an accessory. In America, we don't throw people in jail just because they look guilty, but as they say, where there's smoke, there's usually fire. With all the smoke around Chuck and Tony, why was it so hard to find the fire? Why did it take so long?

Chapter 11

On the Road Again

AROUND THE SUMMER OF 1991, I WAS STARTING TO GO STIR-CRA-
ZY IN LITTLE OLD LEONARD, TEXAS. I was finally feeling good
physically, and I found myself singing in the shower, singing along
with the car radio, picturing myself onstage with a band again.

One morning I woke up singing "El Paso," one of Marty Robbins's classic outlaw ballads. Marty was unique, a great songwriter
with a distinctive voice. His big influence and hero was Gene Autry,
the singing cowboy. In a lot of ways, Gene Autry was the first modern
multi-media star—a huge hit in records, radio, film, and television—
years before Elvis came along.

For Marty Robbins it was Gene Autry, for me it was Elvis. In
Nashville, it always gave me goosebumps to walk by the RCA studio
on 16th Avenue South where Elvis recorded so many hit records.

Considering how relevant Elvis was to Nashville, it's ironic that
when he played the "Grand Ole Opry" in the fall of 1954, they gave
him the cold shoulder. He was never invited back. The Opry people
have been notorious over the years for being on the conservative side.

Down in Shreveport, Louisiana, the folks at the "Louisiana Hayride" were a lot more open-minded--they signed Elvis for a whole year of Saturday nights. When I got the chance to play the "Louisiana Hayride" and they invited me to come back and play again, I couldn't help myself, I just had to say it: Me and Elvis, the "Louisiana Hayride" loved us both.

The morning I woke up singing, I pictured myself onstage with a band in a dimly lit dance hall with a long, oak bar, couples dancing the two-step, and sawdust on the floor. Later that day, those songs were still ringing in my head as I pulled up in my truck on a construction site somewhere outside of Dallas. My Dad and my uncle had a paint contracting business. I'd been helping them out for the past few months.

The sawdust under my boots and the racket of nail-guns and paint compressors that morning must have triggered something in my mind because that was the day I realized it was time to get back to my other profession: singing.

Problem was, I wasn't sure how to get back into the game. At the time, I didn't have a record contract, and the phone wasn't ringing off the wall with offers. For me, the game had always been in Nashville, but I wasn't sure if I was ready to move back there just yet.

Bad feelings had something to do with it, too. I wondered why Music Row hadn't been more supportive of me. If Music Row had been a person, I would've called them on the phone and tried to talk to them. Instead, I just let the bad feelings simmer inside me. Meanwhile, indecision and doubt kept me from moving forward, so I just kept on helping Dad with his business, driving down Highway 121 every day, listening to the car radio, thinking that the voice on there ought to be my own.

June turned into July, July got hotter and hotter, and in August, I was moping around, feeling bitter and cynical. My family and friends got tired of hearing me complain. After heroically assisting and nurturing me during my recovery, they were anxious to see me get moving again.

I remember one night I fell into a real dark mood while watching a nature documentary. Vast herds of wildebeests were tearing across the savannahs of the Serengeti in Tanzania. From what I gathered, these animals spend the vast majority of their time either grazing or stampeding. Whenever predators, such as lions or wild hyenas, come around stalking them, the whole herd takes off running, but they leave behind one or two of the most vulnerable ones to get eaten. A wildebeest never looks back.

Finally, Dad said to me one day, "Son, what do you want to do?"

"What do you mean, Dad?" I said. "Obviously, I want to play music."

"Well, why don't you just do it instead of talking about it?" he said. "Get a band. Get out there and play some honky-tonks and fairs and what-all."

I made some calls, got some good musicians together, hired a booking agent, and headed out on the road. Sammy Sadler & Overdrive was a hard-working band. We wound up going on the road and playing 250—300 or more shows a year. We'd play four or five nights a week. Sometimes they were one-nighters, other times we'd play four or five nights in the same place, have a night or two off, then do it again the following week.

One year, we were only home for about six weeks, the rest of the time we were on the road, either playing somewhere or driving to the next place. We did all kinds of gigs-- no exaggeration. We were playing clubs, casinos, fairs and rodeos, and opening for big-name acts.

Playing in a working band on the road—not a famous one, just a professional musical group—is sort of a cross between going on a long, long vacation trip to a bunch of different places, some glamorous, some really funky, and the hardest, most boring job you ever had. On the other hand, it's a life full of experiences, the gypsy life.

Willie Nelson, whose tour buses have logged a few million miles over the past 60 years or so, captured that feeling in "On the Road

Again," probably one of the most popular road songs in history. According to legend, Willie was on an airplane when he wrote it because one of his friends told him he needed a road song for the movie he was about to star in, "Honeysuckle Rose." Willie pulled the barf bag out of the seat pocket and scribbled down the words. The song is so stripped-down and simple, with bare bones for lyrics ("on the road again... we're the best of friends") that are cut-and-pasted together in different combinations to fill it out. "On the Road Again" could've been the curtain call song for a Vaudeville show over a hundred years ago. My favorite line is where the singer refers to his friends as gypsies "who insist that the world keep turning our way." That's a musician for you. Travel light, expect a lot.

Being a bandleader isn't the easiest job in the world, and it sure isn't the most glamorous. If you're only a performer because you want people to adore you all the time, you'd better be a superstar. You have to find the sweet spot between running a business and being an artist.

I bought my first tour bus from Roy Clark. I didn't know him, but I knew some of the guys in his band. When we went out on tour, we didn't have a big entourage of roadies and guitar techs, friends and groupies. It was usually just the band and the driver. The venues usually supplied people to help us load in and out. Each of the band members took care of their own equipment. My agent made arrangements for hotels and all that, but there were always details that I'd have to handle or ask one of the guys to do it.

Another thrill about being on the road is the level of professionalism you can reach when you have the same people playing together for years at a time. This band became amazingly "tight"—we were able to coordinate well with one another, even anticipating each other's musical direction without much discussion. Sometimes on the bus, somebody would say, "Hey, let's do this new song," and after we checked into the hotel, we'd sit around with guitars, bang it out a couple of times, then play it that night. A couple of the other guys were such good vocalists; they would sing a song or two while I took a break or just sang harmony. We had three or four-part harmonies on some songs. Everybody was a professional.

A funny thing about playing all the time is that you figure out if you don't learn how to have humility, you'd probably never be able to handle success. Some nights we'd play and be treated like big stars, other places, like some of the casinos where we worked, the band is almost anonymous. Some of the casinos, we'd be booked several weeks at a time—four or five sets a night, four or five nights a week. In some places, we would play 75 or 80 different songs. We'd get to play our best stuff, plus the classics we liked, and fill in the rest with the current Top-40 country songs. It was work, but it was easier than laying bricks.

In some of those venues, the audience could be very appreciative. You can make friends all over the country. People come up and tell you that you're the best they've ever heard anywhere. Or they single out the guitar player, the steel player, whomever, and want to talk shop, talk about vintage guitars, amps, or things like that. When people come to hear a band play, they want to be taken out of the daily grind. They are ready to look up to you and admire what you do, so you have an obligation to entertain them and do your best. That's professionalism. At some gigs, somebody tells you that it's their friend's birthday, and we'd sing "Happy Birthday."

Then there are the nights when they treat you like you're a Top-40 band or a human jukebox. Some drunk will come up and make a ridiculous request, like "Smoke on the Water" or a disco song. You must be nice to those people, too.

We played from one end of the country to other and back again, Canada, too. Playing a short set under the big lights for one of the big names was always fun. We played with Willie Nelson, Joe Diffie, Billy Dean, Toby Keith, Steve Wariner, and the Gatlin Brothers. We did radio and TV appearances, too. Once in a while, we'd find ourselves playing in a joint where everybody could've come in one car. That's when you do your best and, inside your head, remember the week before when you played for 25,000 people.

Sammy Sadler & Overdrive experienced different kinds of hazards along the way. Once, as we were driving across New Mexico in the summer, the air conditioner on the bus went out. We had all windows open, curtains flapping like hell, just trying to get some air in there. It felt like torture at the time.

Another time, on what was supposed to be a six-week tour, we left Rapid City, South Dakota, heading for Fargo, North Dakota. We pulled into Watertown, South Dakota at about three or four in the morning and stopped at a truck stop to eat. We had played the casino in that town earlier on the tour.

While we were sitting there eating in the truck stop, we looked out the window and noticed the snow coming down heavier and heavier. The wind started whistling and rattling the windows, and it was really something to see.

It was a severe storm, much more severe than we realized. We just got back on the bus after we finished eating and rolled out of town. Fargo is about 90 miles away. We made it about eight or nine miles out of town when the bus started making this jerking movement.

I told my driver we needed to turn the bus around and head back to Watertown. Looking for a place to turn around, we passed an eighteen-wheeler and noticed that it had snow up to the windows. Finally, we got the bus turned around and headed back when suddenly, it just died. The bus stopped, everything stopped—heater, lights, everything.

We looked up and down the interstate, and there was nothing else around, no life at all. Within two minutes, it was so cold inside the bus you could see your breath. The outside temperature was 30 below zero.

We were sitting there stranded for about 45 minutes, the driver trying to hail somebody on the CB radio. Finally, he got an answer. They said they were going to try to get somebody out to help us, so we figure we'll just have to wait and try to keep warm somehow.

Then, this jeep came down the interstate and drove past us. They were still in sight when we saw their brake lights light up. The Jeep stopped and backed up. They got out and asked us what's going on. It turned out they were Indians from the reservation. They were there when we played the casino on the reservation, and they saw my name on the bus after they drove past us.

They only had room for my keyboard player and me in the Jeep and took us back to the police in Watertown. Later, we got all the guys picked up and brought to town but had to cancel the rest of the tour because of the weather. My bus sat on the interstate for four days before a tow truck could go out there and bring it in for repair. They had to put it inside a big barn to get it thawed out. Everything inside was frozen and broken. We were stuck with a huge repair bill, plus a week in the motel in a town where there was not much at all to do. It's one of the risks you take.

I've owned buses that used to belong to Roy Clark, Barbara Mandrell, and Mark Chesnutt. I'm on my fifth bus right now.

Another town, another casino story: We checked in at the usual hotel near the casino, then that night, we went over to casino, and played all night long, slept late the next day, and started the usual cycle again. We had noticed that the hotel bar opened at nine or ten every morning, and certain people were always there, drinking red beer (beer with tomato juice and salt on the rim). One particular guy stood out--the way he carried himself and the way the others interacted with him. There was something funny about the maids at the hotel, too. I guess we were just a bunch of naïve country boys because it took us a while to figure out that the guy in the bar was running the prostitution service in the hotel. All the women who worked for him either disguised as housekeeping employees or they did double duty—you know, *deluxe* room service. We never took advantage of that service.

The guys in Overdrive didn't set any records for bad behavior or outrageous habits. We were all fairly average guys who loved playing our music, relaxing after the show with a few drinks, and talking to people. We enjoyed female companionship, but in the interest of discretion, I'll leave it at that, except one little story about a situation one of my guys got into.

He had met a girl at one of our gigs, and after we left that town, he kept in touch with her. They were calling each other all the time, while we were traveling one end of the country to the other, playing in Canada, and so forth. This was before the cellular service providers started giving free long distance. When the phone bills started coming in, her husband hit the roof. She never said anything about being married, or at least, that's what my guy said. He'd been calling her collect, and the bill ran up to five or six hundred dollars.

When we came back to that town to play there, it was a prickly situation. Her husband was mad, so were her brothers. They were the ones who showed up at the club, wanting money for that phone bill. I was still on the bus when I heard about the commotion. I got off the bus with one of the guys and asked what was going on. I didn't know the story yet, but the smaller of the two brothers explained it in a straightforward manner.

"Y'all are trying to break up my sister's marriage," he said. "She doesn't need that. You owe her the money for that phone bill. Me and my brother want you to pay it right now."

His brother was big enough to be a repo man for a heavy equipment company. There were more of us, but a fight was the last thing I wanted. "Let's just talk for a little while," I said. "I'm sorry your sister's having marital problems. Believe me I can sympathize with you about that. I've had some experience in that area myself."

A little humility and humor often help in these situations.

"But…" I said, "The way I understand it, she was taking his calls, wasn't she? She was calling him, too. Wouldn't you say she's at least half to blame? If she's a married lady, she shouldn't be calling some guy on the phone that she just met. She was talking to him when we were two thousand miles away from here. That's three-time zones away."

It was a close call. After a little back and forth, the situation was defused, more or less, and the brothers left. Later on, I told my guy, "Listen, dude, don't ever do that again, OK?"

Some musicians will go out on the road with nothing but a van, their instruments, and a couple of changes of clothes. They'll play their hearts out at one joint after another, staying in cheap motels, four guys in one room, or sleep on the floor at some fan's apartment. Even if they realize they'll probably have to get a "real job" someday, it's great to have a chance to live your dream, even if it's only for a little while.

Chapter 12

Bad Boys

ALTHOUGH I MISSED MY FRIENDS IN NASHVILLE, I DIDN'T MISS THE NASHVILLE MUSIC BUSINESS MUCH. Most of the time I was too busy to keep up-to-date with what was going on there. My schedule got even heavier around 1993 when I became the spokesperson for a group called National Organization for Victim Assistance (NOVA). The oldest organization in the country dedicating to helping victims of crime, NOVA pioneered many of the approaches to outreach programs for crime victims and their families, offering services ranging from counseling of crime victims to helping keep the perpetrators of violent crime behind bars. Although it's been called NOVA since 1976, the roots of the organization go back to the work of Rev. Bill Denton, who founded the Furnace Street Mission in Akron, Ohio in 1926.[45]

My experience with NOVA was very rewarding. I got to give speeches to a lot of different groups of people. I think that seeing a country singer, instead of the usual type, like a politician, a doctor, or some other kind of expert, made some people more receptive to the message. You wouldn't believe how many out there are victims of crime, especially violent crime, who find it almost impossible to talk about their experiences and their feelings. Some of them are walking wounded, people whose lives were turned upside down through no fault of their own, and they need help. Some of them don't know where to go to get help. NOVA does great work, and I was proud to support them. I felt like I was giving something back. It did me some good to talk about what happened to Kevin and me, and how the effects lingered on even after my body healed from the gunshot wounds.

It didn't cure me, either. I was still carrying around those nightmares like they were ticking time bombs in my pocket. Guilt and anxiety still haunted me not knowing who had pulled the trigger or why, and when and if they might appear out of nowhere when I least expected it. I think that may have been another reason that most of the time, I kept my distance from Nashville.

Besides giving speeches and photo ops with NOVA, I played music for them, too. Overdrive played shows at the NOVA convention in Rochester, a MADD convention, and played a show in Washington, DC for Janet Reno, who was then the attorney general under President Clinton. I even addressed a special U.S. Senate committee regarding victim assistance. I met with all kinds of people—mayors, governors, senators, members of Congress, and everyday working people.

On February 16, 1993, while doing appearances for NOVA, I made a stop in Nashville to play a little showcase gig at Douglas Corner on 8th Avenue, but then, it was back on the road again with Overdrive.

Meanwhile, back on Music Row, violent crime and mysterious incidents continued to occur. A 26-year-old woman, Janet Riley, had been shot to death during a robbery at the Minit Saver (703 18th Avenue South) in October 1989.[46] In April 1991, a female publicist for Polygram fought off a man who tried to kidnap her in front of the record company office on 18th Avenue. She screamed and struggled, alerting her coworkers. The suspect drove off in the publicist's car but was arrested a few blocks away. The police suspected that the same man had tried to kidnap another female at the same location about nine months earlier.

At least two country singers had been shot outside the Hall of Fame Quality Inn (1407 Division Street) at night since I had first moved to Nashville. Fortunately, neither one was fatal. On July 29, 1986, Paul Davis was shot.[47] He told police that he and a female companion had just pulled up in the motel parking lot next to the Hall of Fame when a robber approached them. Davis said he was shot while trying to escape, and the robber panicked and left the scene. Davis did not want the identity of the woman made public. Several years later, Tracy Lawrence was shot on May 31, 1991, before the release of his first album, *Sticks and Stones*. Lawrence told police that he was escorting a female friend to her hotel room when armed men accosted them. Tracy said he fought to rescue his friend and was shot four times. He required life-saving surgery; the bullet remains lodged in his hip.

Ironically, on September 21, 1992, just four days after I did an interview on a Nashville radio station on the subject, Independent Promoter Gene Anderson was also shot outside the Hall of Fame Quality Inn. Anderson told police that two men had tried to rob him, and then shot him in the back as he ran. A benefit was held in November to help defray the cost of his medical bills. The organizers were members of a group of Music Row residents and business owners called Music Row Victims of Crime Coalition. The group met with police to discuss their concerns: not only recent violence but burglaries and other crime. One member of the group, Steve Bivins, a songwriter for Continental Bear Records, said, "There's been too many people shot in this community, the leading community for bringing money into the city… It's got to stop with Gene."[48]

The independent music community (indie promoters and record labels) was going through a rocky period in the early-to-mid-nineties. Some of them were threatening to run each other out of business, or even do each other bodily harm.

Things got so surreal in the summer of 1991—you wanted to pinch yourself when you heard the latest news. Jason Hawkins, an indie promoter and the head of *Airplay International*/Foxfire Records, called the police on June 20, to report that a suspicious package delivered to his office had contained a dead fish, otherwise known in Mafia lore as a death message or threat. Hawkins and his colleague, Roy Haws, Publisher of *Indie Bullet* magazine, wanted the media to let the public know about the other troubling messages they'd recently received, including the dozen black roses left at the door with a note signed "The Detroit Hit Men." The office had been burglarized; their phones had been tapped. [49]

Haws and Hawkins were taking all this seriously. "I want to brush it off," said Hawkins, "but Kevin got killed."

Hawkins and Hawes told the *Tennessean* and a local television reporter that their livelihoods, as well as their lives, were in danger from rival promoters who were trying to take over Nashville.

Roy Haws had recently filed a lawsuit against Audre Medlock, a former employee, alleging that she and Gary Bradshaw, an indie promoter in San Antonio, Texas, were trying to shut him down, and they both had threatened his life. Until April 1991, *Indie Bullet* had been based in San Antonio. Haws and Bradshaw were friends who happened to be in the same business. What a change from a few months earlier!

Haws moved to Nashville in April and rented office space in the Young Executive Building, just around the corner from Jason Hawkins. Medlock had worked for *Indie Bullet* until June 17, when she left and went to work for a rival publication called *Indie Tracker*.

Haws suspected that Bradshaw had talked Audre into going to work for his rival. In a lawsuit filed in District Court seeking $250,000 in damages, Haws alleged that Bradshaw and Medlock had been contacting *Indie Bullet* customers "in efforts to destroy the business of Bullet Publications, Inc. and ruin the reputation of plaintiff Roy Haws by spreading false and defamatory information relating to them."

Medlock refused to comment on the suit, but Bradshaw told Joe

Rogers, a reporter for the *Tennessean*, that Haws was just upset with him because he wasn't promoting to *Indie Bullet* anymore. The reason he stopped, he said, was he didn't think it was credible. For example, he mentioned a record by Garnet Cooley that had reached No. 1 in the magazine a few months earlier. "I just couldn't find radio stations [that were] playing the record," said Bradshaw. "When I found that out, I looked for another magazine to promote for. I don't need these scumbags. I'm just tired of them."

Hawkins started having problems with Bradshaw after a record on his Foxfire label had gone to No. 1 on *Indie Bullet* without Bradshaw's OK. Next thing you know, he's got dead fish and black roses flopping on the record label's doorstep.

The life of an indie promoter just didn't seem to be worth much these days. Ed Russell was the man behind a little business called Castle Records. Recently, some car with a gun sticking out the window tried to force him off the road. Naturally, he pulled his own gun and returned fire, but the scoundrels got away.

Russell had been on the outs with Bradshaw ever since the latter turned one of the artists on his label against him by convincing her that Russell had overcharged her for recording costs.

Russell didn't bother to deny to Joe Rogers that he had billed the singer for studio time, record packaging, radio promotion, and all other expenses. Castile Records was one of Nashville's infamous "vanity" record labels. It could be said that the major labels typically billed even the biggest stars for their record expenses as well—except that they didn't require Garth Brooks or Brooks & Dunn, for example, to pay those charges up front.

All this feuding seemed kind of like a slapstick comedy, even after the parties took their fight all the way to Circuit Court. Preliminary hearings on the Haws vs. Bradshaw and Medlock case were held in September 1991, and a trial date was set for November 19.

Shortly before the trial, however, Roy Haws agreed to withdraw the suit and moved his *Indie Bullet* operation back to San Antonio.

The judge had dismissed two parts of the case already while agreeing to hear the rest of it, but none of that was mentioned in the sensational report on Channel 2 news (WKRN) that I recently found on YouTube. The date of the original broadcast isn't given, but it would have to be between late September and around November 19, when the case was dismissed. The footage in the YouTube clip begins with Roy Haws having one last smoke in the *Indie Bullet* office, spilling some cigarette ashes on the glass of a copying machine, then disgustedly dusting it off, saying "That's it, I've had enough... I can't take it anymore, I'm moving..."[50]

A bullet hole in the front window of Roy's Music Row office is shown from the outside. Roy and Jason tell the straight-faced reporter that on Friday, a gunman, seen only in a blur, had fired a shot through the window and disappeared. Roy dove under a desk, but Jason wasn't in the room at the time. They tell the reporter about their side of the feud and add one more detail that I haven't already mentioned. On the same day as the reporter's visit, they had received a fax with a message in large, primitively drawn letters that said: "Final warning, get out, Roy Haws & J. Hawkins leave now or your [sic] dead."

After finding the YouTube link, I watched the clip a couple of times, and then on the third viewing, I paused it so that I could study the image of the fax message. The camera zooms in briefly, but the whole page is never on screen, so it took a while to see what I needed to see. The "get out" message had been scrawled on a scan of a Barry Sadler album sleeve or poster.

Barry Sadler (no relation to me) was a decorated Vietnam veteran, a sergeant in the Green Berets who had the No. 1 pop hit of 1966 with the spoken-word song "Ballad of the Green Beret." A follow-up single, "The A-Team" also made the top-30 in 1966, but nothing else he released made more than a blip on the charts. He did some acting in film and TV, and then he moved to Nashville and wrote a series of pulp fiction novels.[51] In 1978, Sadler fatally shot a country music songwriter named Lee Bellamy. Bellamy was the ex-boyfriend of

Sadler's current girlfriend, Darlene Sharpe. Sadler claimed self-defense, but during his trial, it was revealed that Sadler had planted a gun in Bellamy's van to bolster his case. Sadler later agreed to plea to the lesser charge of voluntary manslaughter and was sentenced to four to five years, of which he only served 28 days. Sadler was found shot in the head inside a taxicab in Guatemala City in 1984. The bullet caused severe brain damage that left him a quadriplegic who needed 24-hour care. He died in 1989.

The use of Barry Sadler's image could've been a coincidence, but I doubt it. I think it was supposed to be a clever subliminal message.

There's one other thing about the Roy Haws/Gary Bradshaw feud that says more about the shady business these guys were in than it does about these shady guys in particular. Roy Haws had filed a civil suit against Audre Medlock and Gary Bradshaw claiming that they had damaged his reputation and that of his publication. One of his chief complaints was that they had accused him of chart fixing. He also claimed that they had been telling people that he charged a $750 fee for chart position in *Indie Bullet*.

When Roy Haws spoke to Joe Rogers back in July, he claimed that the fight was all about money, not morals. "The idea is to put *Indie Bullet* out of business and *Indie Tracker* in its place," he said, "such that whoever pays the highest dollar gets the highest chart position."

Which makes me wonder, what was Roy Haws's real grievance against Bradshaw and Medlock? He freely admitted being a chart fixer. I think it was being known as a *cheap* chart fixer that really hurt.

Chapter 13

George, Jim, Chuck, and Tony

THE PEOPLE WHO WORKED CLOSELY WITH KEVIN HUGHES SAID
HE WAS DETERMINED TO PUT A HALT TO CHART MANIPULATION
AT CASH BOX AND HELP RESTORE THE GOOD REPUTATION THE
MAGAZINE ONCE HAD. Then, on March 9, 1989, a man in a black
mask with a gun came up to Kevin's car, wounding me and shooting
Kevin until it was certain that Kevin was dead. So many things
about that night never made sense, but one thing was crystal clear:
The man in the black mask wanted Kevin Hughes dead. No matter
what people in the industry thought about *Cash Box* before Kevin
was murdered, no matter what theories they had about the case,
their impression of the magazine after March 9, 1989 did not improve. Staff morale was in the basement.

Whenever the media asked publisher George Albert for his
comments on the magazine's problems, he lashed out with denial and
counter-attacks. With his approval, the corrupt business practices
continued, and so did the magazine's downhill slide.

Albert was keenly aware that the magazine's ad revenue was
up whenever indie promoters in Nashville found ways to keep their

clients happy. He knew there was a direct correlation between the promoters buying ads for their clients and those clients finding their way onto the *Cash Box* charts.

Cash Box had always been and continued to be a national magazine. The problems that figured into Kevin's murder all had their basis in the country music community of Nashville. But when you picked up a copy of *Cash Box* in Los Angeles, Nashville, New York, Austin, Texas, or anywhere else, the first thing that caught your eye was a story about a gold or platinum-selling artist, usually a pop singer or an artist from the world of rock, hip-hop, or rap. Even though there were platinum-selling country artists, other types of music typically sold more records. To get a quick perspective on that, let's glance at a sampling of the covers over the years.

August 27, 1966 issue, the week I was born, the featured story and cover subject was pop-folk singer Donovan. March 4, 1989, it was Paula Abdul, pop singer and former cheerleader for the Los Angeles Lakers. Smaller stories always appeared next to the charts for each different genre, but over 90 percent of the time, the features were about the giants of pop music, hip hop, R&B, etc.

As much as George Albert enjoyed the revenue flowing out to Los Angeles from indie promoters in Nashville, *Cash Box* depended on the giant stars on the major labels for its existence. If not for them, the magazine would be just another one of those little giveaway publications you pick up as you're leaving the corner store and often as not, end up using it for kindling in the fireplace without a second glance.

As the reputation of *Cash Box* continued to slide, Jim Sharp took notice. "The major labels were starting to ignore it," said Sharp, recalling a painful memory. "They needed to restore their credibility."[52]

By 1991, Jim Sharp and George Albert had known each other for decades, but they weren't exactly close friends. Sharp brought up the subject of the magazine's tanking reputation several times in the late eighties, without positive results. He described a typical dialogue:

"He told me, 'We've got to get back on top, Jim,' but then he wouldn't admit that there was fraud going on at the magazine."

Sharp couldn't help but feel protective of the magazine's reputation and the way business was conducted there. In 1988, *Cash Box* moved from its former quarters in the Joe Talbot Building to the Young Executive Building, located at 1300 Division Street. Bad move, said Sharp. You don't hand a diabetic a pocketful of change and point them toward the Coca-Cola and candy machines.

"I set them up in the Joe Talbot Building," he said. "They were around credible people there. There were law offices there. MGM Records was downstairs. But after I left, they moved over into the Young Executive Building, where all those indie promoters were, like a nest of thieves and scoundrels. They all had offices in that building. The manager of that building also got his hands into the promotion game/racket, so he wasn't the most honest guy around, either."

Over the years, Sharp stayed in touch with several employees and former *Cash Box* employees. Ken Woods, a former intern at *Cash Box* had started a successful promotion company, and his office was next door to Sharp's publishing company.

"One day Ken was sitting in my office," said Sharp, "and he said, 'Jim, do you have any idea what's going on at *Cash Box*?' He was talking about corruption. He said you could hire Chuck Dixon, pay his weekly promotion fee, plus buy an ad in the magazine, and you could get on the chart. Hearing that made me sick to my stomach. So, I talked to George Albert in L.A. and he said, 'Oh, don't worry, they've got it under control.'"

Sharp's network of friends and associates also came to include Detective Bill Pridemore.

"We would have lunch at Longhorn Steakhouse," said Sharp. "We probably met once a month. I wouldn't get much information from him about the Kevin Hughes case. I read about that in the newspaper like everybody else. But he would throw a name at me and ask a simple question. For example, he'd say, 'John Doe, good guy, or bad guy?' Mostly things like that."

In the spring of 1991, George Albert was finally ready to make drastic changes at the Nashville magazine operation.

"George called me and said he had to hire somebody within a week," remembered Sharp. "George had people coming in for interviews, and I said I'd help him evaluate them." After interviewing some of the prospects, Sharp realized he felt a responsibility to do more. He told Albert he'd take the job himself.

"I told George that I'd do a one-year contract," said Sharp. "I wanted to see if he'd changed his ways. He wasn't an easy guy to work with."

Sharp knew that the job wouldn't be easy. Chuck Dixon and his henchmen had wormed their way into the framework of the Nashville office. Even when Chuck wasn't physically present, he was still able to exert his influence.

"The guy who was doing the charts was scared to death," remembered Sharp. "He'd met Chuck, and he'd heard from other people what was going on. He was afraid they were going to kill him." Sharp reassured the chart director that no one was going to come after him while he was in charge.

Then there was Tony D'Antonio.

"This guy, Tony, I never liked him to begin with," said Sharp. "Tom McEntee introduced me to Tony. I started relating to Tony what we needed to do at the magazine. We had different opinions about how to do things. We needed to build up credibility, but this guy was a shyster. I went to Tom and said something about Tony. Tom said, 'He's good. He's honest.' I said, 'Tom, that guy's not honest.' And I was right about that. Sometimes you can just tell about a person."

Tony was a strange bird. He was a thug and a sociopath, but behind his "Music Row dude" outfit of unbuttoned shirts, gold chains, expensive watch, and pinkie ring, The Tone—or whatever hipster nickname he was using at the time—was a walking bundle of insecurities. A friend of mine who worked next door to Tony told me something I'll never forget. "Tony always told people he was related to Jim Croce," she said. "He was only distantly related, a fourth cousin or something, but he would mention it a lot. He was really proud of that."

Jim Croce was a songwriter who had a couple of No. 1 singles in the early 1970s. "Bad, Bad Leroy Brown" took the top slot just before Croce died in a plane crash in 1973.

Croce was a scrappy, street-savvy musician who paid his dues playing gigs for pocket change and working for rent money at everything from construction work to spinning records as a DJ at an R&B station in Philadelphia, where he would spice up radio ads with his own personal street slang. A commercial for Bronco's Poolroom got tagged with, "You wanna be cool, and you wanna shoot pool... dig it!"[53]

Jim Croce's first album was self-produced for $500. The money was a wedding gift from his father-in-law and mother-in-law. The in-laws were betting on the record flopping, which would convince Jim to give up music and get a real job. The gift turned out to be a bad investment for them, however, because all 500 copies of the album sold out. Surviving during lean times, Croce got to know a lot of rough and colorful characters, and he wrote about many of them later on, when his music clicked on Top-40 radio. One of those real characters was "Bad, Bad Leroy Brown," a gambler who wore fancy clothes and a diamond ring— "The baddest man in the whole damned town... Meaner than a junkyard dog."

Did Tony D'Antonio, who grew up in Philadelphia and probably heard Croce as a jive-talking DJ on the radio, identify with those songs? Did he envision himself as a "Bad, Bad Leroy Brown" or perhaps a Don Corleone?

After the newly created Cold Case Unit (CCU) swung into action in early 2002, Bill Pridemore was able to devote more time and resources to the murder on Music Row case. On Friday, February

15, 2002, just one day after the CCU was declared official, Bill Pridemore interviewed a female witness about her experiences with Tony D'Antonio. The witness is a friend of mine, and she asked me not to use her real name, so we'll call her "Jane Doe" and her friend "Jill Smith." Pridemore's report on his interview with Jane Doe is excerpted below:[54]

> I advised Jane Doe that we had learned she had been associated with Chuck Dixon and Tony D'Antonio. She related the following information.
>
> January of 1989, she and Jill Smith started leasing office space in the same building with Tony D'Antonio and Craig Morris. Tony had recently gotten fired from Cash Box magazine and was in the process of promoting artists. During that time Tony requested that she assist him... After completing the job and requesting payment for the work, he refused. He told her that if she tells anyone about it, he has friends who would give her a pair of cement shoes. She considered that a direct threat and never mentioned the money or the incident again. After that incident she never felt comfortable about Tony again and in the early part of 1990, she moved her office out of the building.

Tony was the director at *Cash Box* when Chuck came in and practically took control of the magazine, much like some kinds of predators invade the body of a host species and begin directing its actions. With a friendly director at the helm, Chuck was able to operate a range of different schemes. Hire him as a promoter, and he'd guarantee that your record would make the country chart, but you also had to buy an ad in the magazine. For promoting a record for four weeks, he charged around $2,000. He also bullied the other promoters, saying that *Cash Box* was *his* magazine. If you didn't hire him as a co-promoter, he threatened to keep your record from charting at all.

The fraud became so blatant and tacky; it hurts my eyes to look at the evidence. The 1989 Grammys issue, published on March 11, has Chuck Dixon's grubby fingerprints all over it.[55] On page 43, a half-page ad for a band called Northern Gold has Chuck Dixon and Tony D'Antonio listed as promoters. On page 44 is a full-page for a Chuck Dixon artist named Debbie Sanders, referred to here as the "best female writer since Dolly Parton." Page 46 is a full-page ad for a Waylon Jennings/Paul English look-alike named Hunter Cain promoted by Chuck Dixon, Johnny Morris, and Craig Morris, with "The Tone" (Tony D'Antonio) credited as "Coordinator." Three out of four quarter-page ads on page 49 have one name in common: Chuck Dixon. Page 50 has six ads filling the page. Chuck Dixon and Bill Wence are listed as promoters for a single by Vernon Sandusky on GBS Records. Wence was the promoter who reached out to Bill Pridemore to give him a quick tutorial on the promotions game in Nashville.

On the same page, an ad for Dawn Dorminy's "Mama Didn't Raise No Fool" on Sundial Records, lists Richard F. (Tone) D'Antonio as the promoter. Still on page 50, Marcy Carr has an ad saying "Thanks, country radio, *Cash Box*, for your support, now on the charts with 'Too Many Heartaches.'" The label is Overton Lee Records and one of four listed promoters is Gary Bradshaw, one of Chuck Dixon's cronies at the time.

In the upper right-hand corner of page 50, the band Heartland sends a shout-out to their promoter with a comic book drawing of a muscle-bound mouse pulling a chain that is wrenching a house from its foundations. The mouse, which bears a strong resemblance to the hippie underground comic character Wonder Warthog, wears sunglasses and a tank top where "Dixon 1" is printed on the chest. The caption has a quotation: "If I tell you a mouse can pull a house… hitch him up!" At the bottom: "Thanks, Chuck!"

No wonder people called it "Chuck Box." The ads alone show that something rotten was going on, even without knowing anything about the crooked dealings behind the numbers on the charts. I didn't know about all the scams back then, but it seems so apparent now. That's one of the crazy things about this story—the farce got so out of hand, I guess the culprits thought they could get away with anything.

...

Evergreen Records was a small independent label. Johnny Morris is an excellent record producer, and he was a popular deejay in Missouri years before he started running record labels. Johnny knew what worked on the radio, and he knew talent. He made good records that deserved to get airplay. Listen to the hits he produced by John Wesley Ryles and Narvel Felts. You don't have that kind of success from bribing a few country deejays.

The fact that Johnny Morris contracted Chuck Dixon to promote Evergreen Records probably caused some people to suspect that Johnny, Chuck and *Cash Box* were in cahoots on the chart manipulating schemes. I never knew everything about how Johnny Morris ran his business, but I can tell you right now if Johnny was part of the chart fraud, he didn't exactly get rich doing it. If you want proof, take a drive by the Evergreen Records office. If you look for the shiny high-rise tower with security guards out front guarding the gold bullion inside and a bunch of Mercedes, BMWs, and Lamborghinis in the parking lot, you'll be disappointed. All you will find is a little, green frame house.

A lot of Chuck's power came from his "pocket stations," which totaled about half of the 125—175 stations that reported to *Cash Box*. The total number of reporting stations fluctuated for several legitimate reasons. From time to time, some stations would change their format, go out of business, or begin reporting to *Billboard* (normally, the *Cash Box* survey did not include stations that reported to both publications). Maintaining the legitimacy of the survey was the responsibility of the chart director or someone higher up in the chain of command, which usually meant either the division director or the owner, George Albert. Apparently, when the magazine sank to its lowest moral depths, someone like Chuck Dixon could have stations remain on the list even the chart director had disqualified them. Money talks, and when Chuck was deeply involved in *Cash Box*, the revenue flow made George Albert happy.

Through cash bribes or some other type of exchange, Chuck was able to control those stations and brag that they were in his "pocket." DJ's on Chuck's pocket stations either played the songs he wanted them to play or reported it that way, whether those records were actually getting airplay or not.

The sleaziest part of the deal was the Country Independents chart. As I've pointed out earlier, the top 100 records on the *Cash Box* Country Singles chart didn't look all that much different from the top 100 listed in *Billboard*. An objective study by the *Tennessean* in April 1989 found only about 20 percent variation—20 percent doesn't seem like a lot considering the fact that stations in the *Cash Box* survey were independents, as opposed to those in the *Billboard* survey, which covered non-independent reporting stations. Each magazine had its own brand—*Cash Box* was oriented toward independents; *Billboard* was corporate and mainstream. It seems only natural that you'd find a larger number of records on independent labels on the *Cash Box* Top-100.[56]

The real action for con artists like Chuck Dixon, Tony D'Antonio, and Robert Metzgar (I'll tell you lots more about him later) was in the Country Independent Singles list. This is the one that, according to qualified sources, was up for grabs, provided you had the bribe money. Of the 50 singles on the list every week, a bunch of them probably (knowingly or unknowingly) paid cash to one of those shady promoters for their slot. My records made the Independent chart, but I never asked anybody to put my songs on there, I wanted to make it there honestly. Why would I bother calling radio stations when I was working at Evergreen if I knew all you had to do was pay the right person? Why would anybody work the telephones and schmooze with radio people every day if all you had to do was send them some cash, a hooker, or a trip to Florida?

Ironically, all scams aside, Chuck Dixon was a legitimately good promotions guy, and everybody else I've contacted says the same thing. From what I saw, Chuck did a good job promoting Evergreen Records—my record included. Did he reach out to his pocket stations to push my records higher on the charts? I don't know— I wish I did—but I still made a few dents in the *Billboard* charts, and Chuck didn't report to them.

The *Cash Box* Country Independent chart was placed toward the back of the magazine, following the Top-100 Albums, Top-100 Singles, Top R&B LPs, Top R&B Singles, Traditional Jazz, Rap, Metal, Roots, Country LPs, and Country Singles—just before the "Jukebox" section. The Country Independent chart list took up the top half of the page. In the February 25, 1989 issue, the bottom half of this page had a regular feature called "Rising Stars" which was devoted to a singer named Ross Lewis.[57] Under the "Indie Spotlight" section was a paragraph about a new single by Heartland, a band promoted by Chuck Dixon. Four artists with new singles were listed with a short blurb under "Indie Feature Picks." The first artist was Roy Clark, who was a household name in country music, with a new single on Hallmark. So that could've been legit. The other three artists were Justin Wright, Brian O'Neill, and a duo called Mark Moseley & Marie Lester.

The Justin Wright blurb is the most interesting to me. His new single, on the Bear label, was "Hank and Lefty." A good song called "Hank and Lefty Raised My Country Soul," written by Dallas Frasier and A.L. Owens, is a tribute to Hank Williams and Lefty Frizzell that's been covered by everyone from Moe Bandy to Emmylou Harris. This is not that song, however. Although it's a tribute to the same pair of country legends, the songwriter credits on this cut are J.B. Detterline (Chuck Dixon), Gary Gentry, and Morris Sonny Hall.

It's hard to find much information on this version of "Hank and Lefty." The most interesting thing about it, other than the fact that the Dallas Frasier/A.L. Owens song probably came first, is that Chuck Dixon wrote it with Gary Gentry after the two wrote a much more successful song called "The Ride." This tribute to Hank Williams is about a struggling musician hitchhiking who is picked up by the ghost of Hank Williams.[58] In the end, the musician tells Hank's ghost to drop him off just south of Nashville. Chuck lived south of Nashville, in Mt. Juliet. David Allan Coe released "The Ride" as the first single from his 1983 LP, *Castles in the Sand*. The song peaked at No. 4 on the *Billboard* Country Singles chart. It's been covered numerous times, so it's probably been a good moneymaker.

In Gary Gentry's story about "The Ride," he doesn't say much about the actual contributions of Chuck Dixon, whom he refers to as J.B. Detterline, Jr.

> *I had a co-writer. I had been in a movie called "Hank Williams Tribute — The Man and His Music." We filmed it at the Ryman. And a promoter in town, J.B. Detterline Jr., came to me and said, "Gary, you've gotta write about Hank, man! And Lefty [Frizzell]!" He was a bigger Lefty fan, and I was the biggest Hank fan. I love them both, don't get me wrong. But Hank, I grew up on that.*

> *We got together and wrote a song called "Wherever Hank and Lefty Are, That's Where I Want to Go." At 10, he left, and I said, "It's not enough for Hank." He said, "What? It's a great song!"*

> *He left, and I was drinking in those days, and doing other things. I was living at Country Place Apartments. I lit candles in the living room, and I wanted Hank to show himself. I wanted to write a masterpiece about Hank. And I was mad, and I was drunk. Thank God, I haven't had a drink since 1984, but in those days, it was pretty*

wild. I said, "Hank! Why were you so big? Just because you died young? Show yourself! Help me write this song." I looked down that long hallway, and Hank was sitting there without a shirt on, on my couch, in the living room. And I said, "Hank, we're gonna take a ride. I wanna write about you. I think you're the greatest songwriter and entertainer that ever lived." Thus, "The Ride," at 4 o'clock in the morning.

J.B. Detterline's wife was asleep. She was pregnant. He said, "Gary, don't call late tonight after I leave here." I said, "OK." Well, that morning, about 4 o'clock in the morning, I couldn't even read my own writing. I had the song done and called Chuck ... and I played him "The Ride."

The only thing Gentry says about Chuck Dixon's input on the two songs is that they talked about writing a song—Chuck went home; Gentry did the writing. There could be more to it than that, and over the years, people have gotten songwriting credit for even less input, and sometimes, no input at all. Another songwriter I know who shares a credit on a song with Chuck remembers his experience this way: "Chuck was in the room with us for a little while, then he left, but that's about all I remember about his contributions."

I had known for years about "The Ride" and that Chuck Dixon wrote songs under his birth name, J.B. Detterline, Jr., but I didn't have any notion how many until we were researching this book. The BMI catalog lists 75 titles under his name. You must do more research to sort out the co-writers, but I'm assuming that "The Ride" was the high point of Chuck's songwriting career.[59]

One of the strange things you learn about criminals and con men is that they're often talented, intelligent individuals, but they're also sociopaths, so small achievements and modest rewards aren't good enough for them. They want more. They cut corners and take advantage of people to get it. So, it is surprising to find out that someone is a gifted songwriter after you suspect them of cold-blooded murder.

I felt that way about Chuck Dixon, and I also felt that way about Tony D'Antonio. Maybe they just became twisted after they realized they didn't have what it takes to create something special, so they turned what talents they did have toward low-level grift, larceny, and, when they felt that their evil ways were about to be exposed, murder.

...

Chuck had been in the music business since he was a teenager in the fifties, playing in bands in the Philadelphia area. In 1958 at the age of 18, Chuck was playing in a Coatesville, Pennsylvania-area band called the Rocketones, singing lead vocals as well as playing guitar, trumpet, and piano. He was already a man of many names: John Blayne Detterline, Jr., Chuck Detterline, and Chucky D. The founder of the band, Jim Brown, also went by JB, so that nickname was already taken. According to a source in Coatesville, Chuck had been a ten-year-old talent show winner.[60]

In the late sixties, Chuck was in Nashville, working various angles in the music business, including some cheap scams and probably some that were legitimate. In the summer of 1977, the *Tennessean* ran an exposé on the rampant fraud being committed by small-time music promoters and custom record labels on Music Row, and surprisingly, Chuck Dixon was not mentioned. But he was all over the place in the 1980s.

David Ross, the publisher of Music Row magazine, met Chuck Dixon when he started buying ads and remembers Chuck well.[61]

David said, "Chuck never looked to me like, how can I say this? Over the years, you're in the business, and you don't want to disqualify someone who wants to use your services, but you get a sense of which people are genuine, long-term players, and which people who you really don't want to get to know very well. Chuck always struck me as someone who took the promotion thing a little too far. He was a little too fast, a little too smooth, and he just was not the kind of person I could see myself hanging out with."

David Ross was probably lucky he never hung out with Chuck Dixon, and looking back, I realize I had probably made a good decision to move away from Nashville for a while. When I was on the road playing with Overdrive between 1991—98, it was just a little easier to block out thoughts about the shooting. I still had the nightmares and the other problems, but I had just a little more peace.

I worried a lot about my reputation back in Nashville. I hoped they didn't think I was involved in Kevin's murder, other than being in the wrong place at the wrong time. I just didn't know. The police hadn't done anything to put my mind at ease.

I didn't know who had shot us or why, and that seemed like a good enough reason to fear being shot again if I went back.

In the process of learning all these things about Chuck Dixon, Tony D'Antonio, and the investigations, I've found even more reasons that staying away was a good idea. In Nashville, I would've learned the truth a lot sooner, including the common assumption by so many that Chuck and Tony were behind the murder on Music Row. As I later learned, the police were pretty confident they knew who did it.

If I was living in Nashville at that time and those guys were still walking around free to do as they pleased, it would've driven me crazy.

...

So, while I was on the road playing music, Jim Sharp was at *Cash Box*, trying to clean house.

"Chuck and Tony used to make me sick, hanging around the office, doing all that gangster talk," Sharp told us. "They'd say, 'If that guy doesn't come around, we'll chop his fingers off,' that kind of thing. It was terrible."

Jim Sharp finally did what had to be done. "I ran them off," he said. "I threw him out. I told George Albert, 'We've got to get these guys out of there.' George said, 'Yeah, they're out.'"[62]

For about a year, maybe less, the embargo against the Chuck Dixon crowd held, and George Albert supported Jim's efforts, but then someone let Chuck back into the fold. Sharp himself was the culprit.

"Chuck would still come around, but he knew he didn't have any clout," said Jim. "I brought him back in, I said, 'Chuck, you're a good independent promoter. You can come back if you'll keep it clean. Don't be asking for chart numbers, don't be buying ads to get a record moved up. Any of that and you're out of here.'"

Things were going so well, Jim said, that during the Country Radio Seminar at the Opryland Hotel, he invited Chuck to go with him to visit the record executives upstairs at the RCA/Columbia suite.

"George Albert was in town and thought it was a good idea, too," said Sharp. "I was trying to be a nice guy—big mistake."

Jim's interpretation of what happened is that Chuck became energized by being around the record label big shots. Joe and Chuck were on a first-name basis—Joe Galante, longtime head of RCA Records Nashville, and Chuck Dixon of Morris-Dixon Promotions, that is.

Within days, or so it seemed, Chuck had wormed his way back in again. Jim would call George Albert, and the publisher would use the time to try and impress him with Chuck's brilliant ideas.

At the end of 1991, Sharp sent Albert a letter informing him that at the beginning of 1992, he was going to drop several reporting radio stations. Most of the stations happened to be in Chuck Dixon's pocket. Chuck and some others quickly complained to Albert.

"Chuck was a great schmoozer, he would call George 'G.A.' and build him up, tell him what he wanted to hear," said Sharp. "George started telling me that Chuck said we could do this or that and I said, 'No! We can't do that!' and I said, 'It's my way, or I'm out of here.'"

The press in Nashville quoted Jim Sharp saying that leaving *Cash Box* was his idea. They also quoted George Albert, who said,

"Jim Sharp did not leave my employ. I dismissed him, and I did it myself."

The article in *Nashville Scene* ("*Cash Box* Exodus: Departures Revive Chart Debate," February 13, 1992) gave equal time to both sides of the story, not counting background interviews with employees who left after hearing that Sharp was going.[63] On that subject, an ex-staffer had this to say: "Well, if Jim leaves, only the worst could happen."

Judging from the other responses by the Publisher, he would have done better with "no comment" as his response. According to the article, "Albert says his ex-employees have spoken about chart problems and the Hughes murder as an excuse for their inadequacy."

...

Tom McEntee had many positive things to say about Tony D'Antonio. He told the detectives that Tony quickly grasped the concepts of his position at *Cash Box* and was a hard worker, and a valuable asset. Maybe Tom recognized a little of himself in Tony, a self-starter, a hardscrabble hustler, not unlike Tony's hero, Jim Croce. But Tony also thought of himself as Bad, Bad Leroy Brown, and that was a problem.

In 1972, Croce signed with ABC Records, and his single "Bad, Bad Leroy Brown" took the No. 1 slot on *Billboard*. Croce was on tour in the fall of 1973 when his chartered plane took off from Natchitoches, Louisiana in a dense fog. There was only one tree in the area, and the Beechcraft E18S hit it, killing Croce and five others on board.

I appreciate the fact that Jim Croce worked so hard to make it in the music business. I also admire the fact that he put out his own record and tried to do things his own way. Despite his success, Croce became disillusioned with the music industry. He told his wife he wanted to leave the music business when his tour was over—he just wanted to come home and be with his wife and kid. Shortly thereafter, he died, too soon, at age 30.

Tony might have been interested to learn that I was from Bonham, Texas, which is just a few miles from Sherman where Jim Croce was headed to play his next gig, when his plane crashed. But I never had a single conversation with Tony D'Antonio, so it never came up.

...

When Jim Sharp took the reins at *Cash Box* in 1991 and declared Chuck Dixon "out," the same went for Tony D'Antonio. Both guys had other ways to earn a dishonest living, but Chuck was better at doing so without police intervention. Former *Cash Box* employees mentioned that Tony was constantly talking about his access to illegal drugs. If they mentioned any details in their interviews with Pridemore and Postiglione, they seem to have been omitted from the murder case files. Tony's former drug-dealing partners, however, related some stories to other police agencies, and some of those documents were preserved in the files.

In the spring of 2017, when Bill Pridemore spent an hour and a half with our researcher, he talked about how he had hoped the drug running aspect of Tony D'Antonio's life might eventually provide the lead he was seeking. Periodically, between 1990 and 2002, he would sit down with the Kevin Hughes file and try to give it a fresh look, wondering what he had missed.

In the fall of 1991, in the town of Chatsworth, Georgia, about three hours southeast of Nashville, Tony was involved in what investigators described as "a drug rip-off scheme" with Charles D. Scott and three other partners, which netted them a profit of $34,000.[64] Unfortunately for Tony, his partners decided to cut him out of the deal and keep the money. This betrayal climaxed in an emergency police call on the night of November 22, 1991, from the home of Charles and Frieda Scott. Charles and Frieda, plus two other individuals were present when Tony kicked in the back door and threatened to kill everyone in the house, even the three children if he didn't get his money.

Pridemore didn't learn about the incident until 2002 when he was working with a confidential informant, an aspiring songwriter from Georgia named James Steven Daniel (sometimes referred to as Steve). Pridemore was especially interested in the home invasion incident from 1991. According to the arrest report from Murray County, the gun Tony used in that incident was either a .38-caliber revolver or .357 magnum. For that reason, the documents from the Chatsworth case were added to the Kevin Hughes murder file.

One of the documents is a statement given by Charles Scott, dated January 15, 1992. Scott's statement painted a picture of Tony as someone capable of extreme violence. (Please note: I had to make minor changes to the account to make it more readable because the original was handwritten using a sort of shorthand. Nothing substantial has been changed, however.)

> *Tony came in through the back door… Tommy saw him first, said, "We have company." I didn't know Tony was there until he was in the house. Originally, I thought he was a truck driver. I was sitting on the couch, walked into the kitchen to see.*
>
> *I could smell whisky on Tony. He acted wild.*
>
> *Tony pulled a gun (.357 magnum). Adrian was in the den. He never saw the gun. Frieda was in the kitchen. Tony said, "I'll kill everybody." He made everybody come into the den and sit on the couch.*
>
> *There were three children on the couch, eight-year-old Chad Westmoreland, five-year-old Caitlin Westmoreland, and eight-year-old Lauren Leonard.*
>
> *He separated Charles and Frieda in the kitchen. He put*

the gun up to each of their heads and threatened both of them.

He said he would gouge her eyes out and kill everybody at $5,000 a pop… While he was in the kitchen Tony held the gun to Charles' head and asked Frieda if she believed he would blow Charles's head off.

The telephone rang. Danny Silvers, an employee, was calling. I said, "I've got problems, can't talk." He called back, I said the same thing and hung up.

Silvers called the police. The police came in two or three minutes.

Officers Leonard and Morrison were the first police officers to arrive at the Scott residence. Leonard knocked on the door, Morrison stood back. When Charles Scott answered the door, he told Leonard that the suspect was armed. Morrison described what happened next on the arrest report:

I spotted the suspect outside, the south side of the house. I got closer, then shined my flashlight on the suspect, identified myself as a police officer and told him to stop where he was. The suspect broke into a run. I repeated myself several times during the chase. The suspect attempted to jump over a fence. On his second attempt at the fence, I jumped on suspect's back. In doing so, suspect was struck inadvertently on the side of his face with flashlight.

Tony D'Antonio was taken into custody and booked with six counts of aggravated assault and one count of burglary. He was 29 years old, 6'1" tall, and he weighed 240 pounds. He gave his occupation as "entertainer," his nickname "Dee."

The personal property receipt listed $882.00 in cash, a pocket knife, a Wittnauer wrist watch, a gold nugget bracelet, a 14-karat gold ring, and a gold chain with a diamond piano pendant. But no

.38-caliber revolver or .357 magnum.

One year after the incident, the new residents at the Colonial Hills address called the police to report finding a pistol between the mattresses of a bed. Police officers came to investigate and reported that the gun was a .45-caliber Ruger. For some reason, the police officers didn't even take the gun into custody. Another potential lead in the case came to a dead end.

Chapter 14

Friends in Low Places

Sammy Sadler is a really good meat and potatoes country singer, a Texas honky-tonk singer. He's almost the perfect country singer. He's the kind of guy who could make a living for years playing the honky-tonks of Texas if he wants to. He's always been on independent labels, which is a hard row to hoe. Your chances of success on an independent label are vastly smaller than if you're on a major label, but that doesn't mean it's impossible. Jason Aldean is a perfect example. Jason is on an independent label and he's doing well, so it can be done. It takes a lot of money and a lot of promotional muscle. But Sammy can always make a living in music if he wants to.

–Robert K. Oermann[65]

The first time I heard LeAnn Rimes sing "Blue" on the radio, it was the middle of July 1996, and there was a heat wave in North Texas. The temperature hit 105 degrees in Leonard, my old stomping grounds, and it may have been even hotter in Garland, where LeAnn grew up. "Blue" was the first single, also the name of the album. It sold 123,000 copies the first week of its release. It peaked at No. 1 on *Billboard*'s Top Country Albums chart, debuted at No. 3 on the Top-200 chart, and went on to sell four million copies in the U.S., eight million worldwide. Not bad for a 13-year-old kid.[66]

LeAnn Rimes was the youngest female country star since Tanya Tucker had her first hit "Delta Dawn" at age 13 in 1972.

Everybody said LeAnn sounded a lot like Patsy Cline, and that was no accident. It was exactly what the songwriter had in mind. Bill Mack, a Dallas DJ and promoter, had originally written the song for Patsy Cline in the hopes that she would record it, but her death in a plane crash in 1963 dashed that dream.

The first time I saw LeAnn on stage, we were both guest stars on Johnnie High's Country Music Revue in Arlington. The year was either 1991 or 1992, but I remember LeAnn was nine years old. She was already an experienced performer, having started in local musical theatre performances at the age of five. Three years later, at the advanced age of eight, she switched careers, with the goal of becoming a country music star. During her ninth year, she sang the national anthem at the opening of a Dallas Cowboys game or two, went on the nationally-syndicated talent show, "Star Search," hosted by Ed McMahon, and appeared on the same bill as yours, truly on the "Johnnie High Country Music Revue."

And so, while I was onstage singing, LeAnn and her father Wilbur Rimes were standing next to my father on the side of the stage. Later, Dad told me what Wilbur said to LeAnn as they watched me perform. "See that, LeAnn?" he said. "He's having fun singing. That's how you ought to look when you're up there."

In 1996, LeAnn Rimes was only the latest of a long line of successful country singers whose parents helped them get a start in the business. When I moved to Nashville, my mom and dad came with me, helped me get settled, paid for my first demo recording, and did countless other things to help me get started. It's a tradition there, more or less. You find parents backstage lots of other places—New York, Los Angeles, Chicago, and Austin, to name a few—but it seems to be much more common in Nashville. My personal theory is the relatively wholesome, family-oriented image of country and gospel music.

One of my favorite examples is John Wesley Ryles. Fortune couldn't have smiled upon a nicer or more talented guy—a person I'm proud to call a friend. John's first break in Nashville came through a combination of talent, guts, and luck.

"I came from a musical family and played all my life," said Ryles. "We worked for years and years in the Dallas-Fort Worth area, Big D Jamboree, and all that. When I was 14, I decided it was time to shop my demo tape around Nashville. So, my dad and I came to town and I knocked on doors."[67]

That was in the mid-1960s when it was a little easier to get a walk-in appointment on Music Row. Fortunately, John had a couple of contacts in the business. One of them was Roger Miller. The day John and his dad knocked on the door at Tree Publishing, Roger was in, and so were Buddy Killen and Curly Putman—three legends of country music. They listened to the demo and were impressed. More encouragement came from Harlan Howard, who wrote "I Fall to Pieces" and "Heartaches by the Number." John kept on plugging his songs, meeting people, and getting advice.

At the office of another country music giant, Hubert Long, they met Walter Haynes, who managed Long's publishing company. "Walter listened to the tape and he said, 'I'm gonna play this for my boss. If you'll come back after lunch, we'll see what he thinks.' We came back, and he introduced me to Hubert Long, and they signed me to a development deal with a contract for management and publishing. I guess you'd say that's where I got my start."

Stories about how people got their start in the business always interest me. Talent, a great press kit, and a good demo tape aren't enough. There are always showcase venues, where unsigned artists perform with the hopes that they'll attract a following and someone important, who can help them on their way up the ladder, would take notice.

I mentioned LeAnn Rimes at the beginning of this chapter for two reasons. One is that when somebody becomes a success at age 13, you get the impression that it came easy for them, but LeAnn had been working hard in show business for years before Mike Curb won the bidding war and signed her. The other reason I mentioned LeAnn is that her "debut" album on Curb Records was, technically speaking, not her first.

Nor Va Jak, an independent label founded by the late Norman Petty and based at his studio in Clovis, New Mexico, released the album *All That*, by 11-year-old LeAnn Rimes in 1994. Nor Va Jak was also the place where the Norman Petty Trio had recorded the hit "Mood Indigo" in 1954 and Buddy Holly recorded "That'll Be the Day" in 1957, which featured the Bill Mack composition, "Blue."

LeAnn broke through with a combination of great talent, a great song, and a good recording released on a little indie label. That was the mix that caught the attention of the major labels in Nashville. The funny thing is, Music Row tends to look down on indie labels. There's no doubt about the fact that the major labels are giant corporations and they control the music business. Generally, they control the kind of music you hear on the radio, they release the million-selling records, they subsidize the tours of the acts that sell out the concert halls and arenas, and they have all the big music acts whose latest releases pop up first when you open iTunes or your favorite streaming service. In the music business, bigger is always considered better.

When you're working on Music Row, it can feel like a small town, where you feel as though you know everybody because you're all working in some capacity in the same business. If a friend mentions a conversation he had yesterday with his good friend Joe Galante, the head of RCA Records, you smile as if you know Joe, even if you don't know him personally, because a bunch of your friends know him, maybe even better than the guy telling this story. The small-town aspect also goes for gossip and a tendency for people to think alike, even if it's something negative. A piece of nasty gossip can spread like an epidemic, and almost everybody in town comes down with it. The virus I'm talking about is the bias against small and independent labels, which are often regarded as the "used car dealers of the music industry." A lot of that negative bias is based on fact, but some of it is just unreasonable.

Monte Warden and Brandi Scaife had a unique perspective about the bias against independent labels in Nashville. Monte grew up in Austin, which had solid blues and punk/new wave scenes that caught fire and earned the attention of people around the world. Unlike Nashville, Austin loved everything indie, and that do-it-yourself spirit spawned the Armadillo World Headquarters, Austin City Limits, and the South by Southwest (SXSW) music festival.[68]

"In Austin, back in the eighties, if you signed to Slash Records or I.R.S., or some other cool indie label, and there were lots of them around, it was considered a good thing," said Monte.

"It meant you had a certain autonomy, that you wouldn't get lost in the shuffle like happens at major labels. But in Nashville, it just meant you weren't good enough for the majors."

The first time Monte met his future wife, Brandi Scaife, he told her he was the lead singer for The Wagoneers, that they were on a label she'd never heard of called Watermelon Records. She was less than impressed. Her attitude was, as she described it, "You're on an indie label? So, nobody's signed you, huh?"

Watermelon Records wasn't some fly-by-night operation, however. The Wagoneers sold over 100,000 units on little old Watermelon Records. Label mates included acts as diverse as Don Walser, Carla Olson & Mick Taylor, Alejandro Escovedo, and Santiago Jimenez, Jr.

Brandi might have been teasing Monte because she had encountered her share of snobbish attitudes about Decca Records, where she worked in A&R. At the time, Decca was a smaller, sister label to MCA Records.

"We had distribution through Universal," said Brandi. "We sold millions of records; we had Leanne Womack, Mark Chesnutt… but people would say, Oh, bless y'all's hearts, you're on Decca."

Music people can be like that—putting down this label or that distributor, being snooty about the Bakersfield country scene versus the Nashville country scene, but if you're trying to say that working with an independent label is a losing proposition, you're ignoring a big part of Nashville history. When we talked to Robert Oermann, he was happy to tackle that subject. "Indie labels started right here in Nashville in 1947, with the recording of 'Near You' by the Francis Craig Orchestra on Bullet Records," he said.

That was 70 years ago, and maybe you've never heard of it, even though George Jones and Tammy Wynette also had a hit with the song. The 1947 version, however, wasn't just an ordinary hit record. The original "Near You" was the first record released by Bullet (catalog no. 1001) and it enjoyed the kind of historic success that would be the envy of any record label, even the biggest record label in the world. "Near You" reached No. 1 in the *Billboard* chart and it held that position for a record-setting 21 weeks. Although the hip-hop group Black Eyed Peas came close in 2009, no other song has done better.

The way Robert Oermann sees it, "Near You" was one of a small handful of events that essentially made Nashville the center of country music for the world.[69]

"The record was so popular, they had to build record manufacturing plants here in Nashville to keep up with the demand," Oermann said. "We became a record manufacturing center because of 'Near You.'"

The success of Bullet Records also encouraged all the other independent labels in the 1950s—not only in Nashville, and not only in country music.

"What really gave rise to the birth of rock 'n' roll was the fact that so many of the artists were on independent labels," said Oermann. "Chuck Berry was on Chess out of Chicago, Little Richard was on Specialty in L.A., and Elvis was on Sun, based in Memphis, and none of those labels had distribution deals with a major record company. All of this revolution was started by people who were on independent labels."

I'm not the first nor the last country singer who moved to Nashville with a lot of ambition and very little insider knowledge about the business. Maybe I should've known what terms like "payola" and "chart fraud" meant, but I didn't. Maybe, after graduating from high school in Leonard, Texas, I should've gone off to college and studied the music industry, but instead, I moved straight to Nashville, so I could sing and make records and become a country music star.

Maybe I should have dug in my heels and held out for a deal with a major label instead of signing with Evergreen Records. I know Robert Oermann feels that being on independent labels has made it harder for me all these years.

Up through 1997 or '98, I was still on the road, gigging steadily, playing three to five nights a week. Toward the end of that period, another big scandal about indie labels and promoters erupted in Nashville, but I wasn't keeping up current events on Music Row and I only learned of the sordid tale during the last year or so. It was the kind of thing that does create a dark cloud over independents, but it also makes the whole industry and the city look bad.

There are some so-called record labels that exist just to rip off the naïve "wannabe" country stars that come to Nashville with a whole lot less knowledge about the business than I had when I left home. These people come to Music Row and get dazzled by the "Grand Ole Opry," the Country Music Hall of Fame, and presence of so many of their idols that they become easy pickings for any huckster who brags about having an office on Music Row. It's an old, old story, and it's probably been going on ever since entertainers started getting paid for what they do.

John Wesley Ryles rightly calls the perpetrators of these scams "bottom feeders." John remembers meeting one of these characters not long after he started shopping his music around Nashville.

> *He had gold records on his wall that were fake. He said, "You sound great!" He didn't know if we were good or not, but that's what he did, he bilked people out of lots and lots of money. This guy made so much money he had a house on the lake, big cars, and he had these fake gold records on the wall, but we saw through it right away. Unfortunately, I know a couple of people who didn't. A dentist and his wife in Pennsylvania invested $100,000 and they thought they were getting somewhere, spinning their wheels and spending their money. It's sad.*

The meeting John described happened in the late sixties, and the label was called K-Ark, which had its office at 728 16th Avenue South. K-Ark is also the label Chuck Dixon was working with in 1967 when he was sued by a singer named John Poole for failure to produce the four rock 'n' roll singles for which he had shelled out almost $2,000.[70]

Music Row has been home to this type of shameless, soulless racket for at least 60 years. The victims are plentiful—those who come to Nashville and are so desperate to have a music career or simply naïve about the business that they'll hand over huge sums of money to some shady promoter or vanity record label after being hooked on a bunch of false promises and flattery.

A lot of these pitches happened at the Shoney's restaurant by the old Country Music Hall of Fame. It's all gone now, bulldozed and redeveloped, with a bronze sculpture of naked dancers called "Musica" in the middle of the traffic circle to make the area look more sophisticated. But when I used to come to Nashville as a kid, and up through the late 1980s when I left, country music fans would come to town, stay at the Hall of Fame Comfort Inn, go to the "Grand Ole Opry," visit Opryland and the Country Music Hall of Fame, and go shopping at the celebrity vanity museums nearby. In between jaunts, they would stop in at another original Nashville institution eager for their patronage, Shoney's. There were always tourists at Shoney's, and some of them would be sitting there, daydreaming about becoming a country music star someday.

"A lot of people who came to town, the wannabes, would go to Shoney's for breakfast," said David Ross. "And the promo guys would hang out there, so they could spot them. They'd say, 'Whoa, you're new in town? Yeah, I'm hooked up, I can make you a star.' And the wannabes would go, 'Oh, how much is this going to cost me?' The promo guy would say, 'Well, how much you got?'"[71]

These were the guys who truly gave independent music labels and promoters a bad rap.

In July 1967, a grand jury investigation into a Music Row company called Dino Productions returned indictments against two men on charges that they were bilking victims out of their money using false promises and fictitious connections to the entertainment industry. Carl E. Friend and Lance "Kenny" Roberts were running a diversified operation, seeking gullible would-be movie actors as well as musicians.

The office of Dino Productions was at 812 16th Avenue South. A housewife from McMinnville paid them $660 for an acting course and a screen test for a part in a movie starring the sex symbol Mamie Van Doren, set in the Bahamas. The money was supposed to be refunded if she didn't get the part. After months and months of stalling, the woman filed a complaint against Dino.

Meanwhile, the parents of the five teenage members of TC & the Blue Notes were upset because they paid Dino Productions $2,000 after being promised a deal on London Records, with promotion in 23 major cities. The band was also supposed to get 500 copies of their record within two weeks. After six months and no records, no promo, the mother of one of the boys called the New York office of London Records and was told that London had no dealings with Dino.[72]

"Imagine the hell these kids went through at school," she said, "with everybody waiting for their record."

The Confederates, a teenage rock 'n' roll band from Cleveland, had fallen for the same basic trap. The Confederates were also promised a big dinner party for all the DJs in Cleveland. One of the band members, Joe Bizovsky, sold his motorcycle to help raise his share of the expenses. The young rocker, like the actress, admitted being taken in by appearances. The actress commented that the Dino office was "plush." Bizovsky was impressed that the mother of Hank Williams, Jr. had an office next door. "It looked pretty professional," he said. "Johnny Cash had an office in there, too. It was the last place in the world I would look for a crooked man."

By the time the indictments were returned against Friend and Roberts, the offices at Dino had been cleared out, the phone disconnected. I pored over the back issues of the *Tennessean*, which had been reporting on the case in 1967. I couldn't find anything on how the case was resolved, but I hope Friend and Roberts ended up singing the Hank Williams classic, "In the Jailhouse Now."

One of Nashville's longtime, leading authorities on music fraud in Nashville was the late Robert Douglas Metzgar. Tall, with a head of silver wavy hair and a pair of silver glasses, Metzgar was a former Assembly of God minister who turned music producer and promoter in 1971. Metzgar, born in 1940 and raised in Texas, died a couple of years ago, but www.robertmetzgar.com, was still online during the summer of 2017. When the murder on Music Row case went to trial in 2003, Metzgar was one of the prosecution's star witnesses.[73]

Metzgar's website told me that, as of 2006, he had "produced over 10,000 sides of music in the city of Nashville in both the country, pop, and gospel music fields." By then, he was so busy he was forced to turn down "over a hundred clients a year… who asked for his help in their music career."

Metzgar's first professional career was preaching as an Assembly of God minister, but he found himself at a crossroads in 1983 when the congregation at his church in Hendersonville, Tennessee filed charges against him for 19 counts of larceny, for misappropriating church funds and other financial chicanery to the tune of $96,000. Metzgar's attorneys aggressively fought back against the church in criminal court and in civil litigation. The charges were eventually dropped, but by then, Metzgar had long since been forced to resign from the ministry.[74]

Metzgar moved into the Nashville world of independent production and custom labels. Trouble soon followed. In 1997, attorneys for Garth Brooks and his record label threatened action because Metzgar was using a photo of Garth and his wife, Sandy, in promotions and advertising, including the website for his promotion company, Capitol Advertising & Management. The problem with the photo was that Metzgar was also in it, standing next to Garth and Sandy at a music industry event. The way Metzgar was using the picture implied that he and the country superstar had some sort of professional affiliation.[75]

Furthermore, Garth Brooks was signed to Capitol Records, the real Capitol Records that was founded on the West Coast by Johnny Mercer and two partners in 1942. Judging from the skimpy sales figures of Metzgar's record label, Platinum Plus Records, it was another example of deceptive advertising.

Metzgar caved into pressure, removing the photo from his advertising and web page, and changing the name of his company to Metropolitan Nashville. Despite Garth and Capitol Records not suing him, the Davidson County district attorney's office was investigating other complaints against Metzgar.

Sometimes it seemed like these shysters never got caught or prosecuted, despite the damage they inflicted on people's lives and the reputation of the city. Newspapers and trades dutifully covered stories about events sponsored by shady promoters—talent searches, songwriting contests, showcases, and award shows—without injecting any editorial comment about the legitimacy of those events, or the fact that their primary purpose was tricking clients into spending large sums of money on far-fetched ambitions.

The media—trade papers, radio, TV, and even the city newspaper—often played right along without any commentary on the legitimacy of the events and sponsors. The attendance of a celebrity or two guaranteed photo ops and boldface names for content in the entertainment columns, even if those celebrities were a few years past their sell-by date.

As I explained earlier, I think it's wrong, and it's unfair when all independent labels end up being lumped in with the cheesy vanity labels and fly-by-night promoters. As Assistant District Attorney for Davidson County, Jon Seaborg, said in 1997, "the few bad apples" make it harder on the honest ones. Reporter Sheila Wissner interviewed Seaborg for a two-part exposé published in the *Tennessean* June 29-30, 1997.[76]

"Most of the industry is legitimate and does a real good job of working with people," said Seaborg. "We find these folks who try to take advantage of the unwary and the system, and those are the ones that seem to cause the problems."

Some of the bad-apple stories in Nashville came to light after complaints by a turkey farmer from Tipton, Missouri resulted in a felony theft warrant for Wayne Oliver and a federal lawsuit. Oliver's company, Oliver Enterprises, had an office at 2 Music Circle South. Oliver had assured the turkey farmer, Scott Jurgensmeyer, that he had a verbal agreement from Curb Records that they would sign a country singer named Hawk Montana. The deal hinged on producing a record album and two music videos, which Oliver said would cost $250,000. Jurgensmeyer paid it, but Oliver's claims turned out to be bogus.

Even dead country singers were getting pulled into the scams of what music critics liked to call "the lower reaches" of the music business. Ed Russell, who operated Castle Records from an office at 50 Music Square, was the subject of a cease and desist letter from the estate of Conway Twitty, who died in 1993. The estate's lawyers sought to prevent Russell from continuing his use of an unreleased demo Twitty had recorded with his daughter, Judy Jenkins.

Russell was using an altered version of the recording, one in which Jenkins' voice, the female half of the duet, had been electronically removed. Female singers responding to audition calls were told by Russell that he was searching for the perfect vocalist to complete the duet for release on MCA Records. MCA had already told Russell to get lost, but not many fame-seeking singers realized that. The unluckiest ones signed recording and promotional contracts obligating them to pay Russell thousands of dollars.

Another story about Russell that ended up in the *Tennessean* exposé sounded as if it should have taken straight out of a booklet called "Top Ten Music Row Clichés." Delana Ditto, who already had a career of sorts, singing on cruise ships, visited Music Row for the first time in 1989. Ditto and her drummer, Scott Huber, made the mistake of stopping at Shoney's.

"I was somewhat dressed up, I guess," said Ditto, "and a guy came up to me and said, 'You look like a star.'" The guy was Ed Russell. The address on his business card for Castle Records indicated that his office was right around the corner. They went there, Russell listened to her demo.

"He said, 'Boy, that's great. You've got something here.' Of course, it's everything you want to hear," she said, describing that first meeting when she and Huber fell for Russell's pitch. By the time Ditto spoke to Wissner for the *Tennessean* story, she was older, wiser, and $50,000 poorer. It was all a rip-off. A lawyer told her she had a legitimate case, but that suing Russell might be bad for her career. Besides, she didn't have any money to pay him. Ditto went back to sea, performing on cruise ships.

"We are easy prey," said Ditto. "There are a lot of wannabes. Country is so hot, and we've got stars in our eyes."

Janet O'Hara sang in the church choir in Yankton, South Dakota, and competed in the Miss South Dakota contest. O'Hara spent over a thousand dollars traveling to Nashville in the fall of 1995 after being told at a local audition that she had been selected to perform in promoter Don Reed's "Nashville Starbound Talent Competition." All of Nashville's top record labels had been invited. The promoters urged O'Hara to sell tickets for $10 apiece to help pay her expenses. That should've been one tip-off, but she didn't know.

"I guess the whole thing is that I had never really known how to go about getting started in the business," O'Hara told Sheila Wissner. "I was excited, too. I thought: You never know. You could get down here and somebody could hear you. All kinds of things happen."

What happened was that some 110 participants auditioned from 9 a.m. until late that night, and Janet O'Hara felt she had been conned. She didn't see anyone there who looked important, not even Don Reed himself, who offered to record one of her songs and promote it on the radio for $10,000.

O'Hara said no and went home to Yankton, where no one charged her to sing. Don Reed said she was making a mistake. He had a track record of discovering new talent for 40 years, he bragged. This statement suggested a great opening for a question from the reporter for the *Tennessean*: How many of Reed's clients had landed a major record deal in the last 40 years? The answer: None.

Wayne Oliver, Ed Russell, and Don Reed were all subjects of the 1997 exposé written by Sheila Wissner for the *Tennessean*. The strangest of all may have been the one about a gospel group and their experiences with Robert Metzgar.

In Mebane, North Carolina, two young brothers, Jamie and Jason Dooley, plus their cousin, Eric Dooley, performed in a gospel act called Southern Grace. After playing an audition in a Burlingame motel sponsored by Crystal Image Talent Agency's "Star Seek," the

Dooleys were enticed to play another talent show in Nashville. After that gig, they were ushered backstage to meet Robert Metzgar. The ex-minister told the boys just what they wanted to hear.

Metzgar told them they were so good that they were ready to go directly into the studio to record a professional demo tape that would get them the airplay that would make the labels jealous and hungry to pick them up.

Recording costs for the demo would run $4,000, and they had to do it soon, because, he said, "the major labels [sign] their acts in January." This was in October. Flattered and pressured to make a decision, the Dooleys borrowed the money and recorded the demo. Jamie and Jason's mother, Donna Dooley, the group's manager, told Wissner that when they visited Metzgar's office, they saw "shimmering gold records and photographs of country music stars," and in one photograph, Metzgar standing right next to Garth and Sandy Brooks.

The Dooleys were hooked. After coming that far and paying all that money, the photograph was enough to convince them that Metzgar could do all the things he claimed. So Southern Grace signed a contract with him.

It's such a cliché: The huckster who gives a pitch and uses a fictional connection to a major label or major star as the bait, and the artist dreaming of the day when someone important will recognize their talent and award them with a big, fat deal. But is this music representative really one of those very important people? To erase those doubts, they claim to have personal relationships with music industry big-wigs—"I play golf with so-and-so every Saturday, and he owes me a favor."

After the December 1995 recording session, the Dooleys anxiously waited… and waited. They were still waiting to see or hear the first copy of their record when news came that the Academy of Independent Recording Artists (AIRA) had nominated Southern Grace for Group of the Year, Vocal Performance of the Year, Single of the Year, Singer/Songwriter of the Year, and Song of the Year in the country division.

Robert Metzgar had truly accomplished the impossible: five award nominations before the Southern Grace record had even been released. Donna Dooley demanded an explanation. She was told that 100 CDs had been distributed to 100 stations around the U.S. and the feedback was incredible. Apparently, somehow, Metzgar had forgotten to send any of the advance copies to the artist—if they really existed.

Still dreaming big, the Dooleys forked over another $1,200 to perform at the AIRA awards show in the fall. Tickets were $100 each, dinner $20, and a video of their performance another $19.95. All 12 people in the Dooley entourage had to pay, but it seemed worth it, since Willie Nelson was going to play, and the guest list included fellow award winners Crystal Gayle, Allison Krauss, the Gatlin Brothers, and Waylon Jennings.

The show had just gotten underway when Metzgar announced that Willie's bus had broken down somewhere, after which most of the ballroom became as empty as the promoter's promises. None of the other stars showed up, either.

If Metzgar had a big role in the AIRA awards, the show being such a flop would make him look really bad. Metzgar claimed to have "no affiliation" with AIRA, but since his office phone number and the number for AIRA were the same, the Dooleys had a hard time believing it.

The *Tennessean* didn't offer much advice for the wannabe artists, except to work hard, try to get a following, avoid vanity record deals, and get a lawyer before signing anything. All of the major label representatives the *Tennessean* interviewed seemed to dismiss any alternative to working with them. "If the artist is good enough and pays their dues," said Scott Hendricks of Capitol Records, "they will eventually be discovered and will not have to pay anything."

"If someone is out in some city just burning it up in a club," said

Bruce Hinton, chairman of MCA Records, "sooner or later, we're going to know about it."

In other words, the major labels say, they're the only game in town. Wilbur Rimes, father of LeAnn, went to all the trouble and expense of putting out little independent albums by her, including the one on the tiny label Nor Va Jak, so that the geniuses at the big record companies would sit up and pay attention to her. Wowing audiences at regional shows like Johnnie High's Country Music Revue, Dallas Cowboys games (she sang the national anthem before at least two games), and on national television apparently wasn't enough.

The Davidson County district attorney's office continued to investigate some of the lowest of Nashville's bottom feeders, building solid cases against some of them that would eventually result in convictions.

Although I don't know the number of cases that ended in convictions, Robert Metzgar did sign a plea agreement in 2001 on the condition that he would cooperate with the district attorney in the Kevin Hughes case. When the case came to trial in 2003, Metzgar's testimony proved to be worth its weight in gold. Unfortunately, no one thought to give the ex-minister a gold record.

Chapter 15

Cold Case

The country band BR549 graced the cover of the last issue of Cash Box magazine, which was published November
16, 1996. It was just over ten years earlier that my first single came
out and appeared on the *Cash Box* chart, and also picked up a recommended notice in *Billboard*. Although I knew very little about
the history of *Cash Box* back then, the magazine's reputation had
been declining for years. With the widespread suspicion that the
corruption at the magazine was directly or indirectly connected to
the shooting in the spring of 1989, you'd think that, by summer or
fall at the latest, *Cash Box* would have closed its doors due to either
lack of advertisers, a sense of shame, or both. But no, business went
on, pretty much as usual. The fraud and scams continued. Chuck
Dixon and his tribe were not arrested or run out of town on a rail.
Cash Box continued until November 16, 1996, and five months later
in Encino, California, George Albert died.[77]

Meanwhile, Sammy Sadler & Overdrive turned out to be a pro-
phetic name for me and my band. On the road 300 days a year since
1991, we stopped for a break in 1998, overplayed and overworked. A

couple of guys in the band, including myself, had been burning the candle at both ends, attempting to meet all the women and drink all the beer and liquor in each town we played before moving on to the next. We would do a show and not go to bed till five or six in the morning, sleep all day, then get up and do it all over again. I didn't get into drugs, but I knew I couldn't continue with the drinking and the women. Living too fast, working too hard, chasing a dream, and running from the same old nightmare. No matter what new corner of the world I woke up in, the man in the black mask was always waiting. You can't outrun a ghost.

I still had my musical gift. I had a real good band. We could've stayed on the road forever. We were booked up solid for the next two and a half years. Even when we were at the extreme end of it, performing all night and then drinking and what-have-you till dawn, I was always able to perform, I never lost my voice. I don't want to jinx my gift by claiming to be superhuman, I was just lucky in that regard.

Every now and then, when I had a cold or something, my voice would get a little ragged. The worst instance I remember was in St. Louis, Missouri. About half the band had come down with the flu. The keyboard player and I both had a high fever. I remember my temperature was 102 degrees and I was in bed, just shaking with chills at six o'clock in the evening and we had to go on at 8:30. Somehow, we all summoned the energy to do our show and entertain the people.

That's the power of music and spirit. For seven years, I had pushed myself to the limit, playing as much as I could and maintaining a high level of professionalism, but there's a limit to everything. When I came home, I was so burned out I couldn't see straight. I felt like a hollow log. Everything in my life came screeching to a halt.

Music had been my life, then the murder on Music Row happened, and it took me a year and a half to recover enough to perform again. After that, I went full steam ahead, building up my reputation and fan base all over the country, and then I went silent. I walked away from it. It was a terrible thing to do in a way because I walked away from a lot, but I knew I couldn't continue to live with the alcohol and the women. It wasn't the music, it was the baggage that my lifestyle had accumulated.

For two years I didn't listen to any music. I didn't listen to any music at all at home. I didn't go out to see anybody play. I didn't even listen to music in the truck when I was driving. Music had been my heart and soul all my life, but I'd just lost my joy with it.

I didn't want to be bitter or angry or afraid. I wasn't the type to go around saying "poor, poor me," because that was the opposite of my natural disposition, and I knew that I was blessed with good fortune. No matter how many days I spent on the road, no matter how many incredible experiences I had in my travels, I never forgot the place I came from. I carried a piece of Texas with me wherever I went. I had the best parents a person could ever want.

I still had the same old fears, doubts, questions, and guilt. I never heard anything about the case. We would call Nashville Metro and try to find out if there'd been any progress or developments, but they wouldn't tell us anything. So, we had to assume that the killer was still out there.

Did the murder squad still think I was part of it? Was my family in danger? I could push those questions out of my mind for a while, but they always came back like a barking dog inside my head.

Today, there's a lot of public awareness of Post-Traumatic Stress Disorder (PTSD), which happens when a person experiences a traumatic event, such as being in combat during wartime, or being the victim of a violent attack. The shooting happened in 1989, two years before this country started sending young soldiers to fight in wars in the Persian Gulf countries and Afghanistan. With all the combat veterans returning home suffering from PTSD, there's a lot more treatment for it, a lot more discussion about it. In my case, it was years before it ever occurred to me that I might have PTSD myself, and there might be a kind of treatment that would help me deal with the flashbacks and nightmares.

Music wasn't just my passion or my hobby; it was how I made a living. If I wasn't going to play music, I had to get a job. Here I was, 28 years old, with a high school education, and no college degree.

"I'm not going back on the road," I told my dad. "I don't know what to do."

"Well, son, why don't you come to work for us?" he said, referring to house painting business. "We can use you."

I thought about that for a minute and said, "No, Dad, I want to be in the drywall business."

"All right," he said. "We'll set you up in our office."

I started bidding on drywall construction jobs in our area and the Dallas suburbs and in six months, my business was booming. After two years, I started my own company, and after being in the paint contracting business for over 30 years, Dad left his company and came to work for me.

As I'm writing this, I have about 50 people working for me, not including my secretary. I have people who go out and bid on new sheet-rock jobs, mostly new construction, and I have patch guys, ones who do repair work, patching holes and cracks, things like that. Running this company gets me up early in the morning and keeps me on the road all day long, tending to business anywhere from a mile away to a two-hour drive in Dallas or some small town in North Texas. I carry two cell phones, one for the drywall business, and the other for everything else. The text messages and calls start coming first thing in the morning and keep coming all day long. I guess I'm happiest when I'm busy.

In the last few days of 2001, we got news that Chuck Dixon died. Surprisingly, knowing his reputation, it seems he went away quietly. I never saw an obituary or any notice in the music papers. Later on, I learned that he had cancer. Naturally, a lot of people suspected he had faked his death and gone undercover for the FBI, or simply flew the coop to avoid going to jail. If you brought it up in a conversation, usually, the other person would laugh and say, "Chuck Dixon is dead, yeah, right!"

CHUCK DIXON
Record Promoter

Six months later, I got a call from my old friend, Cheryl Riddle. Cheryl had been cutting my hair since my Nashville days, and always does a great job. She's Dolly Parton's personal hairdresser now.

"Well, Sammy, I just wanted to say congratulations," she said. "It's been a long time coming."

"Congratulations? For what?" I said. "What are you congratulating me for?"

"You don't know? They caught the guy that shot you, yeah," she said.

"Who did they arrest?" I said.

"That guy, that promoter, friend of Chuck Dixon," she said. "Richard Frank D'Antonio."

So, it was Tony, after all. If Tony *was* the man in the black mask, that meant it was likely, that Chuck Dixon was part of it, too. The news stirred so many different feelings, I didn't know whether to be relieved or scared. This thing had had its grip on me so long, it had stunted much of my ability to react and process things without fear being part of the mix. Mostly, I remember feeling kind of numb as I hung up and called Metro in Nashville and asked for Bill Pridemore. He wasn't in, but I left a message, and he called me back.

"Sammy?" His voice had lost none of its cold-edged drawl.

"I heard you made an arrest," I said.

"That's right," he said. "Tony D'Antonio. We're in Las Vegas right now, working on the extradition papers so we can bring him back to Nashville."

Tony and Chuck, the most obvious answer, the conclusion that so many on Music Row had arrived at by default. Why had it taken Metro 13 years to make an arrest? Before I could ask the question out loud, he cut me off.

"Yeah, we got him," he said. "But listen, Sammy, he told us *this* about you…"

I didn't hear the rest of it, didn't want to listen to it. The rage from 13 years ago came back in an instant.

"I don't give a damn what he said about me," I said. "I already told you what I know. That's all there is to it. Whatever he told you about me is a lie, because there's nothing to tell."

I don't remember the rest of the conversation, even though it was really short. Later, I would wonder what Pridemore meant by *this*. Maybe I should've let him say it, whatever it was, but it was too much like the day Pridemore and Postiglione put me in the back of the car in front of Evergreen Records and told me how some anonymous informants had claimed that I had set Kevin up to be killed that night.

Until that moment, I'd never felt that I needed an attorney to represent me in this case. I was a victim, right? But that phone call shook me up, bad. So, I called Ralph Gordon, the lawyer who had represented me when I was on Evergreen.

Ralph's advice was simple. "Don't say another word to nobody," he said.

I never got another call about the case until right before the trial. On March 1, the Davidson County district attorney's office announced that the trial date had been set for August 2003. It was going to be a long five months.

...

No matter where you go in this case, the roads always seem to lead back to Chuck Dixon. Pridemore wasn't shy about offering his opinion. "We couldn't directly indicate that Chuck hired Tony to do it," Pridemore told us. "There was no direct evidence. We all assumed that he did it, but Tony never said that. We didn't talk to Chuck many times because he wouldn't cooperate."

I searched again for any news about Dixon's death. I never found an obituary, but I finally found the official date of his death. The information at *www.obituaries.com* is sparse: *Detterline, John Blayne Jr, age 60, born in Coatesville, Pennsylvania, died in Hermitage, Tennessee, December 26, 2001.* The Social Security Death Index (1935-2014), also online, gives the date of his death and last place of residence, but nothing else. *Findagrave.com* has a photo of his tombstone in the Hephzibah Baptist Church Cemetery in East Fallowfield, Pennsylvania, a town adjacent to Coatesville, where Dixon/Detterline grew up. His wife, Kathyrn A. Detterline, was buried next to the old shyster in 2007.

In 2000, the year before he died, he was still wheeling and dealing, pretending to be a big shot in the music business. That summer, one of his clients was a singer named Jennifer Wall, originally from Colorado.[78] After Jennifer failed to wow the record labels in Nashville, her parents, Bob and Annette Wall, decided to start a label named Jennstar Records. After releasing Jennifer's first single, the Walls planned to help other struggling artists by recording them and releasing their records for a fee, said Bob, a former Elvis impersonator.

"When we first moved here, we got caught up in all the glitz and glamour," Jennifer told a reporter for the *Jackson Sun*. It wasn't long before the Walls got ripped off or, as Bob put it, "We've been taken to the cleaners."

To the rescue came Chuck Dixon, referred to in the article as a promoter with a reputation for being "blunt-but-honest." "In the record business," Dixon told the newspaper reporter, "you have good people and bad people," leaving the reader to guess which one he was. With Dixon's help, Jennifer had released two other songs that placed in the top 10 independent charts published by *Nashville Tracker* and *International Airplay* magazines.

Chuck was riding high at the time, I guess, having recently co-written and produced "Ode to Buford Pusser" with the 66-year-old rockabilly singer Eddie Bond. Buford Pusser was the legendary Dixie Mafia-fighting lawman of the 1974 film "Walking Tall," for which Bond had written the theme song, "Legend of Buford Pusser."[79]

Eddie Bond had recorded for Mercury in the 1950s and toured with Elvis Presley, Carl Perkins, Jerry Lee Lewis, and others, but he's probably most famous for being the guy who told Elvis Presley he couldn't sing. Elvis auditioned as a vocalist for Eddie Bond's band in May 1954 at Bond's Memphis club, the Hi-Hat. Two months later, Elvis and his new trio, with Scotty Moore and Bill Black, recorded late into the night at Sun studio and produced the rough diamond that sparked the Elvis sensation: "That's All Right, Mama."[80]

Elvis became a worldwide phenomenon, and Eddie Bond kept reminding people of his modest association with the "King of Rock 'n' Roll" until he died in 2014. During the late summer of 2000, when Eddie and Chuck were both still alive, Chuck got his client Jennifer Walls a regular guest slot on the Eddie Bond show.

Chuck Dixon died on December 26, 2001, and on January 3, 2002—eight days later, Tom Thurman, deputy district attorney for Davidson County, made a brief announcement to the media. "Details have surfaced in the past few months" about the murder on Music Row, said Thurman. That was all he had to say. So far, no one had been charged or arrested, and Pridemore had no comment. The gears of justice were finally turning.

Chuck Dixon's demise and the announcement must have been related. Some witnesses who'd been afraid to cooperate before were now talking, and others were adding crucial details to previous statements. Several specifically stated to Pridemore that Chuck had threatened them if they spoke to the police.

That didn't come as a surprise. I was more intrigued to learn that back in 1993, four years after the murder on Music Row, Pridemore believed he had assembled a strong enough case to secure an indictment. Unfortunately, the district attorney didn't think the evidence was strong enough to secure a conviction.

As with so many other things in Nashville, this part of the story starts with a songwriter. James Steven Daniel, from Chattanooga, Tennessee, was struggling to make it in the music business in the early 1990s, and at some point, he went from plugging songs to peddling pounds of pot.

In September 1992, Special Agent Del Thomasson of the Georgia Bureau of Investigation (GBI) came calling on Daniel to inquire about the 274 pounds of marijuana stashed in locked steel barrels in his garage.[81] Daniel had come to the attention of GBI during an investigation into a drug smuggling operation called Sandmountain Gloom. Between August and September 1992, 17 individuals from several different states plus two Mexican nationals had conspired to transport 3,000 pounds of marijuana across the border from Mexico. Three separate trips ended at distribution points in Alabama and Georgia where the loads were divided between Daniel and another conspirator for sale to local dealers.

Daniel was one of several individuals whose names were marked "Big Dog" on the list of conspirators. Next to that, someone had added another note: "but first to cooperate." Daniel agreed to turn state's witness and provide evidence against his co-conspirators. With 19 people involved, his statement took some time.

When Daniel was finished giving information about the Sandmountain Gloom conspiracy, he offered to tell the drug agents another story, one that involved one of the other conspirators on the list, Richard F. D'Antonio.[82]

> During further debriefing by GBI, Daniel advised having "muled" several loads of marijuana from Houston, Texas to Nashville, Tenn. for Richard D. Antonio, aka "The Tone," "Tone," 1483 Mt. Juliet Rd, Mt. Juliet, Tenn. Daniel

stated that he would travel to Nashville and obtain the money for the marijuana from D'Antonio then proceed to drive towards Texas. Daniel always stopped in Arkansas to spend the night and would call D'Antonio and advise where he was. The next day, Daniel would travel on to Houston and proceed to East End Auto Parts, a Houston "junk yard" owned by Percy Jerome Grays, Jr.

Daniel would meet with Grays who would have the marijuana hidden in a junk car on the lot. Daniel would put the marijuana in his car and drive back to Arkansas where he would call D'Antonio and spend the night. The next day, he would proceed to Nashville and drop off the marijuana to D'Antonio.

During the investigation, Del Thomasson had several more conversations with Daniel, and at some point, Daniel told him another story about Tony D'Antonio. On March 9, 1989, Daniel had sold D'Antonio a Smith & Wesson .38 caliber revolver for $150. At the time, Daniel had been living in the town of Flintstone, Georgia, a two-hour drive from Nashville.

Del Thomasson called Nashville and relayed the information to Pridemore and Postiglione. Daniel told them he had gotten to know Tony D'Antonio when he was trying to make it as a songwriter. On March 9, 1989, Tony had come to his house in Flintstone. They smoked some pot together, and Tony asked about a gun. Daniel sold the .38 to him for $150. Tony wanted to test-fire the gun, Daniel told them, but he didn't have any bullets, so he went out and bought a box of .38 cartridges, adding that they were the cheapest selection he could find. The two of them went out back, fired the gun a few times, the transaction was completed, and Tony drove back to Nashville.

Something else James Steven Daniel told Pridemore and Postiglione reinforced their belief that Tony was the man in the black mask on Music Row. "The time we met Tony we didn't know for sure that he was the one," said Pridemore. "Sitting back, a couple weeks later, we thought about how witnesses said that the suspect had a funny gait. We thought about how when Tony got up to shake our hands the first time we met, we thought maybe he was just hurt. We thought about that. Many years later, when we were talking to Steve, the first thing Steve said was "Tony walked like a goose" or something like that. Then, I'll never forget, he said, 'Have you ever seen Tony run? It's comical.'"

Pridemore and Postiglione didn't expect D'Antonio to confess if they confronted him with new evidence of his guilt. They had questioned him numerous times already, including once when D'Antonio was in FBI custody during a drug investigation.

I don't remember what the case was, exactly, but the FBI were going to arrest him for weed," said Pridemore. "Pat and I tagged along. While they had him in custody, they allowed me to just talk to him. I told him we were still working the case and we had talked to a lot of people, and that this was the time that he could help himself by cooperating. He never said anything, though."

This time, the Metro detectives tried a different tactic. They contacted D'Antonio and informed him that they wanted to talk. During that communication, they let him know that they had contacts in the Chattanooga area with information on the case, and they were planning to visit those contacts soon.

Meanwhile, Steve started calling Tony. The police were listening in, recording every word. Tony talked to Steve about making another run to Houston to pick up 100 pounds of marijuana. Steve mentioned that two detectives from Nashville were looking for him.[83] Tony then asked Daniel if he remembered one late night four years prior when someone died on Music Row.

> Daniel: *Yeah. Oh, so, what's going on? I don't understand. That's been a long time ago.*

> D'Antonio: *Yeah, I know. Well, see, some of the detectives there in Nashville, they've been talking to everybody in the*

music industry, again, you know, all that shit. Playing it on, um, on Crime Stoppers or "Unsolved Mysteries," some shit.

Daniel: *Yeah.*

D'Antonio: *Now, they're questioning everybody again, in the music industry and stuff.*

Daniel: *Yeah, so... I don't really remember it, OK, to tell the truth, but what, you know, what do you want me to say, or whatever?*

D'Antonio: *I was there till 11:15, or so.*

Daniel: *Oh, you mean 11:30, the news when it goes off?*

D'Antonio: *Yeah.*

Daniel: *OK.*

D'Antonio: *If you... I doubt if you will ever be asked.*

In a later conversation, Steve asked Tony about the gun he had sold him. Tony said the gun wasn't a problem; there was no way it would ever be found, it was gone.

The tape was a valuable piece of evidence in proving D'Antonio's guilt, but in the opinion of the district attorney, they still didn't have a strong enough case to support a conviction. As for the next step, there wasn't one. The murder on Music Row file gathered dust for the next eight-plus years.

Over the years, I wondered if the investigation had been shelved because the FBI, GBI, or some other high-level law enforcement agency wanted to protect James Steven Daniel or, possibly, Tony D'Antonio, as witnesses in other investigations regarded by them as a higher priority. Although Daniel was a valuable informant for the GBI at the time, Pridemore explained that they only asked for some consideration before blowing Daniel's cover.

"Del Thomasson asked us that if we needed Steve, or if we needed to expose him in order to make our case, to let him know," said Pridemore. "He said he'd prefer that we not do anything until they were finished using him."[84]

Pridemore also said that he and Postiglione still weren't "100 percent sure" that D'Antonio was the right suspect.

"We backed off for a while," he said. "We both had other murder cases, so we figured we'd come back to the case when we could. I basically let it go until I found out that Steve had finished being a [Confidential Informant.] He had gone to jail in Georgia and was out. That's when I talked to Del Thomasson and he hooked us up."

...

In a section labeled "Supplemental Reports" of the case files, we found a polygraph examiner's report that fascinated us for several reasons. First of all, it pops up out of nowhere, with no explanation or related documents, but it happens to be part of the background evidence gathered by the police and the district attorney on music fraud in Nashville. Promoter Jason Hawkins is the subject of the report, and his name came up repeatedly over the years in connection in investigations by the district attorney's office and the media for several decades.

The complaint number on the report is 91-196780, which relates to an aggravated assault report filed by Jason Hawkins and Roy Haws in 1991—the year that Haws and Hawkins were having a very public and weird feud with Gary Bradshaw. The date on this polygraph report is January 30, 2001, so apparently, the police wanted to verify some statements that Hawkins had made that linked the 1991 feud to something in the murder on Music Row case.[85]

> *During the pre-test interview... [Hawkins] went on to say that he has had many polygraphs in the past. He stated*

he worked for the Drug Enforcement Agency from 1986—87. He stated that during that time he took approximately 24 polygraph examinations. He stated he was not an agent. He further stated he took polygraph examinations for the Federal Organized Crime Task Force in St. Louis.

He gave me a lengthy list of prescribed medications he is presently taking. He further stated he has a serious heart condition as well as high blood pressure. He stated all his major organs are on the opposite side of his body and that he has, in his chest, a pacemaker. He stated the pacemaker was installed in May of 2000. He also stated he suffers/suffered from congestive heart failure.

Based on the above information no polygraph examination was administered to Powell/Hawkins.

Detective E.J. Bernard, 44830
CID/Murder Squad
Tennessee Polygraph Examiner's License #3

The exam was canceled, and Detective Bernard chose not to mention the exact reason. My own impression from reading the report was that Hawkins came off as a paranoid nut and therefore, the polygraph would be a waste of time. Maybe I'm wrong. I had never heard of someone having all their internal organs on the wrong side of their body, but after a Google search using the terms "when all your internal organs are on the wrong side," I found out that it's a real disorder. Medicinenet. com defines *Situs inversus totalis* as "the complete transposition (right to left reversal) of the thoracic and abdominal organs," with the heart on the right, the stomach on the right, etc., and is believed to occur once in every 6—8,000 births.[86] People who have it usually suffer from a lot of other health complications that would normally affect life expectancy.

Surprisingly, the last time we checked, Jason Hawkins was still alive and well—despite having this strange disorder and having survived working for the DEA and the Federal Organized Crime Task Force. What an adventurous life. At the ripe old age of 76, Hawkins was still promoting, plying the custom label trade, and putting on an annual songwriting contest to help new artists gain entry to the big sweepstakes of fame and fortune. Or at least, that's the general idea.

The January 30, 2001 document is really the only item in our case files that links to a parallel investigation into Nashville music being conducted by the district attorney's office. The two officials who requested the exam were Myra Langlois, an investigator for the Davidson County D.A.'s office, and Pat Postiglione of the Metro murder squad. The D.A.'s investigation would end up playing a crucial part in the murder trial, and Myra Langlois would play a starring role.

...

One after the other, the puzzle pieces were falling into place. One of the first witnesses interviewed in 2002 was Sue Thackery, who started working at *Cash Box* in April 1988 and was terminated a few weeks after Kevin was killed. When Bill Pridemore and Pat Postiglione came to interview her on February 7, 2002, Thackery told them that "she and the other employees were instructed not to speak with the police investigators, but after learning of Chuck Dixon's death, she is willing to speak with us." Other former employees of *Cash Box* told them the same thing.[87]

Thackery told them that Kevin was "a very honest person and tried to keep the charts clean," despite being offered "money and gifts for doctoring the charts." She suspected it was the work of Chuck and Tony for chart fixing. The week Kevin was killed, she said, he confided to her that "something big was worrying him." She asked him what it was, but he told her he wanted to talk to his parents about it first. He was planning to visit them the weekend he was killed.

Thackery believed that the "something big" was connected to

the Country Music Seminar of the previous weekend. Pridemore already knew about the big fuss leading up to Kevin's scheduled address at the seminar, but apparently, it wasn't the only thing bothering him at the time.

The following week, Pridemore interviewed Tony D'Antonio's ex-wife, Carolyn Cox, who had previously told police that Tony was home with her and the kids on the night of March 9, 1989. On February 13, 2002, she told Pridemore the truth:

> When asked about the events the night of Kevin's death, [Carolyn Cox] advised [said] that afternoon when she arrived home from work, Tony was not home. When she went to bed, he still had not gotten home. Approximately 3 a.m., Chuck Dixon called looking for Tony. He still had not gotten home. Minutes later, Tony walked into the bedroom, asking who had called. When told it was Chuck, Tony called and spoke to Chuck for some time. Tony did not tell her that Kevin had been killed until later that morning.
>
> When asked where he had been last night, he told her he had gone to Georgia to buy marijuana from his friend, Steve, who lives near Lookout Mountain.

Lookout Mountain straddles the state line between Tennessee and Georgia. The town of Flintstone, Georgia, is a short drive southeast of Lookout Mountain. Carolyn Cox also told Pridemore that Tony had gotten involved with cocaine and marijuana when he was working at *Cash Box* and that Chuck and Tony "became involved in a recording scam where they would record and promote new artists and use *Cash Box* magazine charts to extort money from the artists."

On Monday, April 29, 2002, Pridemore drove to Flintstone and met up with GBI agents Del Thomasson and Audey Murphy. Days earlier, Del Thomasson had called Pridemore to inform him that he had located the place in Flintstone where Tony and Steve were thought to have test-fired the murder weapon in 1989.

Patricia A. Smith, who had rented the house at 5402 Northwest Highway 341, still owned the property. She met the officers there and gave her permission to conduct a search. Steve had told them that he and Tony had fired the gun in the back yard. Using a metal detector, Del Thomasson started finding bullets in tree trunks, stumps, and in the ground. They recovered a total of 13 spent projectiles.

After photographing and documenting everything according to procedure, Pridemore returned to Nashville. The next morning, Pridemore checked out the Flintstone bullets from the property room at Metro, along with the four bullets recovered during the autopsy of Kevin Hughes. He delivered everything to Special Agent Tommy Heflin at the TBI lab in Nashville and requested Heflin to compare the rounds from Flintstone with the ones from Music Row on the night of March 9, 1989. The next afternoon, Tommy Heflin called Pridemore with some very good news.

One of the 13 projectiles from Flintstone was a match.

Like an artist adding color and features to a stick figure sketch, the Cold Case detectives continued gathering details of the crime that had eluded them for so many years. Wednesday, May 8, 2002, Pridemore and Postiglione returned to Flintstone to meet again with James Steven Daniel. They wanted Daniel to show them the place where he and Tony had test-fired the Smith & Wesson revolver on March 9, 1989. Their meeting wasn't scheduled until noon, but the detectives left Nashville early in the morning to allow extra time for stopping at fireworks stands on the way.

"We went to every fireworks stand up in that area," said Pridemore. "That day, we stopped to use the restroom and decided to just talk to everybody," and this time, they found a place that sold baseball caps that bore the image of a scowling combat solder and the caption *World War II Veteran and Damn Proud of It!!* It was identical to the cap worn by the killer on Music Row.

The seller was happy to cooperate with the detectives, providing the identity and address of the company that distributed the caps. One more piece of the puzzle had been solved.

Arriving in Flintstone just before noon, Pridemore and Postiglione met up with Steve and asked him to show them the spot where he and Tony had test-fired the revolver. Steve walked to the exact location where the bullets had been recovered the previous week and said, *Right here.*

Pridemore and Postiglione left Flintstone around five o'clock that afternoon, feeling satisfied that Daniel had cooperated fully. It had been a very full day.

Back in 1993, when Daniel was in the crosshairs of an investigation into an interstate drug smuggling conspiracy, he was the one who had volunteered to cooperate with the Kevin Hughes case. In 2002, however, Daniel was reluctant and fearful.

"We had to convince Daniel to help us this time," Pridemore told us in 2017. "He was finished being a confidential informant, he'd gone to jail and served his time." In his report on the May 8, 2002 interview, Pridemore added that Daniel "talked about coming to Nashville and meeting with the Deputy D.A., Tom Thurman. He voiced his concern about Tony killing him if he found out, his new life with his girlfriend, and what would happen if Tony was freed from the charges."

On Wednesday, June 5, 2002, Pridemore interviewed Cecilia Bragg again to ask more detailed questions about her experiences at *Cash Box* between 1987 and 1989.[88] In his notes, Pridemore wrote that:

> *When Tony left Cash Box, Chuck Dixon continued to be part of the operation and spent a lot of time with Cash Box and Kevin. During Tony's reign at Cash Box it was apparent he had access to marijuana and cocaine and on many occasions made it available to the employees, as well as music industry leaders.*

Kevin was aware of the accessibility of the drugs but as far as Mrs. Bragg knew, he never took advantage of it. Kevin was known as a clean and religious soul.

During the weeks leading up to Kevin's death, he had been trying to make the charts more realistic, i.e., most of the songs and artists listed on Billboard charts were completely different on Cash Box and he had made it known to all of the independent promoters he was going to change that.

Cecilia Bragg also confirmed the story about Kevin being upset at the Country Radio Seminar when he called George Albert and pleaded to be released from the obligation of making a speech because a group of promoters had plotted to ridicule him. However, there was something else that upset Kevin during the week leading up to his death. As far as she knew, he wouldn't tell anybody what it was.

The following day, Pridemore went to the offices of *Billboard* magazine to meet with Wade Jessen, who had begun his career as a chart director there in 1994.[89] His resume also included a one-year stint at *Cash Box* as a staff writer from 1987—88.

Like Kevin Hughes, Jessen was a country boy, religious, and passionate about music. He grew up on a Utah cattle ranch and worked in radio in Salt Lake City before moving to Nashville, following the advice of some independent promoters he knew.

By the time Jessen started working at *Cash Box*, Tony D'Antonio was in charge and often, high on drugs. Chart positions were being sold off to independent promoters like Chuck Dixon, who was "a regular fixture in the office... spending a lot of time with Kevin and Tony." The magazine had lost much of its credibility within the industry.

Pridemore asked Jessen about possible scenarios in which independent promoters like Chuck Dixon would take advantage of their influence at *Cash Box*, particularly, in dealing with an artist who was, as the expression went, "just off the bus." During the time that the promoter worked a record and the record made the *Cash Box* chart, Jessen said, the promoter would use the chart to convince the artist to continue paying their fee.

What if the chart director at *Cash Box* tried to make the chart "more reliable and in line with other major magazines?" Pridemore asked Jessen. "What effect would that have on the independent promoters?"

"If the stations that the promoters had some influence with were no longer part of the reporting list," replied Jessen, "the artist's songs would no longer be seen on the chart and the artist would seek another promoter."

Wade Jessen died in 2015 of a heart attack, not long after celebrating 20 years as *Billboard*'s chart director. A much-loved and respected pillar of the country music industry, Jessen had helped revamp *Billboard*'s rating system and was also a radio personality on Sirius XM. His funeral was attended by a who's who of country music insiders and celebrities.[90] No one in attendance thought any less of Jessen for having been fired by Tony D'Antonio in 1988 for using the office phone to make personal long-distance calls at *Cash Box.*

The following Monday, June 22, 2002, Bill Pridemore and two other officers came to visit Tony's ex-wife, Carolyn Cox, again—this time, at her home residence, 510 N. Marthona Drive, in the Madison area of Nashville.[91] In an earlier conversation, Pridemore asked Carolyn Cox about the black cat she and Tony had as a pet when they were still together. Cox told Pridemore the cat had been "very partial to a chair and two small, stuffed animals," and that she still had those items in her possession.

The three officers arrived at Carolyn Cox's home at about 11 a.m. and asked to see the items. Officers Blackwood and Bartlett performed a vacuum search of the chair. The stuffed animals were taken back to the CID lab for examination.

The Davidson County grand jury was impaneled and heard the case Friday, July 19, 2002. Bill Pridemore and Pat Postiglione had been subpoenaed to appear as witnesses, along with 18 other Metro Nashville officers, four agents from TBI, one from GBI, and 20 civilians.[92] The first name in the last group was James Steven Daniel. Others included Kevin's parents, at least a half dozen people who witnessed the shooting, and people like Sharon Pennington, Sharon Corbitt, and others who had been close to Kevin and could testify that he was anxious and fearful in the week leading up to his death. Cecilia Bragg was the only former *Cash Box* employee. My name was No. 5 on the list, and in the space after my name giving the address where they sent the subpoena, it said I lived in "Bottom, Texas" instead of Bonham.

There was a town in Bell County, north of Austin, called Bottom. It was founded in the 1890s, and in 1901, about 30 people lived there.[93]

That might have been the high point for Bottom because sometime after World War II, roadmaps didn't bother listing it. My subpoena might have somehow ended up in a mailbox in that area, who knows? This may be the reason I was taken by surprise when the woman who cuts my hair called to tell me they had arrested Tony.

The jurors voted to charge D'Antonio on count one:

> *...Richard Frank D'Antonio, on the 9th day of March 1989, in Davidson County, Tennessee and before the finding of this indictment, unlawfully, willfully, deliberately, maliciously and with premeditation did kill Kevin Wayne Hughes, in violation of Tennessee Code Annotated 39-2-202, and against the peace and dignity of the State of Tennessee.*

And, on count two:

> *...Richard Frank D'Antonio on the 9th day of March 1989, in Davidson County, Tennessee and before the finding of this indictment, unlawfully, feloniously and with malice aforethought, willfully, deliberately, and with premeditation did assault Sammy Sadler with intent to commit murder in the first degree and the assault resulted*

in bodily injury to Sammy Sadler, in violation of Tennes-
see Code Annotated 39-2-103, and against the peace and
dignity of the State of Tennessee.

The following Monday morning, Bill Pridemore, Pat Postiglione, and Assistant D.A. Roger Moore flew to Las Vegas with an
arrest warrant for Tony D'Antonio. Now 56 years old, Tony had gone
full circle, returning to Las Vegas to work as a pit boss at Fitzgerald's
Casino. He'd been living there for the past six years.

The Nashville cops met with Sgt. Manning of Vegas PD and
presented a copy of the indictment. Instead of riding along with
their Vegas colleagues to get their man, they suggested they all go
to lunch, which they did "It was a pretty easy deal," Pridemore said
of the arrest.[94]

> *We were eating lunch and they offered to have their SWAT*
> *team pick him up. They took us to a casino, we ate lunch,*
> *and the SWAT guys brought him back to the homicide*
> *office. He refused to talk. I remember we thought he*
> *would fight extradition. We'd arranged to be out there*
> *for three days. At first, [we were told] he was going to*
> *waive extradition, but then he said he wanted to go now.*
> *So, we stayed another day, then he changed his mind, and*
> *then changed his mind back again.*
>
> *So, we were calling back to see if we could stay the*
> *weekend, because we thought he would probably waive*
> *extradition on Monday, and then he could fly back with*
> *us. But they said "Get your ass back to Nashville. You're*
> *not spending the weekend in Vegas."*

Pridemore and Postiglione had not spoken with Tony D'Antonio since 1989. D'Antonio looked much older than his 57 years.
His thick, black hair had gone grey and thin, and his mustache and
beard were white. He wore glasses.

"Mr. D'Antonio seemed glad and not surprised to see us," Pridemore wrote in his report. "[W]hen [D'Antonio] was told that he was being arrested for murder [he said] he knew it was about Kevin." Several minutes later, he repeated the same thing as the deputy district attorney entered the room.

Arresting the suspect had gone smoothly, but the extradition process between Nevada and Tennessee was complex and slow. Filing the correct paperwork and meeting all the legal requirements was going to take several months.

Back in Nashville on July 31, Detective Pridemore met with Tom McEntee, who gave his own version of the history of *Cash Box* magazine and his impressions of Tony D'Antonio.[95] As McEntee described it, in the 1960s, when he was managing the New York office, times were very good.

"At that time [in the 1960s], it was the leading music chart magazine," McEntee claimed, but in the eighties, it was "nearly nonexistent." When McEntee came over to run the Nashville office in late 1985, "there was only one employee left, Jim Sharp," and he quit as soon as McEntee started.

McEntee remembered his Pac-Man pal, Tony D'Antonio, and called to offer him a job as a chart researcher and assistant. Tony left his ice cream truck route behind and adapted quickly to the job. Soon, Tony was the Nashville chart director, and by "late 1986 or early 1987, business was strong," although Pridemore's notes don't say if McEntee told him from where all the new business was suddenly generated. McEntee suggested hiring a college intern, and that's how Kevin Hughes came into the picture.

> *During that time Tony was doing an excellent job, and other than an occasional free lunch, he felt Tony was an ethical person. [Only later] near the time that Mr. McEntee left, did Tony get involved with Chuck.*

> *Mr. McEntee states the only problem he had with Tony was his relationships with women employees. On several occasions female employees would approach Mr. McEntee telling him about Tony's inappropriate actions and comments. Due to the females' fear of facing Tony, they would not file official charges.*

McEntee had suffered from asthma since childhood. He told people the stress of running *Cash Box* had aggravated his symptoms to the point that he could no longer work. He left the magazine in late July or early August 1987. Was it the stress of being an accessory to fraud, extortion, and other criminal activities, or the legitimate side of the business that aggravated his asthma the most? Apparently, McEntee didn't say.

In most professional business environments, an employee who harassed females and frightened them into silence would have been terminated, at minimum. Instead, McEntee told Pridemore that was "the only problem he had with Tony," and that Tony was "an ethical person."

McEntee did help Pridemore develop a clearer picture of the system of chart fraud that became institutionalized at *Cash Box*, apparently during McEntee's tenure there. In almost the same breath, he gave some insight as to his very loose definition of the term "ethical." [96]

> *After leaving Cash Box, he would speak with Tony and Chuck from time to time. On one occasion, Tony told him about flying around the country providing cash to certain*

radio stations that Chuck "had in his pocket."

When asked about chart manipulation, Mr. McEntee explained there were two ways. One, a promoter would have several radio stations in their pocket and when [the radio station] reported to the chart [director] of Cash Box, they would provide a play list with the clients of the promoter [showing inflated airplay].

[The second way] Mr. McEntee felt was the easiest and most effective. After the office was closed for the day, an employee or others could enter the office with a key and change the reporting list on the chart itself. Due to the [large number of] calls and numbers being manually entered [into the system], it would take a long time before the rater [the chart director] would be able to discover the discrepancy.

After the interview with McEntee, Pridemore went to see Craig Morris. Craig told the detective that he knew me as both a client and a friend. He met Chuck Dixon in "the early 1980s, while working at his father's recording studio." Craig and Chuck decided to go into business together, forming a promotion company in which "Chuck specialized in independent artists while Craig specialized in *Billboard* charts. Even though they shared office space, they did not promote the same artists." Here, I think Craig probably said he and Chuck didn't *necessarily* promote the same artists. In my case, Evergreen Records hired Craig to promote my records to *Billboard*, and Chuck to promote my records to *Cash Box*.

Although Pridemore had probably heard these figures before, Craig told the detective that the fee for promoting a record was $1,500-$2,000, with a bonus of $250-$500 for positive results on the charts. "It would not be uncommon," he said, "for Chuck to have 12 to16 records working at one time."

Pridemore asked Craig about his relationship with Tony D'Antonio. Craig told him that he "did not have much association with

D'Antonio," and that "he did not like Tony and tried to stay away from him."

The last part of the interview was about the shooting. That night, as soon as Craig heard that I'd been shot, he went down to Vanderbilt Medical Center and that's where he first learned that Kevin had been shot and was dead. Then, "while he was at the hospital, he called Chuck, telling him what had occurred."

It was kind of shocking reading the last line. For years and years, I asked myself how Chuck had known my room number, and what was the real meaning of his call that night—to say he was sorry for what happened, or scare me into silence? Craig, his business partner, gave him my number—it should've been obvious, but that's how messed up my thinking was about it all these years. My fear, dread, and paranoia prevented me from seeing things for what they were—I was too close to it, I guess. It's crazy but digging up and clawing through all these murder investigation files helped me find the answers to a lot of complicated questions that bothered me all these years, but they answered some simple questions, too.

The extradition of Richard Frank D'Antonio finally became a fact just before midnight, November 22, 2002, almost five months after he was arrested and charged with first-degree murder and attempted murder. This time, Pridemore was accompanied by Detective Miller.[97]

> *Upon entering the booking/warrant division, Mr. D'Antonio wanted to know what happens next and the type of house situation he would be subjected to. I explained to Richard that … most likely he would be housed in the general population with other inmates with similar charges. Mr. D'Antonio seemed to become upset and worried. Upon entering the commissioner's hearing area and seeing the television news cameras, he turned and stated he would talk to me about the case if I could provide him with a private cell. After explaining I could not do that, he made no other statements.*

I think Tony, like a typical sociopath and grifter, probably just wanted to play Pridemore to see what kind of favors he could get from the cop he'd sat next to on an airplane for the past few hours. Maybe, however, seeing the TV cameras reminded him that he was a big shot criminal, and made him want the kind of treatment they gave Mafia godfathers and serial killers. It's even possible, I guess, that he feared assassination. Chuck Dixon and George Albert were both dead, but Tony might have lived in fear of being hit by one of their friends or ghosts. I sure hope he did, anyway.

Two weeks after completing the extradition, Pridemore got a call from Sharon Pennington, who said she'd just remembered something she wanted to tell him.[98] It was about her phone conversation with Kevin on the night he was killed. "[One of] the reasons he was upset," she said, "he had just discovered the final weekly chart rating he was sending to Los Angeles was not the same when it was published in *Cash Box* magazine."

The short statement on that page of the file gave me goosebumps when I read it. I went back through the files to February 2, 1990, when Pridemore questioned Kim Buckley, who had worked at *Cash Box* as a summer intern in 1988, leaving during the month of September or October. Pridemore asked if she knew of any time that Kevin ever manipulated the charts at *Cash Box*. No, she said, she didn't know of any "voluntary chart manipulation;" however, during her final two weeks at the magazine "Kevin became very upset because he was ordered to change the charts by the owner of *Cash Box*."

George Albert had pressured Kevin into doing it, she explained, because of a deal Tony had made promising an artist a guaranteed chart position. When the record failed to make the chart the previous week, George Albert got an angry phone call from the artist. Now Albert was calling Kevin, telling him that he had to fix the chart for the upcoming issue. Albert promised Kevin it would be "the last time Kevin would have to do this," she said. "Kevin was very upset, but he did change the chart.[99]

On March 6, 2003, Detective Pridemore spoke with Special Agent Kim Reubish at the FBI lab in Quantico, Virginia. Reubish said the package of trace evidence removed from the cap sent from the Metro mailroom the previous week contained the wrong samples. Pridemore apologized for the mistake and told Reubish that he would locate the correct samples and ship them to her.

Pridemore returned to the property room, located the correct samples, packed them up, took them to the Metro mailroom, and from there another Fed Ex package went off to Quantico. A few days later, Pridemore got his report on the cat hair. It was indeed a strand of hair from a black cat. The FBI lab couldn't determine much more than that. The materials vacuumed from the cat toys and furniture didn't turn up any additional identifiable strands of hair.

Pridemore and Postiglione were still confident, however, that "the cat in the hat," or so to speak, was going to help send his old master to jail for a long, long time.

Chapter 16

The Trial

AFTER WAITING 13 YEARS FOR JUSTICE, I PUT MY HAND ON THE
BIBLE, SWORE TO TELL THE TRUTH, THE WHOLE TRUTH AND
NOTHING BUT THE TRUTH, SO HELP ME GOD, AND TOOK MY SEAT
ON THE WITNESS STAND IN THE METRO COURTHOUSE TUESDAY
MORNING, SEPTEMBER 23, 2003, A LITTLE AFTER 10 A.M.

The summer months crawled by with no word about the start
date of the trial of *State of Tennessee v. Richard D'Antonio, case no.
2002-C-1280*. Before the jury could be impaneled, several hearings
took place in July, August, and early September. My presence wasn't
required at any of those.

The trial had been assigned to District Judge Randall S. Wyatt,
Jr., who'd been on the bench in Davidson County for decades. Wyatt
announced his retirement just after I began working on this book.
D'Antonio had entered a plea of not guilty, but since he had fallen
on hard times (perhaps because the Chuck Dixon gravy train disappeared after Chuck died?). He wasn't able to get a high-powered
criminal attorney like Dick DeGuerin to represent him, so his case
was being handled by two attorneys from the Davidson County Public

Defender's office: Ross Alderman and Patrick Frogge. Counsel for the state was Deputy District Attorney General Tom Thurman, aka "The Thurmanator." Assistant District Attorney Kathy Morante was his co-counsel.

Various issues, including discovery, admissibility of evidence, and other points of law and legal precedents were argued in the pre-trial hearings of July, August, and early September. The additional information I'm mentioning here came from the trial transcript. We didn't have a copy of the transcript until late 2017. Many aspects of the case were still a mystery to me until I was able to sit down and read the document from start to finish.

Almost every trial comes down to a story: Who did what to whom and why? The U.S. system of justice is supposed to give every citizen a chance to be equal in the eyes of the law and to have his story heard and evaluated by a jury of his peers. The transcript of *Tennessee v. Richard D'Antonio, 2002-C-1280* tells the story of what happened on Music Row on the night of March 9, 1989, in a unique, vivid manner. It felt a little like watching a movie. Some parts of the story are more detailed, others are streamlined. The motives of the main characters are convincingly revealed.

Back in the fall of 2003, however, news that the trial was finally getting underway took me by surprise. On September 9, 2003, I got a phone call from Deputy District Attorney Thurman. He said I would have to come into his office to talk about my testimony before the trial.

The trial was starting the following Monday, nearly a week and a half from the day of Thurman's call. I told him that this might be a problem for me. I explained that my doctors had just informed me that I had to have gall bladder surgery. The surgery was two days from now, and it was urgent. In a best-case scenario, I'd probably be able to make it, but "probably" wasn't the word he wanted to hear.

The news also caused ripples of tension in the courtroom during the hearings. The transcript for September 10 captured the moment when Thurman informed Judge Wyatt and the defense attorneys about our phone call.

As you read the transcript, bear in mind that, in Tennessee district court, the prosecutor is referred to as "General" and the judge is referred to as "The Court."

The Court: *When is he having the surgery?*[100]

General Thurman: *Yeah, I think he's having it tomorrow.*

The Court: *He ought to be fine by another—*

Thurman: *He ought to be OK, so I just wanted to inform the court that that's a problem. If they get in there and they have to do something else, I don't know, but—*

The Court: *Right.*

Thurman: *He's still planning to be here. He's cooperative. And I just wanted to bring that—*

The Court: *That's good. And I appreciate you doing it. We can be kind of keeping, you know, appraised about that...*

Mr. Alderman (Ross Alderman, counsel for the defense): *If I could respond to that so I don't forget. We have not done an out-of-state witness subpoena on Mr. Sadler because we were sure the state was going to have him here. He is a witness we want to have here. If he is not going to be here, we do not want to go forward without him, because he is an eyewitness to this offense.*

The Court: *Let's just say, if Sammy Sadler can't be available, then we'll—we'll just have to do something. Anything else?*

If I couldn't make it, they'd have to delay the trial. That was obvious to everyone, but Alderman had to make his comments, not only for the trial record but because it gave him an opportunity to needle Thurman about every potential weakness in the state's case against D'Antonio.

In the end, my surgery and my recovery went smoothly. On Monday night, September 22, they flew me to Nashville and put me up at the DoubleTree Hotel. My lawyer, Ralph Gordon, picked me up at 10:30 that night and drove me over to the D.A.'s office to meet with Thurman. It wasn't a long meeting, but it was nerve-wracking. They told me I would be one of the first witnesses to testify. Monday would probably be taken up with some leftover pretrial business and jury selection, so the trial probably wouldn't start until Tuesday morning. The witnesses would be "under rule," a term that means each witness is ushered in and out of the courtroom to testify and is not present when the preceding witnesses are on the stand. The goal is to prevent witnesses from being influenced by the testimony of other witnesses. After my turn on the stand, I had to return to my hotel room and stay there until the jury reached a verdict. That was OK with me.

...

According to the prosecution, Chuck Dixon and Tony D'Antonio were two of the primary conspirators in an ongoing scheme that involved payola, chart fixing, deception, and other illegal and unethical actions. When Kevin Hughes became a threat to their plans, they killed him. Whether the triggerman had shot me on purpose or by accident, that action was also part of the conspiracy. Establishing the conspiracy element of the crime was paramount for the prosecution, because conspiracy law allows more leeway for the introduction of certain kinds of proof—particularly, hearsay evidence. It was also good because it gave Thurman an excuse to portray the late Chuck Dixon for the sleazy character and menace to society that he was.

August 8, 2002, one month after Tony's arrest in Las Vegas,

Nashville Scene published Rob Simbeck's account of the case. "With a bullet: The story of gold chains, doctored charts and a Music Row murder" summed up the "street hypothesis" of the crime in these words: "Dixon—a self-styled godfather of country music—ordered the murder, and D'Antonio carried it out."[101] When the case came to trial, the prosecutor presented basically the same story. Pridemore and Postiglione had also come to the same conclusion. "We couldn't directly indicate that Chuck hired Tony to kill them," said Pridemore in 2017. "There was no direct evidence. We all assumed that Chuck did that, but Tony never said that."[102]

Although D'Antonio had waived his right to testify, it turned out that his own words would be used against him anyway. The two people he relied on to provide his alibi for the night of March 9, 1989, Carolyn Cox and James Steven Daniel, were witnesses for the prosecution. D'Antonio even gave Carolyn Cox (who divorced him in July 1989) one version to tell the police—that he was home with her—while he told her he was with Daniel until 11:30 that night. Cox and Daniel both knew the alibis were fiction and testified to that on the witness stand.

...

Monday night, as we were leaving the D.A.'s office, when we got into Ralph's car, Ralph looked at me and said, "Sammy, they're going to try and sandbag you, son."

"What are you talking about?" I said. "I've told them everything I know."

"They're gonna try to drag you into this," he said.

Not surprisingly, I didn't sleep a wink that night. Ralph came to pick me up early Tuesday morning. After escorting me to the waiting area for witnesses, he led my parents and me to the end of the hallway, as far away from everyone else as possible.

"Sammy," he said, "wait right here. Don't talk to anybody."

"What's going on?" I said, but he was gone. So, I waited. Time ticked by. I've never spent a lot of time in courthouses, but this felt like an eternity.

I saw Kevin's family come and go, but I couldn't talk to them. Ralph finally came back. Almost half an hour had gone by. I asked him what was up, but he just nodded at me.

We'd gone through everything before. Wait until you've heard the whole question before you answer. Don't be in a rush, but don't hesitate, either. Tell the truth, but don't say anything extra.

...

Deputy District Attorney General Tom Thurman gave the first opening statement. He began by reciting the basic facts of the case. For all the ground that it covers, his speech was incredibly short, but effective and moving.[103]

> *Thurman: Good morning, ladies and gentlemen. March the 9th of 1989, Kevin Hughes was 23 years old. He had his dream job. He loved music. He was a chart director at Cash Box magazine. But his dream job turned into a nightmare. His dream job cost him his life. That night, at 10:30, he was at Evergreen Records, with a friend, a business associate, Sammy Sadler. They left to go to his car, which was parked right on Music Row, here in Nashville, Davidson County. As they got to his car, he's approached, I'd submit the evidence will show, by Richard D'Antonio. Mr. D'Antonio had one thing in mind, kill Kevin Hughes. He was dressed all in black. He had on gloves. He had a ski mask. He had a thirty-eight (.38) pistol. As soon as Kevin Hughes and Sammy Sadler got into that car, he fired into the passenger side. Mr. Sadler put his arm up. He was struck in the arm. Kevin Hughes bailed out the other side, started running right down the middle of the street. It's a*

*heavily travelled street. And you will hear from witnesses
who were there at 10:30. He zigzags, trying to get away
from his pursuer, but he's relentless. He follows him down
the road. He shoots him in the back, knocks him down,
walks over Kevin Hughes and pumps two bullets in his
head. There's no more dreams for Kevin Hughes. He's dead.*

In no more than 15 minutes, Thurman related the entire story, setting up the entrance of Tom McEntee and Tony D'Antonio at *Cash Box* in 1985, when the magazine was a mere shell of its glory days in the 1960s and part of the 1970s, and then moving quickly into the "very lucrative business" they were doing after Chuck Dixon became involved.

Thurman pegged the recovery of *Cash Box* magazine to McEntee's creation of the country independents chart. Chuck Dixon took over the chart, and then took over the magazine—even though he didn't officially work there, and even after his main connection to *Cash Box*, Tony D'Antonio, was forced out. The independent chart was dominated by pay-for-play. *Cash Box* became a cash cow, especially for its owner, George Albert, and for its primary promoter, Chuck Dixon.

Thurman returned to the subject of Kevin Hughes, who postponed his college education to work at what seemed like the ideal job for a young man who loved music, who loved compiling charts, who had integrity and honesty. That last pair of qualities, however, put him at odds with Chuck and Tony. After Kevin figured out the chart-fixing scam, he wanted to stop it. He started dropping stations. He refused the bribes offered by Chuck. The scam at *Cash Box*, Thurman said, was "a very lucrative business" that netted Chuck Dixon at least $300,000 a year.

Thurman described the difficulties faced by the police in their investigation, including the long period the case was in limbo until the major breakthrough of 1993, when James Steven Daniel offered his information about Tony D'Antonio. Even after the murder squad concluded that D'Antonio was the killer, there wasn't enough evidence to convict. Finally, in 2002, the case came together with the matching of the bullets in Daniel's backyard, one cat hair found inside a baseball cap, and a distorted audio recording of a phone call between Daniel and D'Antonio. The recording documented one of several times that Tony D'Antonio went over his alibi with Daniel. By meticulously documenting each of these links in the chain of evidence, said Thurman, the detectives "put the murder weapon in Richard D'Antonio's hand."

> *Thurman: That's going to be the proof you'll hear, ladies and gentlemen. And I'd submit, at the end of that proof, you will find Richard D'Antonio is a cold-blooded killer who is guilty of first-degree murder. Thank you.*

Ross Alderman gave the opening argument for the defense, which wasn't much of an argument. The public defender spoke for a little less than three minutes. He didn't say that his client was innocent or that he was a good citizen, but he did say, without offering any substantiating evidence, that the state couldn't prove the defendant's guilt: "As you listen to the evidence, and you put aside the speculation, the rumor, the innuendo, you will realize that there is absolutely no credible evidence linking Richard D'Antonio to a bullet in a backyard in Georgia," he said. "As you listen closely to the evidence, you'll learn that Richard D'Antonio is not guilty."

Larry Hughes, Kevin's father, was called as the first witness and testified for about three minutes, followed by Kyle Hughes, who was on the stand for about 15 minutes. Kyle testified about the last phone conversation he had with his brother on the night that we were both shot on Music Row. Kevin called between seven and eight that night and said he was coming home that weekend. Kyle noted that Kevin "talked about having some things he needed to talk to me about, but he didn't want to talk on the phone… He said they were important."[104]

Kevin had sounded "nervous, almost scared," and before saying goodbye, Kevin told his brother "I love you." Those three words stood out because it was something they'd said to each other in person before, but never on the phone.

When Kevin's belongings were returned to the family, Kyle found various trade magazines (other than *Cash Box*) and copies of Kevin's resume, which proved he was planning to quit and find a position somewhere else.

I was the next witness. It was odd seeing my words typed out on the page, but there they were. [105]

> Thurman: *State your name, please.*
>
> Sammy Sadler: *Sammy Sadler.*
>
> Thurman: *And where do you currently live, Mr. Sadler?*
>
> Sadler: *In Bonham, Texas.*
>
> Thurman: *What's your occupation?*
>
> Sadler: *I own a drywall company.*
>
> Thurman: *OK. Where were you living in March of 1989?*
>
> Sadler: *Nashville.*
>
> Thurman: *What were you doing in Nashville?*
>
> Sadler: *I was recording for Evergreen Records and promoting records for Evergreen.*
>
> Thurman: *And were your records promoted to Cash Box?*
>
> Sadler: *Yes, sir.*
>
> Thurman: *As a result of that, did you know Chuck Dixon?*
>
> Sadler: *Yes, sir.*
>
> Thurman: *Did he, actually, promote you?*

Sadler: *Yes, sir.*

Thurman: *Did you know the defendant, Tony D'Antonio?*

Sadler: *I had met him.*

Thurman: *And you, in fact, were nominated for awards through Cash Box, were you not?*

Sadler: Yes, sir. [I explain that they had featured one of my new records in their "Indie Spotlight" section, and I was also nominated for Independent Male Vocalist of the Year.]

Thurman: *Did you ever sell a record?*

Sammy: *No, sir.*

At this point, the question and answers were a little misleading. I wasn't aware of the extent of Evergreen's record distribution. I knew the label sent out copies to radio stations and reviewers; I saw the packages going out from the office. Could a person in Peoria, Illinois, walk into their neighborhood record shop and buy a copy? That I didn't know. If that sounds naïve and ill-informed about the music business, that's what I was.

Now I realize why some reporters seized on that answer: One of the most potent pieces of evidence of the chart-fixing scams run by Chuck Dixon at *Cash Box* involved his promotion of a wannabe country singer named Mickey Jones. In 1988, Mickey's recording of a song called "Gal from San Antone" started zooming up the *Cash Box* charts, even though, due to a screw-up at the record-pressing plant, no radio stations were playing it. No records had been manufactured. No one had heard it, but it was a hit!

That was one big difference between Mickey Jones and me. No matter what kind of hinky stuff Chuck Dixon had pulled to push my records higher in *Cash Box*, at least I had round, vinyl 45-rpm records to show for my work. People had heard my records.

The next big topic was the night of the shooting.

> Sadler: *I left my house the evening of March the 9th. I was in an argument with my wife*
>
> *at the time. And I was going to leave the house and I picked up the phone to call to see if Kevin was still working. And the phone just rang and rang… I was fixing to hang it up, and I thought I heard somebody say hello and I pulled it back to my ear. And it was Kevin. I said, 'Hey man, are you still working?' And he said, 'Yeah.' And I said, 'Well, I'm gonna come on down and see you.'*
>
> Thurman: *Was that normal for him to work on Thursday nights?*
>
> Sadler: *To my knowledge.*

Next, I told the jury about going in Kevin's car to eat at Captain D's on West End, and then returning to Music Row, stopping at Evergreen Records for a few minutes so I could call my parents before they went to bed, using the office phone. Thurman interjected there, saying, "So you could call on [Evergreen's] dime, basically," which was true, since the average person didn't have free long distance in those days.

I was still on the phone when there was a rattle at the front of the office. Kevin went to check it out. He looked outside but didn't see anything. After finishing my call, we waited a few minutes before leaving. Thurman asked what happened as we got to Kevin's car.

> Sadler: *Well, I walked around in front of Kevin's car and reached for the door, sat down, and started reaching for the door. And I caught something moving out of the corner of my eye. And I looked up. And there was this guy standing between me and the car door with his arms out. And I saw the gun. And I said, 'Oh, my God, this guy's got a gun.' And I threw my arms up to cover my head. And that's when he*

shot me… All I remember was seeing the gloves and a mask.

Thurman: *OK. And you were shot almost [instantaneously]?*

Sadler: *Yes, sir.*

Thurman: *And what did you do after you were shot?*

Sadler: *Well, when I got shot, I fell over into Kevin's car. And I heard other shots, as I*

was laying there. And then I heard a guy in an apartment building or something there.

And he saw my feet moving and hollered down, Hey, do you need some help? And they said I ran up to his apartment.

Thurman: *And do you recall running up there?*

Sadler: *No, sir.*

Thurman: *Do you recall what happened in the apartment?*

Sadler: *No, sir.*

Thurman: *Were you unconscious for some period of time?*

Sadler: *They said—they said I was in and out.*

Thurman asked me about the extent of my injuries and how long I was in the hospital, and then came back to the subject of identification. There was nothing else I could add. I couldn't say if the guy was tall or short, skinny or fat, black or white. When we were still inside the Evergreen office, Kevin had made a remark about what he could see through the window, using the phrase "might have been a black guy," then he remarked that it was so dark outside it was hard to tell anything at all.

After that, Ross Alderman did the cross-examination. I

remember thinking at the time, "*Oh, boy, here it comes…* Alderman started by going back over the subject of what I saw and what I told the police, obviously trying to find discrepancies. Then he asked if I told the police if Kevin or I had any enemies, or if we were involved in drugs. No and no. Then it was the same thing all over again.

> Alderman: *When the police asked you for any information you had…was there anything you recognized? Did you recognize anything about, about the shooter? They asked you did you have any idea who it was? … Did they ask you that?*

> Sadler: *Yes.*

> Alderman: *You said, I don't have any idea.*

> Sadler: *Right.*

> Alderman: *You didn't recognize any features about the person that were distinctive in your mind, at least?*

> Sadler: *Correct.*

> Alderman: *All right. Thank you, sir.*

…

Reading my own words now, it seems like a lifetime ago. I remember the judge telling me I was excused and that I could step down. I remember walking from the courtroom, wondering what had happened, if I had said the wrong thing, because I expected it to be longer and more drawn out, more confrontational, like all my interrogations with Pridemore and Postiglione. I'd expected a lot of questions about Chuck Dixon. When it ended early, I became even more worried. What was next?

I wondered if Ralph Gordon's talk with the D.A. had altered

anything about the way I was treated on the witness stand. I didn't find out anything that day, but I do know that Ralph Gordon and Johnny Morris are still friends today. Obviously, I wasn't the only client Ralph represented that day.

It was hard to believe I'd only been on the stand for 15 minutes or so. Time began playing its tricks after the first few questions. It seemed to go on for hours and hours. But when it was over, time tilted the other way, and it felt like only a minute or two had passed.

After quickly thumbing through all 1,100 pages of the transcript, testimony by all 29 witnesses, I estimate that ten minutes or so was about average time on the stand. Thurman's opening speech wasn't the only economical presentation during the trial. After taking so long to get underway, the murder trial sped along like an efficient, well-oiled machine.

The way I interpret Alderman's cross-examination now, I can see that he was trying to say that if the only survivor of the shooting on Music Row couldn't help the police identify his attacker, then how could we believe the right person had been charged with the crime? Thurman had already exhausted the question, however, which made Alderman bearing down on the same point feel redundant and desperate. Maybe I'm wrong, but I suspect not.

Ralph took me back to the Doubletree after my testimony. It was still early, not even eleven o'clock. He repeated the orders regarding my sequestration: Stay in my room until the trial was over. Don't watch TV, listen to the radio, or read any newspapers that might discuss the trial. They would call me when it was over.

...

Sharon Pennington was sworn in around 10:30. Assistant D.A. Kathy Morante questioned her, focusing on several technical issues. Asked to describe the *Cash Box* Hot 100 and the Country Independent charts, Sharon answered that the Independent chart was "strictly for independent labels." Positions 1 through 40 on the Hot 100 were "spot on with the other trade publications," she said, but the bottom 60 positions on that chart were "not legitimate."

As to the Independent chart, it was not legitimate, she said, but "Kevin was making a real earnest attempt to make it a legitimate chart."[106]

Morante asked how a person would get a song on the Independent chart. Pennington answered: "Some of the [promoters] had starter stations in their pockets. And it was pretty established and known that certain promoters had control of these starter stations." One promoter, above all, controlled the vast majority of those stations, and his name was Chuck Dixon. Here she repeated the colloquial name for *Cash Box* that she had made famous when she was quoted back in 1989. Around the office, she said, they called it "Chuck Box."

She was asked, as a promoter for her father's label, Step One Records, had she ever paid to have a record on the *Cash Box* charts? "I didn't pay any money to promote records to *Cash Box*," she answered. "Our company would buy advertising in *Cash Box*, but we bought advertising in all the trade magazines."

Chuck Dixon had promoted Step One records to *Cash Box*, and on occasion, Tony D'Antonio had worked with Chuck, as his partner, to promote their records. When Pennington was asked, however, if she had ever known D'Antonio to work as a promoter with anyone besides Chuck Dixon, she said no.

During the trial, the prosecution underscored the point that Tony always claimed to be a promoter, even when he was driving an ice cream truck. But did he ever actually promote anyone? It's possible, but the defense never bothered to try and prove it.

After Tony was forced to leave *Cash Box*, he became a partner of Chuck Dixon. The prosecution introduced evidence that Chuck had split his profits with Tony and paid him a weekly salary of $1,000, which was big money compared to the $20,000 annual salary Tony had earned as the division manager of *Cash Box*, where his beginning salary was $150 per week. According to evidence presented during the trial, Tony and his wife Carolyn bought two houses and four cars in a short period of time. After they split, three months after Kevin was murdered, Tony purchased a house, a boat, and a grand piano.

Tony was making $1,000 a week as Chuck's partner, a business relationship that began shortly before Kevin Hughes was murdered. The prosecution maintained that he was paid all that money simply because he had killed Kevin Hughes.

Maybe it was true, maybe it wasn't, but it was a damned good tactic for the prosecution. Just like when you see something grotesque and can't seem to "unsee" it, Thurman wanted the jury to think about the payoff money theory, and then dare them to try and "unsee" it.

...

Sharon Pennington was a great witness. When asked about Tony D'Antonio's "unusual gait," she said she had always assumed it was due to some sort of back injury. Regarding the two memorial services for Kevin Hughes (the first in Nashville, the second in Carmi, Illinois), she said she had attended both. Chuck Dixon, she said, attended the one in Nashville, and "he sat in the back row, the last pew, alone, didn't speak to anyone, and left as soon as the service was over." [107]

Tony D'Antonio, the person who had hired Kevin at *Cash Box* and trained him for his dream job, did not attend either memorial service.

Earlier in her questioning, Kathy Morante asked Pennington about the phone calls she had taken from Chuck Dixon on the day of the murder. The reason Chuck was angry, she said, was because Kevin had dropped more stations that day, including four of Chuck's pocket stations.

Then she testified about going with Kevin to see a movie that afternoon. As they rode to the movie theater, Kevin was "nervous" and "fidgety." She drew a physical picture of his behavior as well, saying that Kevin "would rock back and forth in the car" and that he "kept pushing the sleeves up on his shirt. It wasn't normal behavior," she said.

When she told Kevin that Chuck was upset, Kevin laughed and told her he expected that. Chuck had been trying to reach him all day, but he was dodging Chuck's calls.

The prosecution had entered a list of radio stations Kevin had dropped on the morning of March 9, 1989. Another list showed that Kevin had dropped a total of 42 stations since Christmas 1988.

Nine stations had been dropped because they were reporting to *Billboard*. Kevin didn't want stations that also reported to *Billboard*. Another six were identified as satellite stations that no longer programmed their own music but obtained their programming via satellite or automatic tapes. Yet another six stations that no longer played country music. For 13 stations, no reason is given on our list, which most likely means they were in Chuck's pocket and Kevin had found them out. One station had quit calling reports and the phone at another had been disconnected. The status of three others wasn't known.

Morante asked a final question and passed the witness. Alderman asked a few questions, primarily establishing the fact that the office of Step One Records was in the Faron Young Building, located at 1300 Division, and that Chuck Dixon's office was in the Joe Talbot Building—the former location of *Cash Box* magazine—about a block away.

...

The next three witnesses were all police officers. The first was Sgt. William Kenneth Dyer, who on the night of March 9, 1989, was a patrol officer with Nashville Metro. He was one of the first officers to respond to the 10:30 p.m. dispatch call of a shooting at 1020 16th Avenue South. Under questioning by Tom Thurman, Dyer gave a blow-by-blow account of his actions after he arrived at the crime. [108] After determining that the victim lying in the street (Kevin Hughes) was deceased, a woman told him that there was:

> Dyer: *...another subject who had been shot and he was in her apartment. So, I went with her to her apartment. And he was in the living room area... He was shot and bleeding profusely in the, I believe it was his right arm.*

I was the victim. Someone was attempting to stop the bleeding, Dyer stated, using, he believed, a towel as a tourniquet. Dyer attempted to talk to me. "Was it like a formal interview?" asked Thurman. "No," responded Dyer, "there was nothing formal about it. I was trying to... get some information to put out a suspect description... he informed me that the subject was wearing all black, and that he had a ski mask. And I believe he told me that he thought the subject was a male black."

Thurman asked for clarification. Dyer appeared to have written "male white" on his report and then wrote something else over those words. "I don't know," responded Dyer, admitting that there was some "back and forth between us during the time, and he couldn't decide whether it was a male white or a male black. And maybe we settled on black. I can't recall."

> Thurman: *It was a very brief conversation?*

> Dyer: *It was very brief. It was very chaotic. The subject was bleeding. He was in obvious pain. It was very brief.*

On cross-examination, Defense Attorney Patrick Frogge came back to the same question. Apparently, he sensed a potential crack in the prosecution's case.

> Frogge: *Did you also note that besides saying perhaps that Mr. Sadler said that it was a male black, he also said that the person had a slender build?*

Dyer: *Yes, sir. I believe what I said was to get, like I said, I was trying to get the description. And it was very chaotic. And he was shot, and in obvious pain, that—*

Frogge: *I understand, but—*

Dyer: *The best I recall is I gave him two options, you know. Was he heavyset or was he slender? I was trying to get it out just as quick as I could. The response time was relatively quick. And I though the possibility of catching the suspect in the area would be pretty good. So, I was trying to get out the information as quickly as possible, to get it out.*

Frogge: *Thank you.*

The next witness, Sgt. William Summerlin, was also on patrol that night. When Summerlin arrived, his primary duty was to help secure the crime scene. Summerlin also came upstairs after being told about a second shooting victim. "We followed a blood trail," Summerlin stated, "and found the other victim up there where some people were trying to administer first aid." He did not attempt to interview me or anyone else himself.

The next part of the morning's session in court was probably the most graphic. Officer Charles Anglin, a 30-year veteran of the police department, worked in the Identification Division. On the night of March 9, 1989, Anglin was one of several officers from the Identification who had tagged and bagged evidence from the crime scene and took photographs from every angle that could possibly be utilized in the investigation. Another officer, Ronnie Wilson, now deceased, had drawn a detailed chart of the crime scene.[109]

Under questioning by Kathy Morante, Officer Anglin explained the details of photographs and diagrams of the crime scene, using a laser pointer, a screen, and an overhead projector. There was one photograph of Kevin's body at the crime scene that showed the location of the spent bullet near his head. This was the only crime scene photograph that showed the murder victim introduced into evidence by the prosecution, but the defense contended that it was one too many for the jury.

Previously, in a hearing outside the presence of the jury, Alderman objected strenuously to the introduction of the photo. Thurman explained that the prosecution had chosen that photo because it showed the location of the body, the cap, and the bullet, and by comparison, other photos, including close-ups, were far more graphic, and the state had the right to introduce them. The judge agreed—other photos were far more upsetting to view. Alderman still objected, saying that it was one thing to pass the photo around to the jurors, but to have it blown up on a five-by-seven screen on the wall was too much.

Wyatt overruled the objection once again.

"The Court is going to permit the state to show the pictures," he said. "If this overhead thing is the more appropriate... then they're going to be allowed to do it."

Officer Anglin's testimony was extensive, and it was late in the morning when the judge excused him. Over a dozen items had been admitted into evidence, including bullets, the World War II ball cap, the bloody clothing the paramedics had cut from me, Kevin's clothing, the car keys he had dropped as he fell, and other personal belongings. The projector screen had the photo of Kevin's body, many different views of blood trails, the bloody car interior, and various angles of the 1000 block of 16th Avenue South, including the one looking down from Phillip Barnhart's third-floor apartment. Not that I felt much pity for them, but it must have a grueling 35-40 minutes for the defense table.

If that was tough for their side, sitting through the testimony of the eyewitnesses who came next couldn't have been any easier.

On the night of 1989, Allison Kidd Chimento was in a car on 16th Avenue South with a friend, Robert Lyons III. Both were students at Belmont University at the time.[110] They were on their way to see a movie at Fountain Square. Suddenly, two people ran in front of the car. Lyons, who was driving, had to hit the brakes to avoid hitting them. "One was being pursued," said Chimento, by a man "dressed in all black, ski mask, carrying a gun."

> Chimento: *We swerved at that point and stopped. As I got out of the car to turn around and look back, I saw the man with the gun and the ski mask standing over the victim, shot—firing repeated shots, and then he fled the scene.*

Thurman had the witness point out the location of the car they were driving when they first saw the two individuals, where the victim fell, and which direction the shooter fled. The shooter held the gun in his right hand, was between five-nine and six feet tall, and had "kind of a pudgy belly."

Robert Lyons III gave his own vivid recollection of what he saw that night, at one adding "I remember it just like it was yesterday." Lyons referred to the diagram to indicate where he was as the victim "rolled out in front of me."[111]

> Lyons: *I saw him roll out, didn't, really know what was happening. And all of a sudden, he got up and started running back around this way (indicating on diagram). At that time just as he's getting up, a guy came out from the other side. And they were running in place around the front. At this time, I was, maybe, a car length away. And he shot, I think it was two, maybe three times, at this, at this point. Then the victim came back around and ran up this way. And he was sort of running back. I was looking in the rear-view mirror, as I was going, not really believing what I was seeing. And he fell down back behind the parked cars. And the guy just got over him and went pow, pow, pow, just hit him three more times.*

> Thurman: *So how close did you actually get to the individuals?*

Lyons: *A car length.*

Thurman: *So, they ran, basically, right past your car?*

Lyons: *Yes. I had to slow down to keep from hitting him.*

The shooter, Lyons said, was between five-ten and six feet tall, "stocky," and Caucasian, adding that he could see "around the holes in the eyes" of the ski mask. The shooter's "side to side" running gait "stuck out in my mind."

"So, a very unusual running style?" asked Thurman.

Lyons was definite about that point. "[As] he was running, it was almost, it was almost theatrical to me at the time," he answered. "And I remember it just like it was yesterday, as he ran, ran past."

Lyons supplied another detail I had never heard before. When asked if anyone had tried to resuscitate Kevin, he said yes. "There was a lady that's slender, just from memory," he said. "She pulled up in a purple Volkswagen bus. And she went over and tried to give him mouth-to-mouth resuscitation."

Phillip Barnhart was the guy in the upstairs apartment who was lying in bed with his girlfriend, Connie Gaddis, reading when they were startled by the sound of gunfire on 16th Avenue South.[112] Kathy Morante led the examination.

Did he remember the night of March 9, 1989? "Yeah," he answered. "It was pretty traumatic."

Barnhart stated that after hearing the gunshots, he jumped up and raised the window shade in time catch a fleeting glimpse of two figures running south in a "zig-zag pattern... like a football player runs." After they disappeared from view, he looked down and saw legs sticking out of the open passenger side door of a car parked at the curb, "and that turned out to be the other guy that had been shot."

When Morante asked if he remembered what happened next, Barnhart said he didn't know—which was interesting to hear, because my memory of it is blank, too.

Barnhart: ...*I can't recall if I opened the window and yelled down, 'Are you hurt?' Or if I ran down there. I don't recall.*

Morante: *OK. Do you recall what happened next? You're not sure whether you ran down there, or you called, 'Are you OK?' but what's the next thing you remember happening?*

Barnhart: *The next thing that stands out in my mind is having that guy in the apartment, and he collapsed on the floor.*

Morante: *OK. When you say, "that guy," you didn't know who it was?*

Barnhart: *I didn't know who it was.*

Morante: *What kind of condition was he in when he came into your apartment?*

Barnhart: *Well, he was bleeding profusely.*

Morante: *And when he got into your apartment, did he, did you say that he collapsed?*

Barnhart: *Yah.*

Morante: *Right?*

Barnhart: *And he was bigger than us, than, you know. You know, it was hard to maneuver him.... Connie started calling for help then. And once he was in there, and again, I don't recall how he got up there... But she put ice in a bag. And we held it above the wound. And I think there was a point where I reached in and tried to, you know, hold off the artery, or something...*

Morante: *Was there a lot of blood?*

Barnhart: *Yeah... I didn't know it until the next morning, but, I mean, there was blood, there was a blood trail up the stairs. There was blood on our door. The carpet in the apartment, you know, there was a big spot. There was a lot of blood.*

Morante asked Barnhart if he recalled whether the victim said anything after he collapsed. If the defense table expected to hear evidence of contradictory suspect descriptions, they would be disappointed.

Barnhart: *I don't remember him saying anything. I, you know, I don't think there was conversation... We just kept telling him help was on the way, you know, like, as you would [with] anybody that's been hurt... and... we had no way to know whether this was a bad guy or a good guy. I mean, it's just like, you didn't think about it. You reacted to the situation.*

And, at this point in reading the transcript, I said a little prayer of thanks to the Lord that people like Phillip Barnhart and Connie Gaddis "reacted to the situation" the way they did, whether they knew if I was a bad guy or a good guy. Thank you, Lord.

Two other eyewitnesses were heard that afternoon. Kathy Hunter was visiting Donnie R. Lowery, the professional ichthyologist (fish scientist) and part-time songwriter, when the shooting began. Currently employed as a nanny, Hunter was a singer back in 1989. She had sung on many demo sessions and at the "Grand Ole Opry," she said.[113]

The timing of the events of March 9, 1989, came into sharp focus as Hunter testified she had put on her coat, picked up her purse, and headed for the stairs when Lowery said "he wanted to play me one more song. And about that time, we heard what sounded like firecrackers, pops. But he said it was gunshots."

Hunter and Lowery then stepped to the window, and they saw one person "running and yelling... [and] "stocky-built guy" dressed in all black, ski mask, and baseball cap who shot the victim. After the victim fell, the suspect "walked up... leaned over with his right hand

and stuck the gun up to his head and I guess two to three more shots right into him."

After that, Hunter said, the shooter "casually raised up and just looked both ways and walked straight ahead and disappeared." From the window, Hunter said, it wasn't possible to see where the suspect went from there, but they suspected that he walked between Lowery's apartment building and the one next door.

Donnie Lowery testified next, stating that he was playing his songs for Hunter because she was looking for material to record herself. Lowery's description of what they saw from the window matched Hunter's testimony. He offered that he recognized the noise immediately as gunshots because "I shoot a lot."[114] As to the suspect's strange manner of running as "kind of a loping run/gait, somewhat like a limp, I guess." Lowery also testified that he was on the phone with the 911 operators while the shooting was happening.

The 13th witness was Gene Kennedy, promoter and owner of Door Knob Records. His testimony was pretty much the same story he'd told the reporters who wrote the article "Music Fraud Hinted in Music Row Slaying," which ran in the *Tennessean* on April 9, 1989, exactly one month after the shootings.

That story was the first to publicize the theory that someone inside the promotions-chart-fixing community (and although it wasn't articulated in the newspaper, most Music Row insiders pointed to Chuck Dixon and Tony D'Antonio) had killed Kevin Hughes to prevent him from revealing the chart-fixing scandal to the general public, as well as law enforcement.[115]

Kennedy was one of several Music Row indie record label owners/ promoters who had benefitted from pay-for-play chart fixing in the past, but who came forward, cooperated with the investigation, and told their story to the media. The insider consensus was that Kevin's murder was a paid hit ordered by Chuck Dixon and carried out by Tony D'Antonio.[116]

On the witness stand, Kennedy also testified about Kevin's

behavior in the week before he was killed. When the promoter met Kevin for lunch, Kevin was "very nervous."

Overall, Gene Kennedy helped advance the case for the prosecution, despite the fact that during cross-examination, he provided what was probably the finest hour for the defense. Ross Alderman quickly began chipping away at Kennedy's credibility. Under questioning by Thurman, Kennedy claimed that in 1987, he refused to hire Chuck Dixon to promote Door Knob Records releases; and for the next two years or so, not one of his records appeared in the *Cash Box* charts.

> Alderman: *Let me go through and ask you about a few artists. In January of 1989, were you promoting a record on Door Knob, "Two Hearts," by John Washington?*
>
> Kennedy: *Yes.*
>
> Alderman: *Would it surprise you to know that that was on that day No. 35 on the Cash Box Indie chart?*
>
> Kennedy: *I don't remember.*

About a minute later, Alderman struck again, asking Kennedy about another Door Knob release, "I'm Going Back to Dallas," by Ritchie Valens, which debuted at No. 16 in *Cash Box*. Kennedy said he was unaware of that because, at that time, he was no longer subscribed to *Cash Box*. He didn't pay any attention to it and "it didn't mean anything to anybody," because "it had lost all its legitimacy."

Alderman hammered away at Kennedy, citing four other singles released on Door Knob Records that charted in *Cash Box*, each time, making the question a dramatic gesture, a "Perry Mason" moment. Kennedy's only response was that the records in question had also charted in *Billboard*; therefore, the *Cash Box* rating was superfluous, but Kennedy was now a damaged witness, like a boxer who had taken several falls in the first few rounds of a fight.

Kennedy's claims about his label's releases being blackballed from *Cash Box* had been publicly disputed before. It seems that

Thurman and his people did a poor job of vetting Kennedy's testimony.

The next witness was Tom McEntee, an individual who cast a long shadow over the entire case. If not for McEntee, the Nashville division of *Cash Box* might have gone out of business. If not for McEntee, Tony D'Antonio might have faded from the Nashville music scene completely. Kevin Hughes might have gotten his degree at Belmont and continued working in the Nashville gospel music industry, married, supporting a family.[117]

McEntee showed no remorse for his role in the disasters that followed his imprint at *Cash Box*. He provided expert testimony, however, about the most common technique of chart manipulation, including "false reporting from radio stations controlled by an interested person, for example, a promoter, pocket stations, or [simply] altered by the person compiling the charts." Even when the person compiling the chart was honest and ethical, someone else could come into the office during after-hours and alter the chart before it was printed in the magazine. McEntee acknowledged that possibility. He also said that chart manipulation was common, that it can happen and does happen to at least some extent at virtually every music ratings chart, including the mighty *Billboard*.

As far as I know, no connection between McEntee and the chart-fixing schemes of Chuck Dixon was ever officially established. McEntee did, however, create the independents chart in *Cash Box*, and that's what, for better and worse, started the revenue flowing again.

McEntee claimed that the stress of running *Cash Box* severely aggravated his pre-existing asthma to the degree that he was forced to quit working for a while to regain his health. His illness, in other words, caused him to leave the management of the *Cash Box* operation in the hands of Tony D'Antonio. George Albert okayed the transition. McEntee said that he moved to Florida and was only occasionally in touch with D'Antonio in the years that followed, so he was out of the loop. That's what he claimed in his testimony and in his interviews with Detective Pridemore.

Tom McEntee is dead now, so he's not around to enlighten us on the subject, but I still suspect the story was more complicated than that.

By the time McEntee was excused from the witness box, it was 2:30 in the afternoon. Of the remaining witnesses that day, three were former *Cash Box* employees, two were law enforcement officers, and one was Robert Douglas Metzgar, the disgraced Assembly of God minister turned producer/promoter/grifter. Judge Wyatt excused the jury for a short break.[118] The prosecutor and defense counsel remained for a hearing on the extent and admissibility of Metzgar's testimony. Some parts had to be excluded as being hearsay, but the parts that were admissible were pure dynamite.

...

The jury was seated again at 2:37 p.m. and the trial resumed with the testimony of Robert Metzgar. Metzgar was one of the few promoters in Nashville who may have been as rotten as Chuck Dixon, if not more so. It made sense that they were partners in ripping off some of the most well-heeled suckers who made the mistake of coming to Nashville to make it big.

The bulk of Metzgar's testimony concerned a period from 1988—1989 when he was producing a client named Mickey Jones, a dark-haired amateur from a small town in Louisiana. Robert Metzgar had produced several songs by Jones on his Stop Hunger label and had guaranteed that the releases would become hits on the *Cash Box* charts if Jones hired Dixon for promotion. Metzgar was apparently serving as the go-between on the deal. Dixon's normal fee for promoting a record for a month or so was $2,500. This time he was getting $15,000. They were giving Jones the deluxe package: chart placement on both the independent chart and the *Billboard* Hot

100 Country chart, a story in the "Indie Feature" section, and a hatful of award nominations.[119]

This Mickey Jones, by the way, should not be confused with the Mickey Jones who played drums for Kenny Rogers and others, recorded solo, and acted in film.

At some time in early 1989 or earlier, Mickey told Metzgar that rumors were going around Music Row that Kevin Hughes was planning to go public about the corruption and chart-fixing scams at *Cash Box*. If that happened, certain promoters like Metzgar and Dixon might be going to jail. To find others who might worry about jail time if the scams were revealed, we might consider the names listed on the full-page ad Mickey Jones took out in *Cash Box* near the end of 1989, where Mickey's "promotion team" is listed as:

Chuck Dixon, Tony D'Antonio (*Cash Box* Radio)

Johnny Morris, Craig Morris (*Billboard* Radio)

Tim Fitzpatrick (*Indie Bullet*)

Metzgar went to Dixon's office to discuss the problem. Tony D'Antonio soon joined Metzgar and Dixon. This was the infamous meeting at which Dixon, according to Metzgar, made the following promise: "I will handle Kevin Hughes... And if I, you know, can't handle him, he'll be gone." Although it could be argued that "he'll be gone" meant that Kevin would be fired from *Cash Box*, no one bothered to make that counter-argument.

Even before the trial, Mickey Jones was kind of infamous as the guy whose debut record, "Gal from San Antone," was so good that it was a hit before anybody, except Chuck Dixon and Robert Metzgar, had a chance to hear it. Thurman asked Metzgar to explain to the jury how such a strange thing might happen.

> Metzgar: *It was a record called "Gal from San Antone," and United Record Pressing, here in Nashville, got behind in their manufacturing schedule. And they had not even*

manufactured the record. My client [Mickey Jones] had gone and already paid to have the record promoted. And it was physically in the written, printed chart at Cash Box, and there were no records manufactured yet. They weren't even out.

Thurman: *So, it had already been charted as being played?*

Metzgar: *Yes, sir.*

Thurman: *But there was nothing to be played.*

Metzgar: *There were no records for anybody to play.*

The October 22, 1988 issue of *Cash Box* magazine shows that "Gal from San Antone" by Mickey Jones, the record that didn't exist, made an impressive debut at No. 17 on the *Cash Box* Country Independent Singles chart and No. 89 on the Hot 100 Country Singles chart.[120] During the following week, the ghost record floated up one slot on the indies chart and to No. 83 on the country singles chart.

A week later, roughly the same movement was reported, No. 14 and No. 82, respectively. By week four, however, "Gal from San Antonio" was slipping out of town, dropping to No. 48 on the indies and nowhere to be seen on the Hot 100. Possibly, but it's just a theory, but this could have been the week the records finally became available.

Metzgar became worried about Mickey's promotion goals a week before he met with Dixon and D'Antonio to report the rumors about Kevin. Thurman asked Metzgar about it.

Thurman: *Did you have an occasion to see Kevin Hughes at the [Country Radio Seminar] shortly before he was killed?*

Metzgar: *Yes, sir.*

Thurman: *And who was he with at the time?*

Metzgar: *He was standing pretty close to a booth at the Radio Seminar. And he was having an argument with Mr. Dixon.*

Thurman: *OK. Is that Chuck Dixon?*

Metzgar: *Yes, sir.*

Thurman: *OK. Now, you're saying an argument. Could you just describe what you observed?*

Metzgar: *I wasn't close enough to hear what they said. I just observed that Mr. Dixon was trying to hand him money. And Kevin refused it. He wouldn't take it. And the more Kevin tried to refuse and not take the money, the more heated it got. And it, finally, got so heated I left.*

Thurman: *OK...*

Metzgar: *I didn't want to be involved in it.*

At this point, Thurman asked Metzgar about the meeting he had with Dixon and D'Antonio after witnessing the argument between Dixon and Hughes at CRS.

Metzger: *I told him, I said, "Chuck, you know, I saw you and Kevin having this big argument out at the Radio Seminar." And I said, "you know, he's already dropped some of your pocket stations, which weakens your ability to keep a record in for a long time. And I know he's about to drop a bunch more of your pocket stations." And I said, "Chuck, I'm not going to, you know, give you this $15,000 unless I know for a fact you can handle Kevin Hughes."*

Thurman: *Did you also explain to him something that you had heard?*

Metzger: *I did, General. I said, you know, the rumor is*

*all over Music Row that Kevin is going to go to the media
and expose this chart-fixing scheme you guys are working
at Cash Box. And I said, you know, if he does that, you
know, this is going to look very bad on me and my clients
and everybody involved in this.*

Thurman: *What did Mr. Dixon respond?*

Metzgar: *Well, he was very aware of the rumor. And he
looked at me and he said, "I will handle Kevin Hughes.
And if I, you know, can't handle him, he'll be gone."*

Thurman: *Was Mr. D'Antonio in the room at the time?*

Metzgar: *Yes, sir.*

Thurman: *Did you go ahead and pay the fifteen thousand
dollars?*

Metzgar: *After he assured me that he would handle Kevin
Hughes, I did.*

Over the next few minutes, Thurman introduced several issues
of *Cash Box* into evidence, including one in which a Mickey Jones
single made it to No. 2, and the December 9, 1989 issue with the
Cash Box Nashville Awards Show program listed with all the nom-
inees, and full-page ads taken out by Mickey Jones, thanking *Cash
Box* for its support.[121] The names of many other individuals related
in some way to the strange *Cash Box* underworld appear on these
ads.

One of them is Mark Carman, who took over as Nashville
director of *Cash Box* and was a busy gospel producer and promoter.
Frank Scherman was Carman's partner in Tra-Star Records, which
enjoyed some hits on *Cash Box* charts during this time. Mark and
Frank were the "henchmen" described by Gary Bradshaw whom he
said were twirling their pistols on their fingers the first time he met

Chuck Dixon in Nashville. When Gary walked in, he said, Mark and Frank frisked him for weapons. *(Here's an interesting side note: More recently, Mark Carman has made a name for himself as a lifelong gun-lover who supports common sense gun control legislation.*[122] *)*

Other promoters whose names appeared in the award show congratulations ads alongside Chuck Dixon and Tony D'Antonio were Johnny Morris and Craig Morris.

In the interest of full disclosure, I was nominated for Best Male Independent Vocalist in 1989 but did not win. Mickey Jones got a bunch of nominations and won the award for Best New Independent Male Vocalist. He also performed at the awards show in December 1989. Kevin Hughes had been dead for nine months, and the Dixon-Metzgar-D'Antonio gang was wheeling and dealing as if their scam might go on forever.

The state introduced one other exhibit that was a classic example of the "circumstantial evidence" that helped stitch together their case. It also helped disprove any attempts by the defense to distance Tony D'Antonio from Chuck Dixon. The exhibit was an issue of *Cash Box* that featured several ads and mentions of Metzgar and Dixon's client, Mickey Jones. Somewhere in the pages of that magazine was an ad paid for by Tony D'Antonio, written in beatnik verse by, we can safely assume, D'Antonio himself:[123]

At the sound of the tone, radio listens.

You can hire Tommy Dee or even Robert Gentry

or you can hire Bobby Witt, if you think he's fit,

but if you've got any sense,

forget the rest and hire the best,

A-Tone Productions, Promotions, & Artist Development.

P.S. If my catalog is full, and you can't hire me,

there's only one other. They call him C.D.

He's hardworking, honest, and very sincere.

And besides all of that,

he's Cash Box Promoter of the Year,

Chuck Dixon.

Sometimes, writing a poem is rewarding, sometimes, it can prove to be really embarrassing, and sometimes, it can help send you away to the penitentiary for the rest of your life.

...

Sandra Daens testified about working at *Cash Box* beginning in 1987. Under questioning by Morante, Daens testified that "every now and then" she had overheard D'Antonio "negotiating" with artists and promoters on the phone. "He would just make mention that if the artist or promoter bought an ad in the magazine, then his record may be moved up or debuted early," she testified.[124]

> Morante: *Do you recall when Kevin was murdered in March of 1989.*
>
> Daens: *Yes, I do.*
>
> Morante: *And prior to that time, how was he acting in the office?*
>
> Daens: *He was suspicious that something wasn't right with the charts, that they were being changed… that they were being changed while he was gone for the day.*

Defense counsel Patrick Frogge objected to the witness' answer, and Judge Wyatt sustained the objection as it was "getting into hearsay." Morante resumed her questions, this time asking Daens if she had observed how Kevin had been acting. Daens answered, "He had been a little bit afraid." "Afraid of what?" asked Morante. "Afraid to say anything," replied Daens.

Witness number 16 was Myra Langlois, the investigator for the D.A.'s office. In 2001, Langlois was in the middle of an investigation of Chuck Dixon and Robert Metzgar's promotion schemes. Both men, she said, were "total scumbags." Chuck Dixon, unfortunately, died before the indictments against him could be prepared.[125]

After Langlois was sworn in, Thurman asked her about the search warrant she served on Chuck Dixon's residence in January 2001.

During the search, two payment books containing names and dollar amounts were seized. The entries in one book, dubbed "the orange book," began in 1987 and ended after September 1988. The other one, "the red book," began in 1990 and ended in 2000. There was no record book for 1989 and no record of the last three months of 1988.

The total payments for the nine months in the orange, 1988 book came to $138,747.09. The total payments in the red, 1990 book came to $295,796.57. The orange book also recorded five payments to Tony D'Antonio for a total of $3,499.00. Langlois was not allowed to answer any questions about her speculations as to what the payments were earmarked to do.

The orange and red books were blank ledgers with handwritten figures in them and no explanation. It's hard to imagine any honest businessmen keeping his business records that way. What kind of CPA would accept a ledger like that? Presumably, the men and women seated in the jury box would be able to draw their own intelligent conclusions about it.

Langlois also testified that Dixon's Rolodex was seized during the search. One of the entries in it was Tony D'Antonio in Las Vegas, where he moved in 1995.

Much, much more was learned about that search and the case

against Dixon and Metzgar when Langlois was interviewed for this book in the fall of 2017. [126]

"We took his computer," she said. "The house was a disaster area. He was very, very messy. It wasn't a fancy house, it was a middle-class ranch style house. Although Dixon made a lot of money, I think he squandered most of it on fancy cars, jewelry, and the usual stuff. We found records on *Cash Box*, but by that time, *Cash Box* was defunct, and they were running these fake internet charts."

Apparently, Chuck Dixon had little difficulty transitioning his con games from the vinyl and trade magazine age to the internet and social media age. Decades earlier, victims were often plucked "right off the bus" or when they were spotted at Shoney's. In the 2000s, Chuck and the gang reeled in new marks through online pitches, dazzling them with phony ratings on bogus music sites. The transition was probably quite simple: Pay a web designer for a few hours' work or better yet, cut that person in on the deal and give them a new title: digital music promoter.

The jury was excused for a 20-minute break. Another ex-parte hearing ensued regarding conspiracy law and hearsay rules. Judge Wyatt had been "reading up" on the topic the night before, he said, and now he was better prepared for the issues. The next witness would be Julia Hooper from the Metro Identification Division. Hooper was a frequent expert witness on hair and fiber evidence in criminal trials. Wyatt, always concerned with keeping the trial running on time, asked Thurman how long he expected Hooper's testimony to take.

"Probably not very long," Thurman answered. "She just found a hair in a hat."[127]

As accurate as Thurman's reply was, it woefully understated the importance of the hair in the hat that Hooper had found. As she began her testimony, Kathy Morante first asked Hooper about the technique of finding latent prints on the evidence she examined. The only prints found on Kevin Hughes' car, she said, belonged to Kevin. It was known that the suspect had worn gloves.

Next, Hooper was asked about the ball cap recovered from the crime scene. No latent prints were found on that, either, but that wasn't surprising. "A ball cap is not a good surface for latent prints," she explained. "It's porous. And a better piece for latent prints would be a smooth piece of glass, but, typically, on a porous surface it's difficult to obtain latent prints."

Hooper was then asked about other methods used to search for evidence on the ball cap. "I also processed it with our laser," Hooper answered, explaining that "the alternate light source is used to, really, luminesce evidence, to make things visible that, normally, you wouldn't see with the naked eye. And you use different wavelengths and filters to look at a piece of evidence, to see if you can see, perhaps, a piece of hair or, maybe, a fiber, some cases, a fingerprint."

Using the laser, Hooper testified, she found a hair stuck under the inside flap of the ball cap. The hair was placed inside a receptacle labeled inside with her initials, the date, her employee number, and the case number. She stated that the hair receptacle was given to Detectives Postiglione and Pridemore. In the courtroom, the hair receptacle was assigned the No. 10 and admitted into evidence. The ball cap, exhibit No. 3, was given to Hooper so she could show the jury just where the hair was found.

From here, the prosecution established that the hair had been received by Audrey Shaw, a forensic scientist at TBI. The TBI lab sent the hair to be examined at the FBI lab in Quantico, Virginia. The hair and fiber expert from the FBI, SA Douglas Deedrick, was scheduled to testify Wednesday morning.[128]

The last testimony on Tuesday afternoon from Steve Hess, who had been hired as assistant chart director just before Kevin was killed. Hess had given his deposition earlier, so the testimony—with examination and cross-examination—was shown on video to the jury. Hess, who gave his occupation as "entertainer," is a singer for a contemporary gospel group called Steve Hess & Southern Salvation, a trio of spikey-haired musicians who can be found on Facebook, Twitter, and countless other digital age equivalents of *Cash Box* and *Indie Bullet*.

The testimony offered by Hess was essentially the same as what he told the murder squad in 1989: Tony came in and trained him for the job of chart director. He wasn't told to manipulate the chart information, and as far as he knew, the charts were compiled honestly when he worked there. From his testimony, he seems to have had no curiosity about what went on behind the scenes; he just did what he was told.[129]

Hess compiled the chart data from the reports he was given, he said, although he never personally called any radio stations to obtain reports. He never double-checked the airplay reports he was given.

When Thurman asked Hess if the large number of reporting stations made it difficult to tell if the charts really reflected the information he had compiled once the charts were published, he answered, "Yes, sir. There were almost two hundred stations."

If there were 200 stations in the *Cash Box* survey just a few weeks after Kevin Hughes was murdered, that meant that Chuck Dixon had added the same number of stations that Kevin had dropped in the weeks before his death. Which meant Chuck had reinstated his pocket stations. Steve Hess must have known that, but I suspect he knew a lot of things that he didn't want to mention.

...

The first witness Wednesday morning was Agent Douglas E. Deedrick, the FBI hair and fiber expert. Thurman conducted the first round of questions, taking over ten minutes to establish Deedrick's credentials on the subject, which were impressive.[130] When it came down to the hair found in the World War II ball cap, Deedrick said it was definitely a hair from a black cat, and it probably got there by transfer from another object. The last line of Deedrick's testimony spoke to the ease of transfer. "My daughter has four cats," he said. "So, I see a lot of cat hairs."

On cross-examination, Patrick Frogge got Deedrick to admit that even though the hair appeared to have gotten inside the cap by transfer, no one could say for sure. When all was said and done, it seemed to me that the role of the black cat hair had been just a little overemphasized.

Carolyn Cox testified that her ex-husband suffered from a hiatal hernia. Sometimes, she said, it was so painful for him that he had trouble standing up straight, in addition to his "unusual gait" in walking and running. [131]

She married Richard D'Antonio in 1986 and divorced him in July 1989, four months after Kevin was murdered. After Tony left *Cash Box* and became Chuck Dixon's partner, Carolyn and Tony's lifestyle changed drastically. During their marriage, Tony bought two houses and three cars. Shortly after they split, he bought a grand piano, a motorcycle, and a boat.

With only a few minutes of testimony, she helped shred what may have been left of Tony's alibi for March 9, 1989. That night, she went to bed sometime between 11 p.m. and midnight, and he was not home. At around 3 a.m., she was awakened by a phone call. It was Chuck Dixon, wanting to know about Tony. He wasn't home, she said. At that point, Tony walked in and asked who had called. Tony then instructed her in what to say in case the police asked, that he was there at home with her all evening.

"At first, I complied," she said, speaking of being questioned by Pridemore and Postiglione, "but I wasn't comfortable lying, so I told the truth."

Carolyn also testified that in 1989, she and Tony had a black cat.

The next witness, James Steven Daniel, helped destroy D'Antonio's alibi even further. On the afternoon of March 9, 1989, Tony came to see Daniel at his home in Flintstone, located in the Lookout Mountain region of Georgia. The visit was unexpected. Tony was carrying what looked like an overnight bag, which led Daniel to think he planned to spend the night. Instead, he asked if Daniel had a gun he could buy. Daniel sold him a .38-caliber pistol for $150.[132]

Tony needed ammunition, too, so Daniel went out to a pawn shop and bought a box of cheap target practice ammunition for the pistol. They test-fired the gun in the back yard. Tony went inside and took a shower, changed clothes, and left. Daniel said it was between 7:15 and 8 p.m. Georgia time when he left. Georgia is on Eastern Standard Time, but Tennessee is Central Standard Time, so it was an hour earlier in Nashville. Daniel testified that since there was no interstate highway between Lookout Mountain and Nashville, in 1989 it was a solid 2 hours, 15 minutes to drive from Flintstone to Nashville. That would put Tony D'Antonio in Nashville no earlier than 8:30 p.m. CST.

How was Daniel able to remember the date? Because Tony reminded him of it several times over the years, repeating the alibi that Tony instructed him to tell any detectives who came snooping around, that Tony D'Antonio was at his home in Flintstone until 11:30 that night. Tony also instructed him to tell Carolyn the same story. At the time, Daniel assumed that Tony needed the alibi because he'd been seeing another woman.

At this point, Thurman introduced an audiotape of the phone call made by Daniel in 1994. The jurors were also given a transcription to read. The conversation starts off with coded references to a drug deal; D'Antonio wants to know when the next shipment of pot is arriving. When the talk was steered to D'Antonio's actions on March 9, 1989, Daniel feigns ignorance and poor memory. If possible, he wants to make D'Antonio spell everything out.[133]

> Daniel: *Yeah, so, um, how are you with them, you know? You done them?*
>
> D'Antonio: *Oh, yeah. They're clear. They're all gone.*
>
> Daniel: *Yeah. Well, I probably ought to know something about, maybe, Wednesday morning.*
>
> D'Antonio: *All right.*

Daniel: *If not, I might want to take a trip.*

D'Antonio: *OK. That sounds good, too.*

Daniel: *OK.*

D'Antonio: *We need to talk about something else, too.*

Daniel: *Yeah, what?*

D'Antonio: *You remember four years ago when I was down there till after the 11:00 news, or something.*

Daniel: *Yeah, that was four years ago.*

D'Antonio: *Yeah. Carolyn's asking questions.*

Daniel: *What, now?*

D'Antonio: *Remember when Carolyn and I went down there, and she asked you some questions?*

Daniel: *Yeah, but I didn't know what Carolyn was asking about. I thought, maybe you had a girlfriend, or something.*

D'Antonio: *No, she was asking if I went down there the night before.*

Daniel: *Yeah.*

D'Antonio: *That's when that boy got killed up there.*

Daniel: *Somebody got killed up there?*

D'Antonio: *Yeah, out on Music Row.*

Daniel: *Yeah.*

D'Antonio: *Yeah. She asked where I was. I told her I was out there with you. if she asks.*

Daniel: *What, now?*

D'Antonio: *She asked you if I was with you that night.*

Daniel: *Yeah.*

D'Antonio: *You said, yeah. I left after 11:00 news.*

Daniel: *Yeah. Oh, so, what's going on? I don't understand. That's been a long time ago.*

D'Antonio: *Yeah, I know. Well, see, some of the detectives there in Nashville, they've been talking to everybody in the music industry, again, you know, all that shit. Playing it on, um, on "Crime Stoppers" or "Unsolved Mysteries," some shit.*

Daniel: *Yeah.*

D'Antonio: *Now, they're questioning everybody again, in the music industry and stuff.*

Daniel: *Yeah, so… I don't really remember it, OK, to tell the truth, but what, you know, what do you want me to say, or whatever?*

D'Antonio: *I was there till 11:15, or so.*

Daniel: *Oh, you mean 11:30, the news when it goes off?*

D'Antonio: *Yeah.*

Daniel: *OK.*

D'Antonio: *If you… I doubt if you will ever be asked.*

After this exchange, they return to the drug deal.

As I explained earlier, Daniel volunteered the information about selling the gun to Tony D'Antonio in 1993. He had already named D'Antonio to the GBI as one of his drug smuggler partners when he saw the Crime Stoppers episode about the murder on Music Row.

When the suspect's "unusual gait" was mentioned on the Crime Stoppers episode, Daniel immediately thought of D'Antonio. Daniel contacted his handlers at GBI and shared the information about selling D'Antonio the gun. When Detectives Pridemore and Postiglione came to interview Daniel, he told them Tony "looked like a goose" when he ran.

Daniel was definitely one of the prosecution's most vital witnesses. His direct examination testimony probably lasted over an hour—three or four times as long as most of the witnesses. The logical thing for the defense to do was to attack his credibility. Alderman tried to suggest that Daniel had gotten a sweet deal for testifying, but this attack couldn't have been very effective.

Thurman had already guided Daniel through the admission that he was a twice-convicted drug dealer. Daniel had already turned in D'Antonio as one of his drug smuggling co-conspirators when he saw the Crime Stoppers video. If given the maximum punishment, Daniel could have gotten ten years to life in prison. Instead, he had been sentenced to five months in prison, 30 months at a halfway house, and a $30,000 fine.

> Thurman: *And as far as your federal prosecution, you also lost several things as a result of that, did you not?*
>
> Daniel: *Yes. I lost my house, car, bank accounts, basically, started at zero.*
>
> Thurman: *So, they took everything you had, basically?*
>
> Daniel: *Yes. And left me with a $580,000 in federal tax debt.*

As Thurman pointed out later on, Daniel actually had nothing to gain by testifying in the trial. Since the late 1990s, he had become a successful and respected business owner in Chattanooga, as a long-distance provider.

Postiglione and Pridemore testified next, answering questions about the investigation, the arrest D'Antonio, and the statements he made during his arrest.

The last law enforcement officer to testify, Special Agent Tommy Heflin, answered questions about the projectiles that had been recovered from the crime scene and how they compared to the slug recovered from Daniel's backyard. [134]

"I've been doing this for 28 years," Heflin testified, "and there's no doubt in my mind that these four bullets were fired through the barrel of the same gun."

From what I saw of Tony D'Antonio in the courtroom and in the newspaper photos, he looked shrunken and depleted, maybe even resigned to his fate. I know there was still defiance in him because he never admitted anything, never apologized, never asked for forgiveness or even understanding. He could see that everything possible was aligned against him, that it was time to pay for his crimes. Yet, he was a true sociopath, and if you asked him, he would tell some baloney story about how he'd been framed, and that none of it was his fault. Everyone else was wrong and he was the true victim.

D'Antonio waived his right to testify, so the jury wouldn't be hearing much about his side of the story. The defense was content to simply contend that the state had not proven their case.

At a little after three in the afternoon, the state rested its case. Judge Wyatt turned toward the defense table and said, "OK, we're at the end of the state's proof, Mr. Alderman. Is there any proof to be offered by the defendant?" [135]

Alderman replied, "May it please the Court, ladies and gentlemen of the jury, the defense rests."

The judge thanked the jury and let them go early, advising them to get a good night's rest for tomorrow for the closing arguments and deliberation.

...

The jurors were excused for the day (page 800 of the transcript of Tennessee v. Richard D'Antonio, case no. 2002-c-1280). As I put the manuscript aside for a while, trying to picture the jurors and think about all the things they would be asked to consider as they decided on a verdict, I couldn't help feeling anxious, even though I knew how the story ended.

Tom Thurman and his staff had done a brilliant job of working with what they had. Detective Bill Pridemore and Pat Postiglione, who had by this time been promoted to the rank of sergeant, had put in countless hours pulling together the evidence the prosecutor needed. In the pretrial hearings section, I read over the hearings with the public defender and learned that Pridemore had been, in the months leading up to the trial, searching high and low, traveling hundreds of miles a week, trying to secure more tape-recorded conversations between Daniel and Richard D'Antonio.

These tapes had become the property of various alphabet soup agencies, including GBI, TBI, FBI, DEA, and others, and they were not going out of their way to help convict Tony D'Antonio. In one instance, Pridemore tracked one of the tapes to the Birmingham, Alabama field office of the FBI. In a phone call from Nashville, an agent in the Birmingham office said she would hand over the tape. Pridemore immediately traveled to Birmingham, but when he got there, the agent said no. The FBI wasn't going to release it, after all.[136]

Tapes of the interviews with eyewitnesses to the shooting on Music Row on March 9, 1989, had also disappeared. Pridemore had to testify in the hearings about this matter and provide the best explanation he could. The system of filing and storing tapes at Metro PD kept changing over the years. During active investigations, tapes were often stacked out in the open where anyone who needed access to them could get them. Over the years, tapes simply disappeared. He had searched, researched, and agonized, but there was nothing he could do about it. Fortunately, the written reports by the detectives who conducted the interviews still existed. Ross Alderman complained and questioned the accuracy and veracity of the reports. Pridemore admitted that sometimes, errors made their way into reports, but good detectives did their jobs as best they could.

The state's case was complicated and full of potential landmines such as these. There was no doubt in my mind that Richard D'Antonio was guilty and the jury probably thought so as well, but could they say he was "guilty beyond the shadow of doubt?" If they voted to convict, would the conviction stand up on appeal? If there was a hung jury, D'Antonio could walk away a free man.

Even if they voted to convict, the jury had a wide range of lesser charges to choose from other than the most severe, murder in the first-degree. Clearly, that's what it was, premeditated, cold-blooded, and done with malice and every other evil intent. The jury also had the choice of murder in the second-degree, which applied to a crime of passion (killing someone without planning ahead), or voluntary manslaughter, or even involuntary manslaughter.

On count two, the most severe charge was assault with intent to murder and causing bodily harm. That was for shooting me. Again, the jury could vote to convict on lesser charges all the way down to involuntary assault, which would apply if they decided that D'Antonio had shot me by mistake, or his gun misfired, which was in fact possible. But I hoped for the maximum on all counts.

The discussion of these details in the transcript ran for over 100 pages. When I put the transcript aside to finish in the morning, I imagined the jurors waking up and going back to the courtroom to ponder all the fine points of the law and then sifting through the evidence, the testimony, and the thoughts of each of the 12 jurors. Once again, I tossed and turned all night, wrestling with nightmares and panic attacks, as if the man in the black mask was still waiting in the dark to pounce all over again.

...

Thursday morning's session began at 9:19 a.m. Assistant District Attorney General Kathy Morante gave the first closing argument for the prosecution. District Public Defender Ross Alderman gave the closing argument for the defense, and Deputy District Attorney General Tom Thurman delivered the final closing argument for the prosecution.[137]

Alderman had some valid points. The prosecution's case was mostly circumstantial. He ridiculed the cat hair evidence and questioned the motives of Daniel. He also made light of the chart-fixing fraud at *Cash Box*, saying, "So what? They were influenced by money. That's the way the business world works."

The defense called no witnesses to prove any of these assertions and was not obligated to do so. "What we don't know beyond a reasonable doubt," said Alderman, "is if Richard D'Antonio was the gunman on March 9. I don't know it, they don't know it, and that, ladies and gentlemen, is reasonable doubt."

Thurman wrapped up his final argument with an appeal to the jurors' sense of right and wrong, contrasting the motives of Richard D'Antonio with the character of Kevin Hughes, saying:

"Richard D'Antonio is a cold-blooded murderer. Kevin Hughes died because he did what he thought was right, because he lived by the principles he was raised with. That's really all we're asking you to do, as a jury, is to do what's right, and do what's just, based on the evidence. But it's time for justice after 14 years for Kevin Hughes' murder by Richard D'Antonio."

It was almost noon by the time Judge Wyatt completed his instructions to the jury and excused them. After eating lunch, the jurors deliberated for almost seven hours, and at 6:09, they sent a message to the judge saying that they needed more time. Judge Wyatt had anticipated that and gave the jury the option of going to the hotel to have dinner, then returning to the courtroom to finish deliberating. They went to dinner. At 8:50 p.m., the jury came back, and Judge Wyatt turned to the jury foreman, Corman Hubbard.[138]

The Court: *Well, Mr. Hubbard, has your jury arrived at a verdict in this trial?*

Hubbard: *Yes, Your Honor; we have.*

The Court: *Would you please tell the Court what that verdict is?*

Foreman: *Yes sir. We, the Jury, find the defendant, Richard Frank D'Antonio, on Count 1, guilty of First-Degree Murder. On Count 2, guilty of Assault with Intent to Commit Second Degree Murder. This is our verdict, on the 25th of September 2003.*

The Court: *OK. Thank you.*

The verdict was unanimous. The long wait for justice was over. The district attorney was smiling. Addressing reporters outside the courtroom, he said, "We're happy with the outcome, it was a very difficult case."[139]

In his closing argument, Thurman mentioned that I was simply "in the wrong place at the wrong time" on the night of the murder. I appreciated that.

The official sentencing hearing was on November 7, and I was there. The defense entered a motion to dismiss the second conviction, assault with intent to commit murder, on the grounds that it had expired the two-year statute of limitations. It was the law—the judge had no choice; the motion was granted.

How did I feel about that? Sure, it was a little disappointing that D'Antonio got a "get-out-of-jail-free' card for the violence he had inflicted on me, but it would be ungracious of me to complain about it. The important thing was that there is no statute of limitations on first-degree murder, that a panel of citizens from Davidson County had looked hard at all the evidence in the case and found D'Antonio guilty of taking the life of Kevin Hughes and almost succeeding in taking mine. The judge affirmed the verdict and sentenced D'Antonio to life imprisonment.

D'Antonio had shaved for his appearance, but he didn't look much better than he had during the trial. The *Tennessean* used the same photo of him during their daily coverage of the trial. He was 57 years old. His wavy grey hair was thinning, the sides combed back in an old man's mullet. He reminded me a little of Wile E. Coyote.

D'Antonio was remanded to the Tennessee State Penitentiary at the Turney Industrial Complex in Clifton. Life imprisonment meant he would be eligible for parole in the year 2038. If he lived that long, he'd be 92 years old.

As I exited the courtroom, I was surrounded by reporters. I knew they wanted a statement. I was ready.

"Today has been a very hard day for us," I said. "It's a vindication day for Kevin and me. It's closure for us, and I hope Kevin's family and my family can move on. It's been a long 14 years to have to live with this, looking over your shoulder every day, all your life. And today is the day we can put this behind us and move forward."[140]

I took a breath there, a little surprised at how hard it was to get the first few words out. One of the reporters asked me what it had been like for me these past 14 years. "It's tough," I said. "I lived for five years of my life having constant nightmares. I don't go out at night by myself. It's affected me emotionally, mentally, physically. I'll never have the same mobility and use that I had in my right arm ever again. I've been on medications over the years – at one point close to a nervous breakdown. But you draw strength from God."

Someone asked about my gunshot wound. I gave a shout-out to the people at Vanderbilt Hospital and Dr. Meacham, the surgeon who had saved my arm and did what he could to repair it. "I probably wouldn't have an arm now if not for him," I said.

There were still more questions, about coping with what had happened, so I tried my best to put the years into words. "It's a night I'll never forget," I said. "I'm from a small town in Texas where people know everybody. You know, it's something you see on TV and in the movies. You don't think it'll ever happen to you. One person got shot, one got killed, but it doesn't just affect two people. It affects everybody's lives that are connected to those two people. It's been very hard for all of us."

Someone asked how I felt about the music business after this ordeal. Was I discouraged?

"You get down at times," I said. "But the fire never leaves you. You just doubt yourself sometimes. 'Is this really what I'm supposed to be doing? Do I really want to do this?' But I've got the fire back in me to do it. I'm not doing this just for me, I'm doing it for me and Kevin. Because no telling where both of us would be in our music careers if something like this hadn't happened to us. I just feel like it's something that's meant for me to be doing. God gave me a voice, and I feel like he wants me to use it."

I was only sorry I didn't get to speak to Kevin's family. They were there at the trial every day, and I could only imagine what it was like for them, hearing the testimony, sitting in the same room with the man charged with murdering their son, then hearing the verdict. They hugged each other after the verdict was announced.

The justice system couldn't bring back their son, but it had done what it's supposed to do, give people equal treatment under the law, and punish those who break it. I truly hoped it gave them a measure of solace.

It would have meant a lot to get to speak to them. I knew it might be too difficult for them, so I hoped that they would make the first move. It never happened. Maybe I should've made the effort, but I didn't have the strength to go through with it.

Outside the courtroom, Kevin's father, Larry, told Jim Patterson of the *Tennessean*, "I'm still shaking. It's going to take a while for our bodies and minds to absorb all this."

Kyle told the *Tennessean* that his family had never given up faith that the murderer would someday be caught and punished. "Justice was served today," he said.[141]

My own mother and father were relieved beyond words. After a very long day, I went to bed that night and slept like a baby. It was the first time since the night of March 9, 1989, that I slept without taking sleeping medication.

The blessings kept coming. Over the next few weeks, I took more calls from reporters, and my days were very busy, running my construction business as well as making plans to release an album. Earlier in 2003, I'd been working in the studio with a great bunch of musicians and producer Chet Hinesley. I finished the record that summer, not long before the trial.

The album was being released on a small independent label, Texas Records, on March 9, 2004—fifteen years after the murder on Music Row. After growing up wanting to be a country singer and entertainer, I was finally releasing my first album. There was a song on it written by Tom Paden and Ed Hill about the pain of breaking up, told from both sides of the story. When we finished recording and mixing everything, this song sounded like a single. The title seemed appropriate, so we used it for the name of the album—*Hard on a Heart*.

Chapter 17

The Sun Comes Out

Even if you're a country music fan, you may never have heard of Kevin Hughes. But along Nashville's Music Row, he's a fallen hero.

— "ABC News Primetime," November 10, 2003[142]

Life started to feel a little bit more normal for me. Instead of all that doubt and fear about what happened that night, we had clarity. The fact that Tony D'Antonio had crept up and shot Kevin and me was now part of the official record. From then on, when I was having a hard time sleeping at night (unfortunately, my insomnia returned after that first night of restful sleep following the trial), there was one thought that brought me some peace of mind: I was home in my own bed (or if I was on tour, in my bus or a decent hotel), and Tony D'Antonio was locked up in a cell in the state penitentiary.

After all these years, it felt so normal to go out every day and do the things a musician does without worrying if somebody's going to step out of a dark alley and start shooting at me. Instead of being paranoid all the time, my head was buzzing with the songs on my new album. I had a terrific band in the studio when we made the album: Mike Johnson on pedal steel, Steven Forrest on bass, Dan Justice on guitar, Jason Garner on keyboards, Mark Beckett on drums, David Russell on fiddle, and Roger Williams on saxophone. Working with Chet Hinesley was a real pleasure. He told me I was an "incredible singer" and that I had a "pure voice that flows naturally throughout the mix."

Chet was someone I really respected because he was a performer, songwriter, producer, everything. He had produced a couple of Doug Stone albums that were favorites of mine and a bunch of Jerry Reed records. In fact, we sent a copy of the record to Jerry to see what he thought of it, and he came back with a blurb that said, "I hate Sammy Sadler, because God gave him my voice."

Chet has also worked with Tony Joe White, another person whose music I've loved since I was a kid. Tony is Chet's uncle, and he was married to Jerry Reed's daughter.

The album collected a bunch of fine songwriters, including Tom Paden, who co-wrote four songs, including the title song, and four other songs co-written by John Wesley Ryles. At some point when we were making the record, I spoke to John Wesley, and he told me a couple of things about Chuck Dixon I'd never heard before.

John Wesley's office was right across the street from Emerald Sound, although he wasn't there the night Kevin and I were shot.

"Kevin practically fell in front of our building, you know," he told me, "and when it happened, I was just shocked and horrified that something like this could happen to you. I knew you weren't the kind of person to be involved in something that would cause you to get shot. A few days later, my manager and I were talking, and we came to the conclusion that we might know what did cause it to happen. I didn't know Kevin Hughes, and only met Chuck a few times. I just met Tony once. But we were talking and we just kind of figured it out. It was pretty common knowledge what they were doing, manipulating charts, using the independent chart to sucker these young artists, take their money, and promise them that they would be picked up by the major labels after they appeared on the independent charts in *Cash Box*. Kevin wasn't cooperating with them, so they killed him."[143]

The first time John Wesley ran into Chuck, he said, he bought a car from him. "I bought an '86 or '87 Lincoln Mark VII from him," he said. "It was only a year or so old. I needed a car because I was on tour a lot, and it was a real nice car, with little luxuries like keyless entry on the side, with a push-button code. I liked that."

One of the other times John Wesley ran into Chuck was during a songwriting session.

"A songwriter named Don Goodman got me involved in writing a song with him that Chuck had something to do with. I don't remember the name of it, but I remember writing part of it, and that was one of the first times I met Chuck. I, honestly, don't remember him being much in the room. I think he had the idea for it and he started it with Don. Don and I used to meet and write regularly, so at some point, Don and I worked on the song together, I can't remember any point where the three of us sat down in the room together.

"Anyway, we didn't finish the song, and I didn't think about it again until right after the murder when Don said, 'We need to finish that song,' and I asked, 'Oh, yeah, with Chuck Dixon? I don't want to be around him at all.' Don was a little naïve. He asked 'Why?' I said, 'Don't you think he was involved in this killing?' Don responded, 'Well, I don't think so.' I retorted, 'Well I do.' I think that was the end of it. We just left the song where it was because I didn't want to have anything to do with him."

After the release *of Hard on a Heart* in 2004, I did a radio tour. After that, I went out with the band, though we didn't work as hard as I had with Overdrive in the 1990s. One song from the album, "That Ole Gravel Road," written by Billy Lawson and Roger Murrah, turned out to be a real crowd pleaser at shows.

Hard on a Heart got some good reviews. Writing in *Country Weekly*, David Scarlett said that the album was "worth the wait."

"One thing's for certain, *Hard on a Heart* delivers on all the promise Sammy displayed all those years ago—and then some," said the review. "His vocals are strong and pure, and the obvious joy he takes in singing this great collection of songs confirms that, in spite of the long detour he was forced to take, Sammy's back on the road he was born to travel. He may say this album was nearly two years in the making, but in reality, it was closer to 15."

Writing in *Music Row* magazine, Robert K. Oermann said, "The steel-drenched production is superb, as is [Sammy's] performance..."

We released three singles, and they did well on the Texas charts. In February, I played the Country Radio Seminar in Nashville for the first time, and I played an invitation-only party for the industry at a club called The Trap, owned by Irv Woolsey, George Strait's manager.

That summer, I played in Sacramento and gave a speech at a conference for another big victim support organization, North American Victim Assistance. It was a good gig. When I gave my speech, it was nice to be able to talk about what had happened 15 years ago and, with the conviction, tell a complete story, instead of mystery plot with no resolution, no ending at all.

In the fall, I did an event with Bill Littleton, a unique and talented person who passed away in 2015, leaving a big hole in country music. Bill was an incredibly creative person, a singer/songwriter, music journalist, and a fiction writer, among other things. He was also an actor and had been in movies with Gregory Peck, Alan Arkin, and Tuesday Weld. I'll always treasure the nice piece he wrote for my album.

Sammy Sadler, Hard on a Heart

> *It's kind of hard not to know about this recording, stopped in the making some 14 years ago when Sammy and his friend, Kevin Hughes, were shot down right on Music Row. Kevin didn't survive the ordeal, but Sammy did, and this album*

is soaked with the bittersweet awareness that a great deal of life is "Hard on a Heart." Furthermore, this is an excellent collection of good songs, "good- meaning" songs that delve into life's complications. Quite refreshing, contrasted to the deluge of "You're-so-beautiful-I-can't-stand-it" rewrites we frequently hear on albums geared for today's radio-favored demographics. I'm particularly taken by "No Place to Land," written by Tom Paden and Sonny Steagall. I won't try to list all the songwriters, but they've collectively been delving into human emotions a long time, and Ole Sammy is ready to let the feelings flow. So, we have a very good first album by a guy who is essentially a Music Row legend for reasons that have little to do with singing. OK, it's time for the singing to be what we know Sammy Sadler for.

While I was in Nashville, a reporter for the *Tennessean* wanted me to walk with him down on 16th Avenue South. We stopped in front Evergreen Records, and I pointed out where it all happened, chills running up and down my spine the whole time. "This is part of me now," I told him. "Why one person lives and one dies, only God knows. I'm just glad to be alive and able to see the release of this album. I hope Kevin's up there smiling at us now. He wouldn't have wanted me to give up on my dream."[144]

The story was coming out on March 9, so I had a pretty good idea what the reporter would write. *15 years later... this Music Row victim is back where it began... hopes for a new start...* We both knew why we were here.

"I hope I won't only be remembered as the guy who survived the Music Row shootings," I told him, just before we said goodbye. "I hope to be known as a guy who put out the best country music he could."

I had a very busy summer, touring to support the record. When I finally came home to stay put for a while, I was happy. I spent some extra time with my family, thinking over all my blessings and how lucky I was. Monday morning, I got up early, had a cup of coffee, climbed in my truck, and left the ranch on Highway 121. I was out on the road all day, going from one job site to another, dealing with all sorts of issues. Work was just like I remembered it: one little knot of problems, one after another and laborious as hell. I loved it.

It was still sometime later that I finally got up the nerve to read the memorial page they printed in *Cash Box* after the shooting. Despite all the years, the weight of loss instantly returned, and I felt bad not just for myself and Kevin's family, but for the people who had written these heartfelt lines.

> *Kevin loved his job because he loved music. Among the tapes in his collection, one would find everything from Barry Manilow to Metallica. He was a devoted employee who spent endless overtime hours perfecting the country charts each week.*[145]

> *But more than that, Kevin was an All-American young man who dreamed of marrying a nice girl, having a few kids… white picket fences and all. He was not an advocate of vice—he championed the good things in life. He emanated an inner strength that is rarely found and, in his own special way, imparted it to others.*

> *It is with tremendous sorrow that we say goodbye to Kevin. However, we know that he has moved on to a greater existence and that it is we who are left to carry on in this imperfect world, having benefited from his generous spirit. We will miss him greatly.*

I put the old magazine down and brushed away a tear or two, thinking about how Kevin's friends and coworkers said he was "just a sweet kid," that he was "an innocent farm boy, honest and good," and it was all true. It's easy to exaggerate the good points of a person after they're dead, but Kevin's case, he was all those things.

I know it's one of the reasons the story of the murder on Music Row caught the attention of so many people because the contrast was so stark. It was good vs. evil, honest vs. dishonest, the corrupt vs. the straight arrow.

This was the theme in story after story in the media, and it came out loud and clear in one true crime show after another. Kevin's brother, Kyle, appeared in several of those programs, describing what Kevin was like, where he came from, and the kind of values he had. Dixon and D'Antonio were almost the perfect villains if you think about it. They came along and tempted Kevin, attacked his values, threatened and bullied him, and when he didn't break, they killed him. It took too long, but finally, they were found out, and now, the whole world knew what kind of men they were, along with the blatant corruption that had existed for so long—apparently, with very little outrage on the status quo from the public.

When Kyle was interviewed on "ABC Primetime," he explained that Kevin was murdered because he was trying to make *Cash Box* legitimate. "My brother was trying to clean it up and make it a reputable chart," he said. "That's what he was trying to do because he didn't want to work at a place where his integrity would be questioned at all."

When the producers of *Fatal Encounters* interviewed Kyle, he told them about the time Kevin called him and said he was troubled because a promoter wanted to take him to see a basketball game. Kevin loved basketball and really wanted to go, but he struggled with the ethics of accepting a ticket to a sports game from a promoter. It didn't seem that bad of a conflict, but Kevin decided not to go.

Just by knowing him, Kevin brought brightness into people's lives--like a good song, like the sun coming out on a cloudy day. I feel blessed just to have known him for a little while.

Chapter 18

Moving Forward

Toward the end of summer 2010, my mother, Juanita Sadler let go of her ailing body and went home to the Lord at the age of 77. Services were at our church, Living Word, in Bonham, and we laid her to rest at a little community cemetery a few miles south of Bonham out on Highway 121. She and Dad had been married 46 years, and other than Dad and God, she had been my best friend and biggest supporter all my life. I miss her every day. It took forever to get used to the idea that I couldn't pick up the phone and talk to her, no matter where I happened to be. As time went on, I realized I didn't need a phone to talk to her at all—she was with me all the time, and that made my grief a little easier to bear.

Ever since the release of *Hard on a Heart*, I'd been on the road a lot. Texas radio stations were supporting the record, but my label just didn't have the resources to take it nationwide. It was the same old story you hear from other musicians: Great record, and everybody who heard it, loved it. Too bad more people didn't hear it, but we didn't have the distribution or the promotion we needed.

Meanwhile, on the road, we were having a ball with fans. Starting in 2011, Doug Stone and I rolled out a long string of shows billed as *The Real Country Music Tour.*

Doug was a genuine platinum-selling artist, with eight No. 1 singles, including the Grammy-nominated song, "Better Off (In A Pine Box)." We both had our survival stories. Doug lived through a heart attack, a stroke, and a plane crash; I survived the murder on Music Row.

Another friend of mine in music, a great entertainer and survivor, T. Graham Brown, had joined me on an album called *What About the Victims.* "His T-ness," Mr. Brown, had survived alcoholism and being a wild man. "If right was right," he once said, "I'd be dead by now, but God has taken care of me." We all felt that way. As I told one interviewer, "It's a cliché, but between the three of us, our lives are like a bunch of beat-up old honky-tonk songs." I loved touring with these guys.

T. Graham Brown is a one-of-a-kind country/soul/gospel singer. From his early career up to his recent hit album, *Forever Changed*, Brown had done everything from Taco Bell and Kentucky Fried Chicken commercials to a duet on "Don't Sit Under the Apple Tree" with Broadway icon Carol Channing.

Doug and I went out on a second leg of *The Real Country Tour* in 2012, playing stages in Texas, Arkansas, Oklahoma, Louisiana, Missouri, Tennessee, Kentucky and then some. Starting in the early spring of that year, we were promoting my second album, *Heart Shaped Like Texas*—the beginning of another crazy chapter in my adventures with the record industry.

I was on a new record label. In 2000, Koch Records bought out the shares owned by the original founders of Audium Records, and the label became the Nashville division of Koch Records. Koch was one of the largest independent labels in the country. The Nashville division was no small operation. They released about 75 records and signed deals with Daryle Singletary, Cledus T. Judd, Deborah Allen,

Charlie Daniels, Dale Watson, Ray Benson, and Sammy Sadler. Not long after I signed with Koch, it was sold to a company called Entertainment One Music, which later changed its name to E1 Music. So far, so good.[146]

The A&R (Artists and Repertoire) man who signed me, Chuck Rhodes, was a Texan who grew up in Corpus Christi and had worked in radio in Dallas for over 11 years before he moved to Nashville in 1987. After we started getting to know each other, he told me he'd been following me for a good while and was a huge fan. I thanked him for that, and he responded, "No, I really mean it."

Chuck said to me, "Sammy, I'd love to work with you because, in my opinion, you have one of the few amazing voices left in our business. Pure and just amazing."

No matter how good you think you are, if you have a humble bone in your body, it sends a chill down your spine when someone you respect pays you a compliment like that, and I'll never forget it. So, we both had high hopes. The first single we released was a song by Steve Wariner and Bill Anderson, "I'll Always Have Denver." Steve Wariner came in and sang harmonies, which was another memorable experience. I'd been in awe of Steve's talent for years by then, and then he not only sang on my record but turned out to be one of the nicest guys I'd ever met. John Wesley Ryles—my friend as well as one of the most sought-after vocalists in the business--also sang harmonies on the record.

Jerry Cupit, the producer, was at the helm on Ken Mellon's first album, the one with the truly classic tune "Jukebox Junkie." Besides his gift for producing, Jerry was a songwriter, author, inventor, and a fountain of talent. He'd worked with Tim McGraw, George Jones, and John Anderson, to name a few. Cancer took him in 2014—too soon—he was 60 years old.

I've always loved gospel music, and on this album, we recorded "John 3:16," a song by Doug Deforest that really connected with me. "Thank God" originated when we were in Jerry's studio one day, and he said, "We need to have a song about your experience on Music Row, Sammy." So, Jerry picked up an acoustic guitar, and in about five minutes we wrote the first part of the song. It came to us so naturally; it felt like God just wanted us to write this song.

We had to put it aside to finish later, though, because I was heading back to Texas later in the day, and there was still work to do on some of the other tracks. After I left, Jimmy Carr came by the studio and picked up a tape of what we had so far and said he'd work on it that weekend. Jimmy was driving home to Hendersonville when the song started coming to him. The inspiration was so strong he had to pull over on the side of the road. He said he felt like God was talking to him.

> *I'll never forget, the house caught fire*
>
> *As I lay asleep the flames burned higher*
>
> *Ole Danny Boy jumped on my bed*
>
> *Barking so loud he could wake the dead*
>
> *Thank God, He was there, or I might not be here…*

A friend of Jimmy's had been saved from burning up in his house during his sleep because his dog started barking and got him up. Then there's a verse about being a ten-year-old and jumping out of the barn, thinking you can fly like Superman. It's only a miracle that you didn't break your neck. And the last verse is about the murder on Music Row, how God was there that night, and He saved my life, like so many other times. Otherwise, I wouldn't be here today.

> *Then one night down on Music Row*
>
> *A shot ran out, my blood ran cold*
>
> *Thank God, He was there, or I might not be here*
>
> *He's always been a friend down through the years*

He ain't the kind to turn and run, he never shows no fear

Thank God, He was there, or I might not be here

When Jerry called me the next day, he told me the story about Jimmy having to pull over and write down the rest of the song. In a way, I wasn't surprised to hear about it. I knew God wanted us to write this song.

After doing a radio tour, I went out with the band on the road again. We were getting radio support in both the U.S. and European markets. The title single, "Heart Shaped Like Texas," quickly made it to No. 5 on the European Top-40 Country Hot Disc chart. "Trying to Get the Girl" (written by Kim Tribble, Keith Follese, and Wade Kirby) made No. 5 on the Country Independent Top-20 and No. 5 on the European Top-40 Country Hot Disc chart.

There are more country music lovers in Europe than most people realize. In 2012, I was invited to play the British Country Music Awards. The event was at the Concorde Club at Heathrow, London's biggest airport. Playing for a crowd of country music fans over there, I couldn't help but pinch myself. This country boy had come a long, long way.

As an artist, you always remind yourself that you can't be discouraged by the bad things they say about you, and you can't get too puffed up by the good things they say, but it does feel nice when they recognize the good work you've done. Mario Tarradell of the *Dallas Morning News*, for example, doesn't go out of his way to praise just anyone, but he was very generous in his comments about the new material. "*Heart Shaped Like Texas* reminds me of the warmth and honesty country-pop music had in the early eighties, before mega-bucks and mega-sales turned much of it into slick rock disguised as country," he wrote. "When he sings 'I'll Always Have Denver,' it sounds like it was meant for him to croon."

In 2009, I played the CMA Music Festival again, riding high on the release of "I'll Always Have Denver." The festival originally started in 1972 as the CMA Fan Fair, but by the mid-2000s, it had become a four-day festival with multiple concert stages. The fans also get to meet the artists for autograph sessions inside the Nashville Convention Center. It's an incredible, one-of-a-kind opportunity for both the artists and the fans, and it's one of my favorite gigs every year. In 2009, we had crowds of 60,000-65,000 a day.

...

As it is with fish in the deep blue ocean and companies in the corporate world, the big ones are always gobbling up smaller ones. Sometimes the artists and other entities lower down the chain don't even notice the difference, and sometimes they end up getting left by the side of the road. We heard that a company in Canada was interested in buying E1 Music, but we didn't know for a while how it might affect the Nashville record division. Eventually, E1 sold for $81 million and, six weeks later, they shut down the country division.

My album was lost in the shuffle. Here was a record company that used to have Joan Baez and Ringo Starr, and had Nashville buzzing with excitement about Dale Watson, Cledus T. Judd, and Daryle Singletary, and then the new owners come in and decide to put their money into other kinds of music. It's their money, right? They saw big profits in pop, rap, hip hop, and metal. They signed up acts like Tupac, Crowbar, Black Label Society, and Big Moe, and began gobbling up television and film production companies. They also shut down the whole Nashville office and dumped us like yesterday's donuts, but again, it was their money and their right to spend it however they want to spend it.

I recently looked it up on Wikipedia and the list of film and movie properties they either bought outright or acquired large stakes in made my head spin. Nowadays the corporate entity goes by the name Entertainment One or eOne.

Long story short, the album *Heart Shaped Like Texas* got released, but in a more modest fashion than we had hoped. I had to put together deals for distribution and promotion through my own production company, S Records, and I was disappointed, but I had come too far to quit now.

So, I went out on the road doing what the Lord put me here to do: Sing, entertain, and tell my story.

...

One day in 1999, Nashville disc jockey Carl P. Mayfield received a package wrapped in crime scene tape. Inside was an unlabeled cassette tape of a new song by Larry Cordle and Larry Shell. When Mayfield heard the song, he liked it instantly, particularly the lyrics. [147]

> *Nobody saw them running*
>
> *From 16th Avenue*
>
> *They never found the fingerprints*
>
> *Or the weapon that was used*
>
> *But someone killed country music*
>
> *Cut out its heart and soul*
>
> *They got away with murder*
>
> *Down on Music Row*

Mayfield gave the tune a great introduction to the public. "He made a programming decision on his own without consulting anybody... He decided to let his listeners see if [the song] was right," said Larry Shell. "The first day he went on with it, he played it seven times from beginning to end, and it jammed his phones."[148]

Naturally, the first time I heard the title of the song, I thought it was going to be about Kevin and me. The song does start out that way, but then it does a neat trick, which is something that songwriters have done since the beginning of songwriting: A real event is used as a metaphor in another story. In this song, the "murder victim" isn't a human being, it's traditional country music, and the murderers are "the almighty dollar / and the lust for worldwide fame."

> *Steel guitars no longer cry*
>
> *And the fiddles barely play*
>
> *But drums and rock 'n' roll guitars*
>
> *Are mixed up in your face*

The song makes a valid point, and these two guys have the authority to make that point. Larry Shell and Larry Cordle are a couple of bluegrass pickers and traditionalist songwriters with a bunch of hit songs to their credit. Shell has co-written songs for Reba McEntire, Merle Haggard, Ricky Skaggs, Charly McClain, and others. Cordle has written songs for Ricky Skaggs, Alison Krauss, Garth Brooks, George Strait, Trisha Yearwood, Alan Jackson, and many more names. According to Cordle's website, his songs have sold "a combined total of more than 55 million records" at last count.[149]

"We actually noticed [the spurning of traditional country music] around 1994 or '95," said Larry Shell. "We noticed that our country songs were not being accepted very well. A&R people were starting to call us back and using the phrase 'too country.' I guess the song was written out of that frustration."

Ironically, lashing out with a bitter ballad turned into a good career move for Shell and Cordle. The first version of the song to be released was the one Larry Cordle recorded with his bluegrass outfit, Lonesome Standard Time, on the eponymously titled album, which was also the first record released by his label, Shell Point Records. The buzz of controversy and gossip added up to brisk sales and helped get Shell Point off to a running start. The original version of "Murder on Music Row" went to No. 1 on the Americana single and album charts and No. 1 on the bluegrass single and album charts.

That was just the beginning. Tony Brown at MCA played the song for George Strait, who invited Alan Jackson to record it with him. Released as the B-side to Strait's single "Go On," as a single, "Murder on Music Row" made it to No. 38 in the *Billboard* country singles chart. The Country Music Awards of 2000 put another feather in Cordle and Shell's hats when their song about the country music business having gone to hell was recognized with the award for Vocal Event of the Year and Song of the Year.

...

Sometimes, as the success of the song "Murder on Music Row" proves, it pays to put all your bitter lemons in a juicer and make lemonade. I guess you could call this book a barrel of lemonade. I thought about writing it for a good while before I sat down and wondered where to start: beginning, end, or middle? The disappointment I had with my second album gave me a chance to sit down and think about that.

I also wondered, for about the millionth time, how things might have gone differently if I hadn't gone by to visit Kevin that night? For one thing, he might still be alive. What about me? Without the stigma of that tragedy and scandal, I might be living in a mansion with gold and platinum records wall-to-wall. Putting it that way, it sounds like a petty, selfish dream. So, to heck with it, I don't ask that question anymore. I'd rather concentrate on moving forward, so that's what I do.

When I started writing this book, I realized that it couldn't just be a recitation of facts, dates, and people. A huge part of it was the equivalent of a murder mystery. As time went on, I found out who had shot us, and then, 14 years later, he was convicted and sent to the penitentiary with a life sentence. Why did it take so long? Who were the people who already knew who was guilty before the police knew? What was the killer's motive? Was it really all about chart fixing?

Seriously, toward the end of a lengthy interview with Robert K. Oermann on this subject, he threw his hands up in the air and said, "A murder over chart fixing? It's cracked, it's weird!"[150]

Why did so many people act as though they thought I was involved somehow in the motive or even the planning of Kevin's murder, if not the actual carrying out of the plan? The process raised a lot of questions that deserved answers. There is no statute of limitations on the truth.

I knew I had to go back there, physically and mentally, and attempt to see things as others might have viewed them, starting with the view from Music Row on that fateful night in 1989.

Everybody on Music Row knew the name Chuck Dixon. You could throw a rock in the air, and there was a good chance it would land on somebody who had done a piece of business or two with Chuck. On the night of March 9, 1989, when they looked out their windows and saw Kevin run down like a stray dog and shot to death by a masked man with a strange limp, a lot of them were probably able to put two and two together and reach a near-instant conclusion that Chuck Dixon was behind it all. Perhaps that knowledge made some of them feel not only fearful but guilty and ashamed. Those emotions created a toxic cloud that would cling to all of us for years and years to come.

Kevin's friend, Sharon Corbitt was at the top of my list of people to contact for interviews. "If there were weird feelings toward Sammy, or feelings of taint from the crime and corruption, it's only because of the uncertainty, the trauma of what happened," she said. "Kevin was innocent and kind and good, and Sammy was a good guy, talented and focused, and I liked him."

Sharon also praised the work I've done with victims' organizations like NOVA. "Survivor's guilt is hard to bear but, as Sammy has done, it's better to use what you've learned working as an advocate for victims of crime and violence," she said. "There couldn't be a better way to honor Kevin's life."

The survivor's guilt I carried for so long was, as Sharon said, hard to bear, and even harder to get beyond, and so was the "victim mentality" that afflicts people who have been struck by death, illness, war, and other traumatic experiences.

Sharon's words were wise and thoughtful, and I took them to heart. I sincerely, absolutely agree that it's better to be a survivor and an advocate for others who are suffering than to hang your head, cry about your troubles, and seek someone to blame.

Another person at the top of my list to talk to was John Wesley Ryles. John and I kept in close contact when I was writing this book. I asked him if he thought my career had been negatively affected, or tainted, by the murder on Music Row.

"Tainted is probably the best way to describe it, Sammy," he said. "I think most of them knew about the *Cash Box* situation and who the likely culprits of this terrible crime would be. It's such a shame, because there were a lot of people who did know what was going on, and they weren't going to talk. They were terrified."[151]

John seemed eager to get it off his chest, having thought about the case constantly over the years. "It was shocking to everybody," he said. "Nobody knew at the time if it was a robbery gone bad or a random thing, or what had happened, but look at the people who got hurt. You two guys were kids, basically, and I knew you didn't do anything to cause that to happen. When you told me [that] you were afraid to come back to Nashville because you didn't know what might be waiting there for you, I felt so bad for you. It was all just a terrible, terrible thing."

...

One night when I was on tour with Ken Mellons, he said he had a friend who wanted to meet me. "His name is David Williams," he explained. "When I told him [that] I was touring with you, he told me he was the first policeman on the scene the night of the shooting."

"I'd like to meet him, too," I said.

What an unexpected gift this turned out to be. Yes, of course I was interested in meeting David, but it worked out to be a great deal more than a simple meet-and-greet after 27 years.

David and I talked a little and hit it off immediately. He was eager to meet and explain a few things about what happened that night on Music Row, beginning with—of all things—an apology. Meeting David was the beginning of a very special relationship.

David had retired in 2006, after serving more than 20 years as a Nashville policeman. He told me he was still haunted and disturbed by his experiences on the night of March 9, 1989. As you may recall, earlier in the book, I quoted David extensively on his experiences as the first cop to arrive at the scene of the crime.

When he arrived at the crime scene on 16th Avenue South, David saw the blood in the street, the growing crowd around Kevin's corpse, and the trail of my blood that led up the sidewalk and then up the stairs to Phillip Barnhart's apartment. As the first cop on the scene, David found himself in "a hell of a quandary," as he put it. He was faced with an active shooter on the loose, an unsecured crime scene, and a wounded victim. David chose the higher responsibility, which was to render aid to the wounded (me).

After David found me and ascertained that I was in good hands and an ambulance was on the way, his next duty was to secure the crime scene. Simultaneously, I was going into shock, and when he tried to tell me he had to leave my side, I went into what he called "full-blown panic mode," and begged him not to go.

David was full of guilt as he told me these things when we met. "You don't remember any of this, do you?" he said.

"No, not really," I said. "I don't remember you at all."

What I could not remember, he had been unable to forget. "You were going into shock," he explained. "You hadn't said anything to me up until that point, but I kept talking to you. Meanwhile, I'm thinking, I've got to get an ambulance here and get the crime scene under control. The woman was still applying direct pressure, so I thought, 'He's conscious, losing blood, but I can't do anything about that. I told her to keep applying direct pressure while I would go get the crime scene back under control, but when I told you I was leaving, I'll never forget it, you just went into a complete freakish panic mode. You were reaching out toward me, saying, 'No, you can't leave me. He's gonna come back and finish me off…'"

Hearing David share his side of the story, the source of his own traumatic memories, was a surreal experience, and totally unexpected. Here was a former Nashville cop, 27 years later, asking me for forgiveness and understanding.

"You don't know how bad I felt when I left you there," he said. "I knew how scared you were, and I was your protection, and I had to leave you there. I can just imagine how scared you were. I just felt bad."

I'd been angry with the Metro police ever since the murder. They seemed to have no empathy, no understanding, and no ability at all to see things from my side. On top of that, I had never understood why it took them 14 years to solve the crime. All those years I had those bad feelings in my heart, David Williams was with suffering regret and remorse for doing his duty in a complicated situation. Time and time again, he said he'd thought about what it must have felt like to feel the terror and the pain I was in. Now, at last, he was able to reach out and ask for my understanding.

I told him I understood. I also told him I was thankful that God had brought us together.

We met several times again and talked at length. He was shocked and disappointed when he heard how I had been treated by Pridemore and Postiglione, that I was always treated either as a suspect or as a hindrance to their investigation and suspected of withholding vital information about the case.

"I never asked them about the case," David explained. As a patrol cop, he said, "You normally turn things over to the detectives assigned to the case. Most of the time, you never hear about it again."

"I can't believe they never apologized to you," he said. "After having put in 20 years as a policeman, I have to say I feel ashamed. I mean, not only did you watch your friend die, you were shot and almost died."

Through my ongoing friendship with David, I gained a lot of insight and knowledge about the case. David helped me obtain the police files, a process that turned out to be more laborious than it should have been, but the trouble was well worth it. He also repeated his story for the taped interviews, going over his experiences that night in detail. He also shared insight into the history of the Metro Police Department for the decade or so prior to the shooting.

...

By the time I started writing the book, Tom Thurman had retired from the D.A.'s office. Pat Postiglione had also retired. Myra Langlois and her husband had moved to Colorado. Judge Randall S. Wyatt, Jr. announced his retirement shortly after the book got underway. Between people changing addresses, going on vacations, and other complications, it wasn't easy to track down everyone I wanted to hear from. I felt awkward about asking some of them to communicate with me directly, not to mention the fact that interviewing people isn't one of my skills.

Bill Pridemore serves on the Nashville Metro Council now, representing the Madison and northeast Davidson County areas. I wasn't surprised to hear that Bill still thought I had not been completely honest with them, but I was relieved to learn that he was considerably more put off by Chuck Dixon.

"Chuck and some of the others used both violence and intimidation," he said. "These independent promoters reminded me of used car salesmen. Chuck's tactics were a little bit underworldish, and I guess some of the people in the business he was dealing with, even though they're bottom-feeders too, were afraid of him. Chuck was bigger and badder than they were, but he operated in the same filthy world."[152]

Pat Postiglione retired from the force in the last year or so with a list of some of Nashville's most sensational criminal cases solved under his leadership. He also has a reputation for being a really nice guy.

"We had to, you know, kind of push his buttons, because, in order to clear someone, you've got to get them to tell you what they know," Postiglione explained to the interviewer. "We didn't think Sammy was guilty of anything, except maybe unknowingly being used by someone so that they would know where Kevin was going to be, because, how did they know? Did they follow them? And why did he let Sammy go? We had to ask that question? It was a big question."

Both detectives were deeply concerned with the question of how the shooter had known where Kevin would be that night. For some people, including me, it's not a hard question to answer. As I've stated earlier, following us would have been relatively easy. Hiding in the shadows, waiting for Kevin to return to his car would also have been a simple thing to do.

"Now, Bill may have pushed him a little harder than I did, but he was the lead detective," said Postiglione. "You have to remember, we had a killer running around who shot Sammy and then went up to Kevin and coldly shot him and then walked up to him and shot him several more times in the head. I mean, I hope we left it on good terms."[153]

Near the end of writing this book, we managed to speak with Myra Langlois, the former investigator for the Davidson County D.A. I had seen Langlois in brief scenes from an undercover video in the "Cold Case Files" episode "The Hitmakers." Unfortunately, the narration in the show doesn't explain where the video came from, except to say that it's from a "separate investigation... a sting on an operation similar to the one they claim was run at *Cash Box*... to illustrate how shady promoters work, bribing chart makers... [and] making no-talent singers believe they're about to become a star."

Later, I learned that the subjects of the sting operation were Chuck Dixon and Robert Metzgar. Langlois's performance in the video also made me look forward to hearing her recollections of the case. In the video, she plays an amateur country singer who is extremely ungifted and tone deaf, but very enthusiastic. She puts herself at the mercy of a white-haired producer in a recording studio, and the producer repeatedly assures her that she sounds great and she's going to be a big success.

The producer offers encouragement and offers the following advice: "Can you give me that kind of laid back, kind of sloppy approach, like you did on the last song? It's kind of like a person who's had one drink too many and really feels good?"

The following are excerpts from the interview our research team arranged.[154]

> Interviewer: *What was the set-up in this sting operation?*
>
> Langlois: *I was supposed to be a country music singer, represented by Robert Metzgar. He had promised me that Chuck Dixon was the big promoter that was going to make me a star.* Cash Box *was defunct by then, and they had these faked internet charts where they promoted my songs. They got me up to No. 3 with a bullet.*
>
> Interviewer: *They thought they had you hooked?*
>
> Langlois: *Oh yeah, we paid them about $10,000. I had done three songs and they wanted me to do an album. My stage name was Beth Watts.*
>
> Interviewer: *Did they actually distribute records or CDs?*
>
> Langlois: *Back then they were cassette tapes. They just made cassette singles.*

Interviewer: *Who is the producer in the studio with you on the video, the white-haired guy?*

Langlois: *That's Robert Metzgar, he's the one who said, "sing drunk." He's just a sleazeball. He was bilking a lot of people out of their life savings at the time. That's why we opened the investigation. We had so many complaints against him and Chuck Dixon. Unfortunately, Chuck died before we could press charges.*

Interviewer: *I've been told by another detective that you can't sing a lick.*

Langlois: *Oh God, no, I can't. That's why they picked me for the job. I can't sing worth a damn. I sound like three cats in a burlap sack. And because my husband, Bob Langlois, was in the music industry, we ran in music circles, those parties and stuff, so I knew the lingo, I could pull it off. Nobody else in our office at the time could've done that.*

Interviewer: *As I understand it, Bob worked for a production company in Nashville, working for touring bands?*

Langlois: *When I met him, he had just gotten off the bus with Conway Twitty. He worked for Reba McEntire and others. Now he owns an audio company.*

Interviewer: *The songs you were performing sound pretty bad, too.*

Langlois: [laughs] *My cousin had written those songs when he was a teenager and kept them in his underwear drawer. "Every Time I Look for Love I Go Blind" was the one that went to No. 3 with a bullet on Metzgar and Dixon's chart. The others were "Love Enough for Two" and "When Hell Froze Over."*

Interviewer: *We didn't realize there even was an investigation into Chuck Dixon before he died.*

Langlois: *There definitely was an investigation. Chuck didn't know he was being investigated until he found out about the search at his house. He threatened to kill me when he found out.*

Interviewer: *How did that come about?*

Langlois: *Metzgar told me. Chuck told Robert Metzgar I was just trying to "make my bones," you know, that old mob expression. Metzgar came and told us that Chuck had threatened to kill me, and he said that since he had known Chuck, he had had other people killed. Now, this is before he told us what he knew about Kevin Hughes. But later, we got him to tell us about it, and with all the other evidence we had against him, he pled to a reduced charge, and agreed to provide testimony for the Kevin Hughes trial.*

Interviewer: *There's a theory that since so many people on Music Row did business with Chuck Dixon, the overall community felt a shared sense of guilt about the murder on Music Row. Unfortunately, those people recovered from their sense of shame, but Sammy's career did not, even though he was innocent.*

Langlois: *Sammy Sadler didn't do anything. He didn't have anything to do with his murder. He was just there. Kevin was murdered because he threatened to expose Tony and Chuck Dixon's scamming at* Cash Box. *Sammy had nothing to do with it.*

Everybody on Music Row benefitted from the scamming because all the tiny labels had Chuck promoting them. That's how anybody got anything in Cash Box.

Interviewer*: If you look at the old issues of* Cash Box *(available online at www.americanradiohistory.com), you can see all the different artists being advertised in* Cash Box *and promoted by Chuck Dixon and his cohorts, and a lot of those artists went on to become gold and platinum selling artists.*

Langlois: *Everybody started out that way. Pay for play. It's just the way it was back then. It just so happened that Chuck Dixon was a mobster. A lot of people in the industry were mob-connected back in the* Cash Box *days, but D'Antonio and Dixon were real mobsters.*

Interviewer: *Do you mean that in the sense of "Nashville Mob" or the real mob?*

Langlois: *No, the Italian mob, the Mafia. They were from the Philadelphia Mob.*

Interviewer: *So, it was basically payola, or one form of it, anyway.*

Langlois: *Pay for play, the mob shit, it still goes on today. It's more sophisticated than in the* Cash Box *days. Back then you actually had to spin a record on a radio station to get a rating on a legitimate chart. Licensing companies like BMI could document how many plays a record got and so forth, but with* Cash Box *you just took your money to Chuck and paid for your ad. It was more a complicated process at Billboard, but they did pay-for-play, too.*

It was a cesspool that bred the kind of thing that happened to Kevin. He was a Christian boy who went to a Christian college and was outraged when he found out what was going on and wanted to do something about it. He didn't have the good sense to keep his mouth shut, telling them that he would turn them in, and it got him killed. The whole thing resulted from that.

Interviewer: *This is great. Do you have anything else to add?*

Langlois: *I don't know if it means anything to Sammy, but I was deeply involved in that case for a long time, and you can tell him, he had nothing to do with it, he has nothing to feel guilty about. It was a horrible situation that resulted in Kevin Hughes' death, and what happened to Sammy Sadler.*

It's not part of my life now, but at the time, for a year or two, that was my whole life...that industry.

Chapter 19

Blessings

Nashville legend Owen Bradley had nothing against independent record labels and promoters. In 1946, recording under the name Brad Brady and His Tennesseans, he released a single
called "Zeb's Mountain Boogie" on his own label, Bullet Records,
and later, his band had two hit records on Coral, a subsidiary of Decca. Bradley had deep scorn, however, for the independent promoters
and custom record label operators who scammed Music City visitors
with rip-off record deals and bogus schemes. [155]

In the late 1970s, during Owen Bradley's fourth decade in the
music business, he was on a board of music industry leaders committed to ridding Nashville of the scourge of these "parasites" through
increased prosecution, oversight, and public awareness. Bradley, along
with Dutch Gorton, Secretary-Treasurer of Local 257 of the American Federation of Musicians, and Rose Palermo, an attorney who
represented a number of victims of the rip-off artists, and others, were
actively discussing solutions to the problem with Assistant District
Attorney General Bob Strong.

Attention to music fraud seemed to be peaking in 1977 when the state Division of Consumer Affairs was investigating 50 complaints by songwriters against a single producer, and the Davidson County D.A.'s office, the FBI, the SEC, and several other agencies were pursuing action against various other producers and companies. The *Tennessean* ran one of their periodic exposés on the prevalence of music fraud, including one article titled "How Not to Become a Star in Nashville's Record Industry." The CBS program "60 Minutes" aired an investigative report. One of the most egregious of the rip-off promoters was convinced to get out of the music business entirely. Another one agreed to move to Florida.

According to the state attorney general's office, in the pre-Chuck Dixon era, Glenn "Tex" Clark was the most prolific of the rip-off artists on Music Row. Undeterred by a prior conviction for mail fraud, Clark had been peddling his services in Nashville since 1966. Clark's Brite-Star Promotions, along with 11 other dodgy music enterprises, operated from an office above Spanky's Sandwich Shop at 26 Music Square East. Clark was one of four promoters who split the profits from a deal in which they charged Mr. and Mrs. Kenneth Kirby, from Orlando, Florida $15,980 to press 34,000 copies of their record "One More Whiskey, Please," after convincing them it was a hit.[156] Six months later, the Kirbys received a check for $18.33, representing their royalty share on the sale of 87 records.

Grifters like Tex Clark, Cliff Ayers Ostermeyer, and Robert Metzgar found their victims not only by trolling Shoney's but through classified ads ("Singers Wanted"), songwriting contests, and talent shows in towns that were hundreds of miles from Nashville, sending out "talent scouts" who would build up their victim's hopes, lure them to Nashville for demo sessions, and often, take them and their families for every cent they could lay their grubby hands on. In one of the most common pitches, the promoter would offer to produce a demo session (costing up to $1,500—$2,500 or more) and send out 100 copies to deejays and/or record companies, after assuring the victim that effort was an almost sure-fire way of securing a contract with a major label. The victim was also often induced to sign a management contract, and it would cost them additional thousands of dollars for "management services."

Many of these victims should've known better, but still, I felt terrible for the guy who giddily told a reporter that he'd signed a deal with Capitol. After the story was published, an employee at the real Capitol Records office had to phone the poor guy with the bad news, saying, "I'm sorry to tell you this, but no one at Capitol Records has ever heard of you. Unfortunately, you apparently signed a contract with that white-haired parasite, Robert Metzgar, who calls his company Capitol Management and Promotions."

All these practices were common in the pre-Chuck Dixon era, that is, before Tony D'Antonio took the helm at *Cash Box* magazine in the late 1980s with the blessings of Tom McEntee and George Albert. When Chuck Dixon hooked up with Tony D'Antonio and basically took over *Cash Box*, their brand of pay-to-play benefitted from the reforms that went into effect after the first big payola scandal of the 1960s. That is, the decision-making power at radio stations was taken away from the individual deejays and given to the station programmer. Thus, promoters only had one person to promote to (or bribe or extort) for their clients.

In 1986, "NBC Nightly News" did a big report on a federal investigation of what they called "The New Payola." It was touted as the most intense investigation of the music industry in 25 years.

According to the NBC report,

> *A small but powerful group of perhaps 30 independent record promoters can influence which records get played on Top-40 radio.*

> *These promoters, known in the business as 'The Network,' used cash payments, cocaine, women, free trips and even threats to get their records played on the radio...*

Allegedly, "The Network" was being paid up to $80 million a year to get their clients' records on the radio.

Indictments were being prepared against some of the biggest names in the independent promotion business: Joe Isgro, Ralph Tashijian, and Frank DiSipio, to name a few. Joe Isgro was credited with making the careers of Michael Jackson, Madonna, Elton John, Billy Joel, and other megastars. Isgro, DiSipio, and others were also alleged to have ties to organized crime.

The record labels reacted in a chorus of knee-jerk reactions. Almost every major label, including Capitol-EMI, WEA, RCA, CBS, PolyGram, MCA and A&M, dropped their independent promoters. The labels issued statements saying they had "no knowledge of any wrongdoing or illegal activity" committed by the independent promoters in their employ. But, don't believe it for a minute. No one pays $80 million without knowing where that money is going and how it's being handed out.

A few promoters swept up in the "New Payola" wave ended up serving prison time. Joe Isgro's case was thrown out of court, but a few years later, he served time for loan sharking and extortion. Isgro was back in court again in 2014, answering charges that he was part of a sports betting operation run by the Gambino organized crime family.[157]

Another aspect of the "New Payola" years was the practice of including a budget for radio promotion or tour support in artist contracts with the major labels. A longtime friend of mine who managed several rock bands in the seventies and eighties explained how that budget was dispersed. "When we signed the contract with CBS, they told me, 'This $80,000 is for radio promotion,' and told me to hire these guys," said my friend. "'That's a lot of money,'" I told them. 'I'll have to ask how many spins this amount of money is going to buy.' The record company guy shook his head and said, 'Oh, no, you don't want to be asking these guys questions like that. Just give them the money, they'll know what to do.'"

In the 2000s, the practice of pay-to-play got a new name, "Corporate Payola." Napster and other new technology offered new, cheap alternatives for listening to recorded music and sharing it, often in ways that were technically illegal. The big record companies freaked out, went to court, lobbied Congress, and finally settled for adapting these technologies for their own enrichment.

The recording industry survived, payola evolved, and despite the new technologies, commercial radio was still the most effective way to get people to love your records.

In 2004, New York Attorney General Eliot Spitzer and the Federal Communications Commission were investigating record companies and radio stations suspecting of engaging in various pay-to-play practices. Feeling the heat, many record labels announced policy changes before the investigation was completed. Infinity Broadcasting, the second-largest radio broadcaster in the country, fired a programmer who had been exposed for accepting gift certificates from record companies, which had become a convenient substitute for cash. One label admitted that $1,000 worth of Best Buy certificates had recently been sent "in care of" the programmer. They were supposedly for promotional giveaways at radio stations, but it's doubtful that anybody at the label was checking up on that. Promoters had also adopted a practice of paying radio stations $100,000 or more annually. The promoters claimed that the money wasn't payola, just a fee to get sneak peeks at their playlists.[158]

In 2005, Spitzer nailed the hide of Sony BMG to his trophy wall. Among other things, Spitzer had unearthed a treasure trove of damning emails, including one from an executive complaining "Two weeks ago, it cost us over $4,000 to get Franz [Ferdinand] on WKSE. That is what the four trips to Miami and hotel cost." And another sleazy promotion by Epic (owned by Sony BMG) from 2002 came to light. Epic had sponsored a contest in which listeners of Infinity Broadcasting stations could win a trip to see Celine Dion play at Caesars Palace in Las Vegas. Infinity's part of the deal: 13

of their stations had to add Dion's new single, "Goodbye's (The Saddest Word)."

In July 2005, Sony BMG agreed to a settlement under which they acknowledged they had broken the law and agreed to pay a $10 million fine. Spitzer said the funds would benefit, in part, independent musicians who had been frozen out by the record label's payola schemes.[159]

It's been 12 years now, and I'm still waiting for my cut.

Satellite radio, which first came online in 2001, meant hundreds of additional channels for listeners to choose from, but not necessarily more places at the table for lesser-known artists. Sirius Satellite Radio launched the year after its bigger rival, XM Radio, merged with the latter in 2008 to become Sirius XM. According to their Wikipedia page, their business strategy is largely built around "exclusive deals with big-name entertainers and personalities to create and build broadcast streams from the ground up." That's why the big names in satellite radio are Howard Stern, Martha Stewart, Steven Van Zandt, Jimmy Buffet, and so on. On SiriusXM, you'll find a handful of channels devoted to country music, including Willie's Roadhouse and Outlaw Country, and several devoted to country hits.[160]

Today, music streaming services have become the big, new thing, or if you want to use a snappy cliché, "playlists are the new radio." You don't have to worry about scratched vinyl or misplaced CDs, plus subscriptions are relatively cheap, and some of them are free. Spotify is the biggest one by far, leaving its rivals Apple Music and Pandora far behind.[161]

The music industry is currently recovering from a 20-year slump, thanks largely to Spotify and other streaming sites. Record companies saw streaming sites bring in $3.4 billion in 2016, which was more than half (51 percent) of their retail music income that year. In the first six months of 2017, the figure rose to 62 percent--a 17 percent increase. According to *Variety*, "digital music is reversing the fortunes of an industry that has seen more than a decade of revenue declines. On a retail basis, music industry revenue grew 11.4 percent in 2016."

Aside from the royalties that trickle down to the music creators, streaming has the potential for helping artists reach new fans and build a following, but it's also open to a new and legal form of pay-to-play called "playlist payola." According to an article in *Digital News*, "the biggest playlists on Spotify aren't organic, they're bought-and-sold like radio playlists of old.[162] Which means it's nearly impossible to get discovered with great music alone (just like before)."The power to draw up those playlists, according to *Digital News*, is "increasingly controlled" by Universal Music Group, Sony Music Entertainment, and Warner Music Group. The three labels collectively own "a very substantial" share of Spotify, and they either own or control other streaming services.

A 2014 article in *Billboard* by Glenn Peoples gave the following menu of prices: $2,000 for a playlist with tens of thousands of fans, and up to $10,000 for the bigger ones.

The major labels control the playlists, and they're not embarrassed about it. In May 2016, Warner Music Group became the first major label to announce that streaming was its primary revenue source. Just in case you were thinking that playlists might give the little guy a better chance of making an impact without a big record deal, Warner CEO Stephen Cooper has news for you:

"Playlisting," he said, "is one of the big reasons why artists need record labels today."

The major labels have the money and the power, and they're not shy about using it. These giant corporations have to tell their stockholders and Wall Street how much their earnings are going to be a year in advance. You may ask, "How can they know how many records they'll sell that year?" A record label CEO might say they know a hit when they hear one--they're the tastemakers of the world.

A friend who was an executive at MCA Records who once told me, "We can take a bum off the street and put him in the studio singing 'Old McDonald Had a Farm,' and we can make that bum famous, make him No. 1 around the country." He said it would cost them $500,000, but that was in the 1990s so it would cost two or three million or so today.

...

As dismal as all that sounds, I still believe that the little guy has a chance to make it in America. It does seem to have gotten a lot harder, but as long as there's business, there's going to be corruption. Sadly, that's just the way it is. Some of us have to make an honest living and make the best of whatever breaks come our way.

As awful as the music business is, I still love Nashville and the people there, and I love making music more than I ever did.

The last few years have been good to me, and I've been on the road a lot. After the *Real Country Music Tour*, I took a short break to record with producer Greg Cole (Aaron Tippin, Daryle Singletary, and Rhonda Vincent) and started a national tour with Ken Mellons called *Takin' the Country Back Tour*. Our first show in 2015 was in Nashville at the Station Inn, broadcast live around the world on 650 AM-WSM. We began the tour as a double-bill with Ken and me, and later, Jeff Carson joined us to make it a triple-trouble bill.

Playing shows with Jeff Carson was a real treat. First of all, he's a star and a fantastic performer who's had a bunch of hits (including the No. 1 single "Not on Your Love"). Poor management and lack of radio support caused Jeff to retire from the music business and take a job as a full-time police officer in Franklin, Tennessee. Ken and I were able to coax him out of his musical retirement to join us on tour. We put on a 90-minute, high-energy show, and every night, we closed the show trading lead vocals on Ken's signature hit, "Jukebox Junkie."

We played to crowds of 300 to 8,000, in all kinds of places—The Barn, in Dixon, Missouri; the grand Texan Theatre in Greenville, Texas; Tater Melon Day in Fayetteville, Tennessee; and back to Nashville for the CMA Festival again. What a thrill, playing on the banks of Cumberland River for a sea of country music fans, on the same bill with longtime friends and personal heroes.

...

In the summer of 2013, the *Fatal Encounters* episode on the murder on Music Row aired for the first time on the Discovery Channel. The producers did an okay job, but by this time, I had lost track of all the different true crime programs that had told our story. They all seemed to get a few things right and a few things wrong. I guess that's another reason I wanted a crack at telling it myself.

In 2014, I learned that Richard F. D'Antonio had died in prison.[163] By that time he had been incarcerated in the special needs section of the prison. I don't know what kind of illness he had, but the producers of "Fatal Encounters" used portions of a prison interview with him in the program. Even from what I knew about D'Antonio, I was a little surprised to hear him claim he was innocent. He said that the police had framed him.

Instead of feeling anger, I felt pity for him. I also felt bad for his son and the other family members he left behind. I sincerely hope that in last year or so remaining of his life, he found the wisdom to admit his guilt and ask the Lord for forgiveness.

When I was looking through the songwriter catalog on BMI recently, I remembered that he was supposedly an aspiring songwriter for a while, and I was startled to find at least 65 songs registered under his name and an alternate spelling, which could be his son (There are three entries, "D Antonio, Richard Frank; Guitarus Maximus (Tony's publishing company), and D Antonio, Richard Anthony. The apostrophe in "D'Antonio" is missing).[164] Some of the song titles, such as "Penitentiary Blues," "City Where the Deals Go Down," "Angry Young Man," and "Marijuanaville," suggest that the songs might be autobiographical. After spending more time doing online searches, I learned that Tony D'Antonio's son, Rick D'Antonio, has released some of his father's songs through CD Baby and other sites, performing under the name "Rich Rhocks." In his bio, he says he's been influenced by the country music he grew up with in Nashville, as well as Stevie Ray Vaughan, Metallica, and Ozzy. He mentions that he played guitar on his father's demos.

In the year 2017, he turned 40. That's all I know.

...

For years and years, between the sleepless nights and PTSD panic attacks, I was full of anger and resentment because the murder on Music Row had, I believed, taken my shot at success away from me. Some of that resentment was targeted toward the Nashville music business (the big labels, the CEOs, and the decision-makers), the community of Music Row (who seemed to view me with suspicion and doubt), the Metro detectives (who never took my word when I proclaimed my innocence), the media and the rest of the community (who never rallied to my cause), and countless other groups and individuals. Resentment is a radioactive emotion, however. After a while, it does more damage to you than the target.

No doubt about it, the .38-caliber rounds fired from that stubby revolver on the night of March 9, 1989 traveled a long, long, long way—not only piercing my body and taking the life of a good and innocent man, my friend, Kevin Hughes, but ricocheting throughout Music Row and beyond for years and years to come.

But today I realize that those bullets did not steal my career away from me; the stigma from that night did not take away my shot at success. There's a much bigger picture to look at, and with God's help and mercy, I've been able to take the longer view, and I've been blessed with greater peace and humility.

And, as I said at the beginning, no bullet is going to stop me from pursuing my dream and my inspiration. Corruption in the music business isn't going to discourage me, either. I'm going forward with my life, and I feel good about it. I feel blessed.

Like everyone else, there are times when I get down and question everything. One day, in the middle of working on a new record, I suddenly stopped and asked myself what I was doing. Was it worth it to continue putting myself out there, touring and recording? Considering all the odds stacked against me, I became depressed and surly, like the old days. At some point I talked to Chuck Rhodes and got it off my chest.

"Is it worth it, Chuck?" I said. "I mean, who needs another country singer? Maybe I should just concentrate on the construction business, take it easy, and leave the music business behind."

"Sammy, listen to me," he said. "I've told you before what I think of you, but I'll tell you again. Yours is one of the few amazing voices left in our business. You're a great entertainer."

Chuck went on, and I listened. He reminded me that when I put a record out, I'm on the same playing field as Tim McGraw, Alan Jackson, and Brad Paisley. Those guys happen to be on major labels, which means they have tons of money behind promotion, distribution, and tour support.

"You went out on the road and work over 200 days a year and you've kept that pace up," Chuck added. "Over the years, you've built a really, really big fan base, loyal fans, people who love your music. Those people will buy a ticket to see you whenever you come to their town."

I thanked Chuck for the pep talk and got back to work on my album. I think it's going to be my best work yet. When I selected the songs, I searched out my favorite songwriters, like John Wesley Ryles and Steve Wariner, and came up with "Louisiana Rain" and "Everything is Gonna Be Alright." I wanted some old favorites, too, and I recorded "I Can't Get Close Enough," a song by the band Exile that was always on the radio the year after I moved to Nashville.

I knew I had to put "Takin' the Country Back" on this album. Curtis Wright and Marty Stuart wrote it, and John Anderson had a huge hit with it. When I play it at my shows, it always brings the audience to their feet, stomping and hollering. I think we did the song justice this time in the studio, too. We even brought John Anderson in to sing with me on it.

Finally, I always knew I wanted to come back to "Tell It Like It Is." It was the record I had out in March 1989, and I think it could've been a big hit for me. It's a classic, beautiful song. Today I'm a little older and, I hope, a little wiser. When I play this song in my shows, I hope what I've lived through will touch people who might benefit from hearing my story.

As I look back on my life and everything I have been through, I honestly know God has had his hand on me and has been carrying me every step of the way. I gave my life to Christ over 20 years ago, and because of my faith and trust in Him, I can live and move on. When Jerry Cupit, Jimmy Carr, and I wrote the song "Thank God," I realized it was more than just a song to me because without Him I really wouldn't be here today—I am nothing without Him.

To all those I have met along life's highway and have had the chance to play for and meet, I want to thank you for the opportunity. I hope to be releasing new music and touring when the time permits. Until then, may God bless and keep you all.

About the Author

In 1989, country newcomer, Sammy Sadler, had already charted several critically-acclaimed singles and was ready to release his first album on **Evergreen Records** when he was shot during the assassination of then *Cash Box* chart-manager, **Kevin Hughes—an incident known around the world as the "Murder on Music Row."**

The police had no suspects, and even though Sammy suffered a nearly fatal bullet wound, the officers kept him under suspicion during the 13-year investigation. Evidence would eventually reveal a "payola" scandal that would bring down the magazine and rock the music industry.

Vindicated, in 2004, Sadler rebooted his career, releasing *Hard On A Heart* (Tri label), yielding a top-10 single on the Texas charts and topping the charts in Europe for multiple weeks. In 2009, *Heart Shaped Like Texas* (Audium) produced rave reviews for the two lead singles, "I'll Always Have Denver," featuring Steve Wariner and "No Place to Land," but the label was in transition, selling to Koch and then to E1, which ultimately shuttered leaving Sadler's promising album shelved.

Still determined to pursue his dream, in 2012, Sammy launched the hugely successful **"Taking the Country Back Tour"** package with **Doug Stone,** and later **Jeff Carson & Ken Mellons** (2015-2016), yielding over 200 dates and giving rise to a book deal with **Indigo River Publishing**. A follow-up retrospective EP, *1989,* to be released shortly thereafter.

ENDNOTES

1   Trust, Gary. "Happy 75th Birthday, Billboard Charts!" Billboard. July 27, 2015. http://www.billboard.com/articles/columns/chart-beat/6634627/happy-75th-birthday-billboard-charts.

2   Simbeck, Rob. "With A Bullet," Nashville Scene, August 8, 2002.

3   "Remembering Tom McEntee," Country Air Check, Sept. 28, 2009, https://www.countryaircheck.com., Sarah Skates, "Lifenotes: CRS Founder Tom McEntee Passes," MusicRow, Sept. 28, 2009, https://musicrow.com/2009/09/lifenotes-crs-founder-tom-mcentee/.

4   Interview with Jim Sharp, 2017.

5   Frances Preston, BMI 50th Anniversary Book, https://web.archive.org/web/20030412122819/http://www.bmi.com:80/library/brochures/history-book/index.asp

6   https://web.archive.org/web/20030412110201/http://www.bmi.com:80/library/brochures/historybook/creative.asp

7   https://web.archive.org/web/20030219015942/http://www.bmi.com:80/library/brochures/historybook/rock.asp

8   Interview, David Williams, May 1, 2017.

9   Bill Pridemore interview May 22, 2017; Pat Postiglione interview, May 23, 2017; Supplemental Reports, Case no. 89-59058.

10   Medical Examiner's Report, Supplemental Reports, Case no. 89-59058.

11   Supplemental Reports, case no. 89-59058.

12   Sheila Wissner and Robert Oermann, "Music Row becoming Murder Row," *Tennessean,* March 11, 1989.

13   Oermann, Robert K. "Highwaymen Rendezvous for Second LP," *Tennessean,* March 10, 1989.

14   Wikipedia contributors, "Berry Hill, Tennessee," *Wikipedia, https://en.wikipedia.org/wiki/Berry_Hill,_Tennessee.*

15   Wissner, Sheila. "Music Row friends heading home when shots started, survivor says," *Tennessean,* March 15, 1989.

16   *Cash Box*, March 25, 1989.

17   Various details regarding the investigation, such as the polygraph

exam questionnaire in this chapter and throughout the book were documented in the criminal files of Case no. 89-59058.

18   Bill Pridemore interview, May 22, 2017.

19   Sheila Wissner, "Cap may hold clue in Music Row killing," April 13, 1989.

20   Sheila Wissner, Thomas Goldsmith, Robert K. Oermann, "Music Fraud Hinted in Music Row Slaying," April 9, 1989.

21   "Man carrying 2 guns arrested," *Tennessean,* April 6, 1989.

22   Here and throughout the book, details from the homicide investigation are documented in Supplemental Reports, case no. 89-59058.

23   Sheila Wissner, Thomas Goldsmith, and Robert K. Oermann, "Chart fraud hinted in Music Row slaying," *Tennessean,* April 9, 1989.

24   Jim Sharp interview, May 23, 2017

25   Gary Bradshaw interview, May 9, 2017.

26   Kirk Loggins, "100 Ticket Raffle Price for House," *Tennessean,* Feb. 20, 1985.

27   Tom McEntee to Bill Pridemore, *Supplemental Reports,* Case no. 89-59058

28   "Remembering Tom McEntee," Country Air Check, Sept. 28, 2009, https://www.countryaircheck.com, Sarah Skates, "Lifenotes: CRS Founder Tom McEntee Passes," MusicRow, Sept. 28, 2009, https://musicrow.com/2009/09/lifenotes-crs-founder-tom-mcentee/, Rob Simbeck, "With a Bullet," Nashville Scene, Aug. 2, 2002.

29   Pat Postiglione, interview, May 23, 2017

30   *Supplemental Reports,* case no. 89-59058.

31   "Dave & Sugar," AllMusic.com, https://www.allmusic.com/artist/dave-sugar-rowland-mn0001411997.

32   *Supplemental Reports,* case no. 89-59058.

33   *Tennessee v. Richard D'Antonio,* case no. 2002-c-1280."

34   Todd Eisenstadt and Sheila Wisser, "Music link lacking in Music Row slaying," *Tennessean,* June 6, 1989.

35   *Lab Reports,* Case no. 89-59058.

36   Sheila Wissner, Thomas Goldsmith, and Robert K. Oermann, "Chart fraud hinted in Music Row slaying," *Tennessean*, April 9, 1989.

37   Todd Eisenstadt, "Music Row slaying on TV draws tips," *Tennessean*, Feb. 5, 1990, "Namedropper," *Tennessean*, July 23, 1989.

38   "Kevin Hughes," *Unsolved Mysteries Wiki*, http://unsolvedmysteries. wikia.com/wiki/Kevin_Hughes.

39   *Supplemental Reports*, case no. 89-59058.

40   "Local News top stories 1989," *Tennessean*, Dec. 4, 1989; Robert K. Oermann, "Familiar names dominate '89 in Nashville music," Dec. 30, 1989.

41   Todd Eisenstadt, "Murder in Music City," *Tennessean*, Jan. 7, 1990.

42   Todd Eisenstadt, "The dead and difficult murders populate police reporter's turf, *Tennessean*, July 15, 1990.

43   *Supplemental Reports*, case no. 89-59058.

44   Pridemore in *Supplemental Reports*, Feb. 2, 1990, case no. 89-59058.

45   "Our Proud History," Victim Assistance Program, http://www.victi-massistanceprogram.org/who-we-are/history.aspx; "National Organization for Victim Assistance," https://www.trynova.org.

46   Todd Eisenstadt, "Rewards offered in slaying of market clerk," *Tennessean*, Oct. 10, 1989.

47   Harwell Wells, "Gunman fired, then robbed, detective says," *Tennessean*, July 31, 1986; "Police ask help in finding shooting, robbery suspect," *Tennessean*, Sept. 2, 1986; Brad Schmitt, "Music Row publicist attacked," *Tennessean*, April 11, 1992; Robert K. Oermann, "Tracy Lawrence aims sky high," *Tennessean*, Feb. 8, 1992.

48   Benjamin Tate, "Music Row businesses band together to stop crime," *Tennessean*, Oct. 29, 1992.

49   Joe Rogers, "Chart fix charges stir up a stink" and "Ill wind: Jitters spreading down Music Row," July 17, 1991; and "Music magazine publishers settle dispute out of court," *Tennessean*, Nov. 20, 1991.

50   "Attempted Murder on Music Row," YouTube, published Jan. 9, 2014, https://www.youtube.com/watch?v=Hq0HgXBKm9A.

51   Wikipedia contributors, "Barry Sadler," *Wikipedia*, https://en.wikipedia. org/wiki/Barry_Sadler - mw-headhttps://en.wikipedia.org/wiki/Barry_Sadler .

52   Jim Sharp, interview, May 24, 2013.

53   Wikipedia contributors, "Jim Croce," *Wikipedia, https://en.wikipedia. org/wiki/Jim_Croce.*

54   *Supplemental Reports*, case no. 89-59058.

55   *Cash Box*, March 11, 1989.

56   Sheila Wissner, Thomas Goldsmith, and Robert K. Oermann, "Chart fraud hinted in Music Row Slaying," *Tennessean,* April 9, 1989.

57   *Cash Box*, Feb. 25, 1989.

58   "Songwriter says he talked to Hank Williams' ghost," http://www. tennessean.com/story/entertainment/music/2015/08/13/songwriter-says-he-talked-hank-williams-ghost/31534161/.

59   "Songwriter/composer, Detterline, John Blayne, Jr.,» BMI repertoire, http://repertoire.bmi.com/Catalog.aspx?detail=writerid&keyid=89014&sub-id=0&page=4&fromrow=51&torow=75.

60   "Ladies And Gentlemen....The Rocketones!" *Parkesburg Today,* Oct. 27, 2013, http://parkesburg.today/ladies-gentlemen-rocketones-part-1/.

61   David Ross, interview, May 24, 2017.

62   Jim Sharp, interview, May 24, 2017.

63   *Cash Box* Exodus: Departures Revive Chart Debate," *Nashville Scene,* Feb. 13, 1992.

64   *Supplemental Reports*, Case no. 89-59058.

65   Robert K. Oermann, interview, May 24, 2017.

66   Ron Kinner, "Classic Tracks: The Making of LeAnn Rimes' 'Blue,'" http://www.mixonline.com/news/classic-tracks/classic-tracks-making-leann-rimes-blue/423305; Wikipedia contributors, "LeAnn Rimes," *Wikipedia,* https://en.wikipedia.org/wiki/LeAnn_Rimes.

67   John Wesley Ryles, interview Aug. 16, 2017.

68   Monte Warden and Brandi Scaife, interview, May 31, 2017.

69   Robert K. Oermann, interview, May 24, 2017.

70   "Record company sued by singer," *Tennessean,* Aug. 20, 1969.

71   David Ross, interview, May 24, 2017

72   Pat Welch, "Grand jury probes music fraud claims," June 29, 1967, and "Surrender slated in music fraud charges," July 1, 1967, *Tennesean.*

73   "Robert Metzgar, Legends Hall of Fame Music Producer," www. robertmetzgar.com.

74   David Jarrard, "Church, minister remain embattled," *Tennesean,* June 23, 1985; Ellen Margulies, "Questioning of deacon to resume," *Tennesean,* Nov. 7, 1986; Ellen Margulies, "No ill feelings says ex-pastor," *Tennesean,* Sept. 29, 1987.

75   "Label weaves a different web site," *Tennesean,* July 10, 1997.

76   Sheila Wisser, "Keep your money, execs say," "New pitch, do a duet with Conway," and "Lower reaches of music business under new scrutiny," *Tennesean, June 29, 1997;* "Few disheartened musicians file complaints," "Major stations, labels, ignore independents, writers learn too late," *Tennessean,* June 30, 1967.

77   *Cash Box,* November 16, 1996.

78   Kim Thomas, "Local singer sets new path in country scene," *Jackson Sun,* Aug. 24, 2000.

79   "Eddie Bond to Release New Single," www.rockabillyhall.com/Eddie Bond.

80   Peter Guralnick, *Elvis Day by Day* (New York: Ballantine Books, 1999).

81   *Supplemental Report,* Case no. 899-59058.

82   *Miscellaneous Reports No. 3,* in *Supplemental Reports,* case no. 89-59058.

83   *Tennessee v. Richard D'Antonio,* case no. 2002-c-1280.

84   Bill Pridemore, interview, May 22, 2017.

85   "Polygraph report," in *Supplemental Reports,* case no. 89-59058.

86   Situs inversus totalis, http://www.medicinenet.com/script/main/art. asp?articlekey=5499.

87   *Supplemental Reports,* case no. 89-59058.

88   *Supplemental Reports,* case no. 89-59058.

89   *Supplemental Reports,* case no. 89-59058.

90   Tom Roland, "Wade Jessen, Billboard Senior Chart Manager," Dies at Age 53, *Billboard,* March 5, 2015, http://www.billboard.com/articles/news/6494333/billboard-senior-chart-manager-wade-jessen-dies-aged-53.

91   *Supplemental Reports,* case no. 89-59058.

92   *Tennessee v. Richard Frank D'Antonio,* Criminal Court No. 2002-C-1280, Grand Jury Subpoena for July 19, 2002.

93   *Handbook of Texas Online,* Mark Odintz, "Bottom, TX," accessed September 07, 2017, http://www.tshaonline.org/handbook/online/articles/hvbcg.

94   Bill Pridemore, interview, May 22, 2017.

95   *Supplemental Reports,* case no. 89-59058.

96   *Supplemental Reports,* case no. 89-59058.

97   *Supplemental Reports,* case no. 89-59058.

98   *Supplemental Reports,* case no. 89-59058.

99   *Supplemental Reports,* case no. 89-59058.

100   *Tennessee v. Richard D'Antonio,* case no. 2002-c-1280, pp. 152-54.

101   Rob Simbeck, "With a bullet: The story of gold chains, doctored charts and a Music Row murder," *Nashville Scene,* August 8, 2002.

102   Bill Pridemore, interview, May 22, 2017.

103   *Tennessee v. Richard D'Antonio,* case no. 2002-c-1280, p.255-271.

104   *Tennessee v. Richard D'Antonio,* case no. 2002-c-1280, p284-87.

105   *Tennessee v. Richard D'Antonio,* case no. 2002-c-1280, p288-300.

106   *Tennessee v. Richard D'Antonio,* case no. 2002-c-1280, p303

107   *Tennessee v. Richard D'Antonio,* case no. 2002-c-1280, p303-15.

108   *Tennessee v. Richard D'Antonio,* case no. 2002-c-1280, p317-324.

109   *Tennessee v. Richard D'Antonio,* case no. 2002-c-1280, p337-70.

110   *Tennessee v. Richard D'Antonio,* case no. 2002-c-1280, p373-80.

111   *Tennessee v. Richard D'Antonio,* case no. 2002-c-1280, p397-402.

112   *Tennessee v. Richard D'Antonio,* case no. 2002-c-1280, p384-96.

113   *Tennessee v. Richard D'Antonio,* case no. 2002-c-1280, p403-407.

114   *Tennessee v. Richard D'Antonio*, case no. 2002-c-1280, p407-411.

115   Sheila Wissner, Thomas Goldsmith, Robert K. Oermann, "Music Fraud Hinted in Music Row Slaying," April 9, 1989.

116   *Tennessee v. Richard D'Antonio*, case no. 2002-c-1280, p412-27.

117   *Tennessee v. Richard D'Antonio*, case no. 2002-c-1280, p429-44.

118   *Tennessee v. Richard D'Antonio*, case no. 2002-c-1280, p450-64.

119   *Tennessee v. Richard D'Antonio*, case no. 2002-c-1280, p464-86.

120   *Cash Box*, Oct. 22, 1988.

121   *Cash Box*, Dec. 9, 1989.

122   "Gun owner Mark Carman makes plea for modest regulation," *The Trace*, Nov. 16, 2015, https://www.thetrace.org/2015/11/gun-owner-mark-carman-makes-a-plea-for-modest-regulation-is-pilloried-online/.

123   *Tennessee v. Richard D'Antonio*, case no. 2002-c-1280, p736.

124   *Tennessee v. Richard D'Antonio*, case no. 2002-c-1280, p493-97.

125   *Tennessee v. Richard D'Antonio*, case no. 2002-c-1280, p512-20.

126   Myra Langlois, interview, Sept. 7, 2017.

127   *Tennessee v. Richard D'Antonio*, case no. 2002-c-1280, p533-40.

128   *Tennessee v. Richard D'Antonio*, case no. 2002-c-1280, p589-603.

129   *Tennessee v. Richard D'Antonio*, case no. 2002-c-1280, p562-75.

130   *Tennessee v. Richard D'Antonio*, case no. 2002-c-1280, p589-601.

131   *Tennessee v. Richard D'Antonio*, case no. 2002-c-1280, p604-21.

132   *Tennessee v. Richard D'Antonio*, case no. 2002-c-1280, p664-705.

133   Transcript of the taped phone conversation between D'Antonio and Daniel, *Tennessee v. Richard D'Antonio*, case no. 2002-c-1280, p776-84.

134   *Tennessee v. Richard D'Antonio*, case no. 2002-c-1280, p754-68.

135   *Tennessee v. Richard D'Antonio*, case no. 2002-c-1280, p785.

136   *Tennessee v. Richard D'Antonio*, case no. 2002-c-1280, p75—84.

137   *Tennessee v. Richard D'Antonio*, case no. 2002-c-1280, p815-79.

138   *Tennessee v. Richard D'Antonio*, case no. 2002-c-1280, p942.

139   Colin Fly, "Judge upholds life sentence of 'Music Row' murderer," *Associated Press, Tennessean*, Nov. 3, 2003.

140   Ron Wynn, "Sadler finally resumes career," *Nashville City Paper*, Nov. 7, 2003, Colin Fly, "Judge upholds life sentence of 'Music Row' murderer," *Tennessean*, Nov. 8, 2003.

141   Jim Patterson, "Music Row slaying suspect found guilty," Sept. 26, 2003.

142   "The dark side of Nashville's music business," *ABC News*, Nov. 10, 2003, http://abcnews.go.com/Primetime/story?id=132437&page=1.

143   John Wesley Ryles, interview, Aug. 16, 2017.

144   Tim Ghianni, "15 Years Later, Sadler Back Where It Began," *Tennessean*, March 9, 2004.

145   "We Mourn the Passing of a Colleague and Friend," *Cash Box*, March 25, 1989.

146   Chuck Rhodes, interview, Aug. 16, 2017; Wikipedia Editors, "E1 Entertainment," *Wikipedia*, https://en.wikipedia.org/wiki/Entertainment_One, "Another Label Bites The Dust: Koch Shuts Nashville Branch," *Celebrity Access Media Wire*, Oct. 18, 2005, http://www.hypebot.com/hypebot/2005/10/another_label_b.html.

147   To come: publishing info and permission note here.

148   Edward Morris, "It's Still 'Murder on Music Row,' Songwriters Complain; Shell, Cordle Unfazed by Award Nominations," CMT, June 11, 2003, http://www.cmt.com/news/1472512/its-still-murder-on-music-row-songwriters-complain-shell-cordle-unfazed-by-award-nominations/, accessed Sept. 21, 2017.

149   Larry Cordle's website, www.larrycordle.com, Larry Shell, *All Music*, http://www.allmusic.com/artist/larry-shell-mn0000782959.

150   Robert K. Oermann, interview, May 13, 2017.

151   John Wesley Ryles, interview, Aug. 16, 2017.

152   Bill Pridemore, interview, May 22, 2017.

153   Pat Postiglione, interview, May 23, 2017.

154   Myra Langlois, interview, Sept. 7, 2017.

155   Kirk Loggins, "How Not to Become a Star in Nashville's Record

Industry," *Tennessean*, Dec. 25, 1977, "State Censures Record Company for Stock Fraud," *Tennessean*, Nov. 3, 1977, "Music Industry Cons, 'Ripoffs,' ; Tex Nobodies,'" April 28, 1977.

156   Kirk Loggins, "Producer Claims Four Promoters Shared Profits," *Tennessean*, May 16, 1977.

157   Desson Howe, "Payola Probe Deepens," *Washington Post*, March 4, 1986, Jacqueline Trescott, Richard Harrington, et al., "Pay-to-Play Record Scandal? Safeguards Working, Local Stations Say," *Washington Post*, March 5, 1986, Penny Pagano and Wm. Knoedelseder, Jr., "Senate Plans Record Industry Payola Probe," April 3, 1986, *Los Angeles Times*, Mark Schwed, "Payola probes under way," *UPI*, April 19, 1986, and "Figure in '80s Payola Scandal Now Faces Mob-Linked Charges," *AP*, July 30, 2014, http://www.billboard.com/biz/articles/news/legal-and-management/6203073/figure-in-80s-payola-scandal-now-faces-mob-linked, accessed Sept. 21, 2017.

158   Jeff Leeds, "Radio programmer fired for dealings with promoter," *New York Times News Service*, November 21, 2004, Charles Duhigg and Walter Hamilton, "Sony BMG said to be near settlement in payola investigation," *Tennessean*, July 23, 2005, and Lorne Manly, "How Payola Went Corporate," New York Times, July 31, 2005, Caroline Cakebread, "Spotify and other streaming services are finally giving the music industry something to cheer about," *Business Insider*, http://www.businessinsider.com/one-chart-shows-the-rise-in-revenue-from-music-streaming-charts-2017-9, *Janko Roettgers*, "Streaming Services Generated More Than 50% of All U.S. Music Industry Revenue in 2016," *Variety*, *http://variety.com/2017/digital/news/streaming-services-us-music-revenue-2016-1202019504/*.

159   Dean Starkman, "Sony BMG Settles Radio Payola Probe," *Washington Post*, July 26, 2005.

160   Wikipedia contributors, "Sirius Satellite Radio," *Wikipedia*, https://en.wikipedia.org/wiki/Sirius_Satellite_Radio.

161   Paul Resnikoff, "Major Label CEO Confirms That 'Playlist Payola' Is a Real Thing," *Digital Music News*, http://www.digitalmusicnews.com/2016/05/20/playlist-payola-real-killing-artist-careers/, Glenn Peoples, "How 'Playola' Is Infiltrating Streaming Services: Pay for Play Is 'Definitely Happening,'" *Billboard*, , Aug. 19, 2015, http://www.billboard.com/articles/business/6670475/playola-promotion-streaming-services, Andrew Flanagan, "'Music Isn't a Commodity': Warner Music CEO Stephen Cooper on That

Streaming Milestone, the 'Value Grab,'" *Billboard*, May 13, 2016, http://www.billboard.com/biz/articles/news/record-labels/7370414/music-isnt-a-commodity-warner-music-ceo-stephen-cooper-on.

162   Paul Resnikoff, "Major Label CEO Confirms That 'Playlist Payola' Is a Real Thing," *Digital Music News*, http://www.digitalmusicnews.com/2016/05/20/playlist-payola-real-killing-artist-careers/.

163   Jessica Nelson, "Man convicted in 1989 Music Row murder dies," MusicRow.com, Sept. 18, 2014, https://musicrow.com/2014/09/man-convicted-in-1989-music-row-murder-dies/.

164   "D Antonio, Richard Frank," "Guitarus Maximus Music," and "D Antonio, Richard Anthony," BMIrepertoire.com.

CPSIA information can be obtained
at www.ICGtesting.com
Printed in the USA
FSHW022107040621
82096FS